Library of
Davidson College

VOID

CHRISTIAN INFLUENCE
UPON THE IDEOLOGY
OF THE TAIPING REBELLION

1851–1864

Frontispiece—
Title page of the *T'ai-p'ing chao-shu* (Taiping Imperial Proclamations), a typical rebel religious publication, photographed from an original in the New York Public Library. Notice the Chinese style dragons on either side of the large characters of the title. The characters across the top inform the reader that the book was printed in 1852, the second year of the Taiping Heavenly Kingdom.

太平天國壬子二年新刻

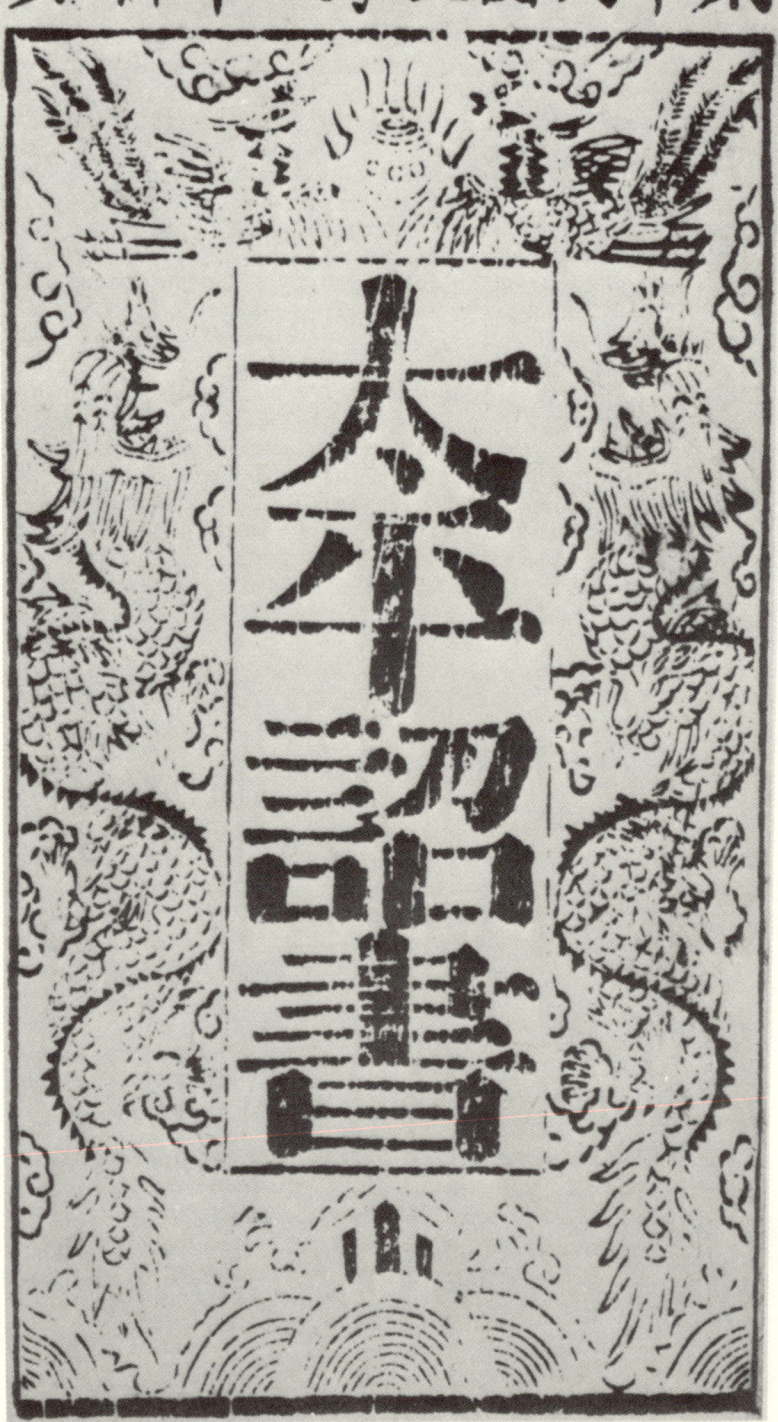

太平詔書

CHRISTIAN INFLUENCE UPON THE IDEOLOGY OF THE TAIPING REBELLION

1851–1864

Eugene Powers Boardman

1972
OCTAGON BOOKS
New York

Copyright, 1952, by The Regents of the University of Wisconsin
Copyright, Canada, 1952

951.03
B662c

Reprinted 1972
by special arrangement with the University of Wisconsin Press

OCTAGON BOOKS
A DIVISION OF FARRAR, STRAUS & GIROUX, INC.
19 Union Square West
New York, N. Y. 10003

LIBRARY OF CONGRESS CATALOG CARD NUMBER: 71-159168

ISBN 0-374-90697-1

Manufactured by Braun-Brumfield, Inc.
Ann Arbor, Michigan

Printed in the United States of America

To
Charles Watkins and
Irmgard Heth Boardman

Preface

In presenting this study I am obliged to point out that the picture I give is intended to apply to the Taiping religion as it existed until 1854, that is, during the first three years of the Rebellion.* Central features of Taiping doctrine and practice that I describe persisted after 1854 and are recognizable to the end of the regime in 1864. The acquaintance of Hung Hsiu-ch'üan and other Taiping leaders with the New Testament improved conspicuously as the Rebellion went on; in the latter part of it they refer to passages never mentioned in documents of the years before 1855. For example, Hung Jen-kan had engraved on stone the Beatitudes, a portion of the Sermon on the Mount never alluded to before 1855. Likewise, tendencies toward the accommodation of Chinese concepts and political necessities were in the religion at the beginning. The years that followed the capture of Nanking, however, saw extensive elaboration of these tendencies, increased fanaticism, and perversion. These later developments await separate treatment.

A comprehensive investigation of what Taiping leaders learned of Christian ideas after 1854 and of what their religion became later requires full study of rebel writings after 1855 and full use of the North-China Herald, British Parliamentary Papers, and, if obtainable, official French reports for the period 1856-64. It has seemed unwise, meanwhile, to postpone further the appearance of a study already long delayed.

* Except for the transliteration of Chinese titles, the simpler form Taiping is used throughout the book in place of T'ai-p'ing, the correctly romanized term.

Preface

The use of Medhurst's extensive translations of the principal Taiping documents has made it possible to handle more readily the principal religious ideas of the Rebellion and to find more quickly passages in the original Chinese. English translations of Chinese given, however, have all been checked with the originals and in many cases are as much my own as Medhurst's.

In the earlier stages of this study I was of the opinion that not enough of the doctrines of Christianity was borrowed to justify the term "Christian Influence" in the title. In the Harvard doctoral dissertation from which this has come, I used the phrase "Biblical Influence". But later reflection upon the sterner nature of the 19th century fundamentalist Christianity to which the Taipings were exposed has caused me to choose the term "Christian".

My thanks for continued encouragement and suggestions go first of all to John King Fairbank, Professor of History at Harvard, under whose direction I first became interested in the Taiping religion. Professor Derk Bodde of the University of Pennsylvania read the entire manuscript and made many corrections and helpful comments. My residence in Hongkong as a Fulbright scholar the second semester of the academic year 1950-51 made possible contact with Mr. Jen (Chien) Yu-wen, one of the leading Chinese scholars of the Rebellion. Mr. Jen also read the manuscript and suggested improvements. I am indebted to him for the hand-written title page which appears on the back cover.

The trustees of the Rockefeller Foundation furnished support for the completion of the manuscript in its dissertation form after five years of interruption during World War II. This later revision and smplification was greatly facilitated by grants from the Research Committee of the Graduate School of the University of Wisconsin which provided support during the summer of 1947 and the services of a research assistant. The United States Educational Commission in the United Kingdom facilitated my enjoyment of a Fulbright grant for Hongkong.

I am especially indebted to my erstwhile research assistant So Kwan-wai and, in lesser degree but just as gratefully, to Robert Boardman, Kuo Chung-ying, Li Dun-jen and to Irving Antin, Richard Wilde and other student members of my history seminar.

The Library of the Harvard-Yenching Institute, the libraries of the Yale and Harvard Divinity Schools, the American Board of Commissioners for Foreign Missions, the American Bible Society, the New York Public Library, and the Division of Orientalia of the Library of Congress have been most helpful in making available Taiping and 19th century Christian materials.

The University Library and the Fung Ping Shan Library of the University of Hongkong were most helpful in affording me facilities for putting the manuscript into its final form. My thanks go to Paul Frillman of the United States Information Service in Hongkong and to members of his staff for assistance in arranging for the printing of the Chinese characters.

Finally, gratitude is due my wife who has lived with this book from the time when the first research for it was under way.

July 1952   E. P. B.

Contents

1. Introduction — 3
2. The Story of the Rebellion — 9
3. The Taiping Appeal to China — 33
4. The Christian Component
   What Was Available to the Taipings — 41
5. The Christian Component
   What the Taipings Took — 52
6. The Christian Component
   What the Taipings Failed to Take — 106
7. The Role of the Christian Component
   in the Outcome of the Rebellion — 116
8. Bibliographical Appendix — 130

Index — 173

CHRISTIAN INFLUENCE
UPON THE IDEOLOGY
OF THE TAIPING REBELLION

1851–1864

I

Introduction

The ideology which forms the subject of this volume was created by the leaders of an uprising in nineteenth century China known to the outside world as the Taiping Rebellion (1851-64). This was certainly the largest internal upheaval of its century and it ranks with the greatest uprisings of Chinese history.

The Rebellion drew favorable foreign attention early in its course because its public pronouncements were rumored to have a Christian flavor. Members of the foreign communities in the treaty ports actually knew little or nothing of the quasi-Christian character of the rebels until the Taipings took Nanking March 19, 1853.

News of this event spread to the outside world through Shanghai. Shanghai was a community vitally concerned with the uninterrupted flow of trade in the Yangtze Valley. How was the presence of the Taipings there to affect trade? In view of the interest of its readers it was natural for the North-China Herald, the leading English language newspaper in Shanghai, to begin the publication in translation of a number of official Taiping documents as they found their way into the hands of foreigners along the China coast. These translations appeared in the columns of the Herald from time to time throughout 1853 and 1854. Most of them were made by Walter Henry Medhurst, an experienced missionary sinologue. The rest were supplied by Dr. Mac-Gowan, a missionary to Ningpo, and appeared under the serial title, "Dr. MacGowan's Notebook." These English translations were copied widely. They became a subject of general comment among Christians in China. Word of what was happening there soon reached home mission boards in the United States and England and on the Continent.

Except for one brief episode involving two of the leaders only, Western Christian missionaries never preached directly to the Taiping rebels at the time when the movement was in its initial stages. After their formal expulsion from China in 1724, Roman Catholic priests continued to visit their scattered flocks in the interior under risk of death or imprisonment if detected and reported.[1] But there is no textual evidence or contemporary mention to the effect that Chinese Catholic communities existed in the neighborhood of the first Taiping communities in Kwangsi. All Western missionaries including Protestants were forbidden access to the interior of China, even after the Emperor had decreed toleration for Chinese and foreign Christians in connection with the treaties of 1842-44. Missionaries were forbidden to travel outside the five recognized treaty ports. In 1847 the founder of the Taiping religion came for his brief personal instruction to an American missionary in Canton, one of the treaty ports.

Despite this lack of Western tutelage, the more enthusiastic of the Western missionaries in China permitted themselves to see in the beliefs of the Taipings a miracle of what the dissemination of the Scriptures unaided by instruction had performed.[2] The missionaries were glad to hear of the attitude of the insurgents toward various forms of heathen worship and idolatry. Their ruthless iconoclasm was constantly reported. When Issachar Roberts (1802-71), the only missionary who had ever talked with the Taiping chief, received a letter from Hung inviting him to Nanking, he was eager to renew the association and asked permission of the American commissioner Humphrey Marshall to do so.[3] What an opportunity for evangelism! How much more might not personal instruction on the part of trained missionaries accomplish! The report that the rebels opposed the use of opium also attracted favorable attention.[4] Missionary interest was a factor in the general eagerness of Westerners to effect an understanding with the rebels.

Interest among Christians abroad seemed to match that shown in China. In the summer of 1853 a campaign was begun in England to raise funds for the printing in China of a million Chinese New Testaments. Within six months the necessary amount, about 16,000 pounds sterling, had been raised. By June 1854 40,901 pounds sterling had been subscribed.[5]

As matters turned out, Western attempts to effect an understanding with the rebel leaders were based on hope and little else.[6] Taiping Christianity was discovered to be unlike anything anticipated. The Scriptures unaided had wrought no miracle, and in their Chinese context many Scriptural ideas had been misapplied if not perverted. What astonished and then angered the foreign visitors most was the presumption with which their allegiance to the Taiping religion was demanded. Had not their Heavenly King, Hung Hsiu-ch'üan, had a later revelation from God than his

Introduction   5

elder brother Jesus? The efforts of individuals, like the
Rev. C. Taylor and Dr. E. C. Bridgman, came to nothing.
The hopes of the missionaries afterward were never as high
as they had been in 1853 and 1854.
  The Taiping Rebellion was put down in 1864. Rebel records were destroyed or censored by official order but the
Taipings were not forgotten. The time came when a more
successful movement than theirs disposed of the Ch'ing
dynasty. Then a school of publicists for Dr. Sun Yat-sen's
revolutionary movement found in the earlier rebellion a
prototype of the Revolution of 1911.[7] More recently the
Taiping Rebellion has become in rather uncritical fashion
part of the revolutionary heritage of the Chinese Communists.[8] Chinese Communists have given especial attention to
the tactics of the rebels.[9] At the same time the official
histories of the Kuomintang neglect mention of the Rebellion.[10]
  The supposedly Christian element in Taiping apologetics
continued to be of interest long after the suppression of
the Rebellion. Missionaries for years afterward referred
to mistakes in evangelization methods in the light of the
Taiping experience. "Christianity still suffers from the
travesty," wrote the editor of a mission year book.[11]

". . . it is better for them (i.e. Chinese Christians)
not to be thrown entirely on their own resources.
They might fall into error as did the Kwangsi Christians, who began so well and so seriously with reading
the Scriptures and prayer-meetings. There was no one
to tell them that our religion is peaceful, and that
the weapons of our warfare are not carnal. The zeal
of these men which, untempered by an enlightened prudence, led them to the brink of destruction, would have
wrought wonders for the spread of Christianity if
rightly directed."[12]

  An experienced missionary is authority for the statement that the Taiping Rebellion made the Chinese government fear religious propaganda as politically dangerous.[13]
As a result, even after Christianity had acquired an international legal status in China and missionaries were permitted to travel and even to reside inside the country,[14]
officials were instructed to prevent missionaries from
settling in the interior lest they should win the hearts
of the people. In his opinion, the great number of lives
lost during the thirteen years of Taiping rule rolled up a
"legacy of hatred against Christianity, a hatred which has
scarcely yet melted away."[15]
  Interest in the Taiping experience with Christian ideas

has not been confined to missionaries. Historians, students of revolution and cultural diffusion as well as novelists have been attracted to the exotic features of the Taiping religion, but until very recently little effort has been directed by either Chinese or Westerners toward an exact determination of the quality and extent of borrowing from Christian sources. Few Chinese Taiping historians have read or paid much attention to the set of pamphlets first seen by Hung, the Ch'üan-shih liang-yen 勸世良言 despite their obvious importance for fixing the sources of Christian influence.[16] Little has been attempted by Westerners along this line since the labors of Medhurst and his contemporaries.[17] Yet several important questions have never been fully answered. What Christian religious literature was available to the Taipings between 1835 and 1853, the formative period of the religion? Which of this did they see? What part of the material reaching them did rebel leaders accept and use? What parts of what they saw did they discard? What was the basis for selection?

The original religious writings of the Taipings and a representative collection of early Chinese Bibles and tracts are now available. It is possible, therefore, to attempt a textual comparison of the principal Taiping religious documents with Protestant missionary materials accessible at that time. Such an examination may go far toward answering the questions of all who are interested in the Taiping religion.

Footnotes.

1. William Dean, The China Mission (New York, 1859), 82.
2. John B. Littell, "Missionaries and Politics in China -- The Taiping Rebellion," Political Science Quarterly, XLIII, 4 (Dec.,1928), 566-99. This is a thorough study, drawn from letters and contemporary reports, of missionary attitudes, principally of Americans. Littell reports little direct evidence of missionary influence on the policy of the United States regarding the Taipings.
3. Permission was refused. This was done because Humphrey Marshall felt that Roberts' request that he be allowed to "assist that the gospel may be made plain" to the insurgents at Nanking constituted unneutral action. Marshall was also inclined to support the Manchu government as a means of countering the British, who gave indications of recognizing the rebels. Enclosures 1 and 2, Humphrey Marshall to Marcy, June 21, 1853, Dispatches from United States Ministers to China, Vol. 8, Aug. 5, 1852 - Feb. 22, 1854.

Introduction

See also Tyler Dennett, Americans in Eastern Asia (New York, 1922), 216 ff.
4. The Rev. Frank L. Norris, China (London, 1908), 43.
5. W. Canton, History of the British and Foreign Bible Society (London, 1904), II., 448. The enthusiasm coincided with the completion of an improved translation of both Testaments called the Delegates' Version, based on the collective work of the best missionary scholars of Chinese. The Rev. William Muirhead, China and the Gospel (London, 1870), 141-2.
6. The hopes of the foreign community at Shanghai at the beginning of 1854 are summarized in the following. "We regard him (Hung Hsiu-ch'üan) as the instrument in the hands of God for accelerating, perhaps by ages, the civilization and Christianization of the Chinese; we regard him as hastening forward, with rapid strides, the real opening of China, and her union with the Western world; and we trust that under his more enlightened sway our merchants will speedily exchange present difficulties and impediments for all the advantages of a free, reciprocal, and unblemished traffick." Editorial, North-China Herald, 180 (Jan. 7, 1854), 90. Italics unaltered from the original.
7. Ssu-yü Teng, New Light on the History of the Taiping Rebellion (Cambridge: Harvard University Press, 1950), 1-2. A more detailed account of the Taiping influence on Sun Yat-sen is found in P'eng Tse-i, T'ai-p'ing t'ien-kuo ko-ming ssu-ch'ao (The dynamic thought of the Taiping Rebellion) (Shanghai: Commercial Press, 1946), Chap. 6. Characters for authors and titles such as this appear in the bibliography.
8. The first volume of a Communist history of recent Chinese revolutionary movements devotes its first section to the Rebellion; also, a Communist source book for the study of modern Chinese history reprints a lengthy selection of Taiping originals. Group for the Study of Recent Chinese History, Chung-kuo hsien-tai ko-ming yün-tung shih (History of recent Chinese revolutionary movements) (Hsin Hua Shu-tien, 1942), I, 1-24. Yang Sung and Teng Li-ch'ün, Chung-kuo chin-tai shih ts'an-k'ao ts'ai-liao (Materials for the study of modern Chinese history) (Chieh-fang She, 1942), I, 126-222. Three recently published works of note are the following. Fan Wen-lan, T'ai-p'ing t'ien-kuo ko-ming yün-tung (The Taiping revolutionary movement) (Shanghai: Hsin Hua Shu-tien, 1949); Fan Wen-lan, editorial director, Hua-pei ta-hsüeh li-shih yen-chiu (Historical research group of North China University), T'ai-p'ing t'ien-kuo ko-ming yün-tung lun wen-chi (Centennial volume, collection of writings on the Taiping revolutionary movement) (Peking: San Lien Shu Tien, 1951); Hua Kang, T'ai-p'ing t'ien-kuo ko-ming chan-cheng shih (History of the Taiping revolutionary war) (Shanghai: Hai Yin, 1949).

9. Teng, op. cit., 65, and references cited under under his footnote 16.
10. See Feng Tzu-yu, Chung-hua min-kuo k'ai-kuo ch'ien ko-ming shih (History of the revolution preceding the foundation of the Chinese Republic)(Chung-kuo Wen-hua Fu-wu She, 1944, 1946); Tai Chi-t'ao, Kuo-min ko-ming yü chungkuo kuo-min-tang (The people's revolution and the Chinese Kuomintang) (Chung-kuo Wen-hua Fu-wu She, 1943, 1946); Tsou Lu, Chung-kuo kuo-min-tang shih lüeh (Historical sketch of the Chinese Kuomintang) (Chungking: Commercial Press, 1945); and references given in P'eng, op.cit., 136-7.
11. D. MacGillivray, ed., The China Mission Year Book 1915 (Shanghai, 1915) 434.
12. Joseph Edkins, The Religious Condition of the Chinese (1859), 285-6. Vigorous and searching criticism of indiscriminate use of the Bible in evangelical work in China may be read in Bertram Wolferstan, S.J., The Catholic Church in China--from 1860 to 1907 (London, 1909), 74 ff. On page 105 appears the following: "There can be no doubt that the indiscriminate circulation of the Bible, aided by the 'inalienable right of private interpretation' thereof, is capable of producing the most disastrous material results. Of such a nature was the T'ai-p'ing Rebellion. . . . We also see in this movement the effect of the distribution in that country of Bibles and Christian tracts."
13. Timothy Richard, Forty-five Years in China (N.Y., 1916), 158.
14. This refers to the Treaties of Tientsin, June 26-29, 1858, which, when ratification was finally obtained, opened the interior of China to missionary enterprise. Harold M. Vinacke, A History of the Far East in Modern Times (N.Y.: Crofts, 1946), 50-1.
15. Richard, op. cit., 186.
16. Teng, op. cit., 75. See also the account of the influence of Christianity in Hsieh Hsing-yao, T'ai-p'ing T'ien-kuo ti she-hui cheng-chih ssu-hsiang (Social and political theories of the T'ai-p'ing t'ien-kuo) (Shanghai: Commercial Press, 1935), 23-33.
17. Recent Western studies that discuss Christian influence are the following: W.J.Hail, Tseng Kuo-fan and the Taiping Rebellion (New Haven: Yale University Press, 1927), Chap. 5; K.S.Latourette, A History of Christian Missions in China (N.Y.: MacMillan, 1929), 297-302; G.E.Taylor, "The Taiping Rebellion: Its Economic Background and Social Theory," Chinese Social and Political Science Review, 16.4 (January, 1933), 545-614; C.C.Stelle, "Ideologies of the T'ai-p'ing Insurrection," Ibid., 20.1 (April, 1936), 140-9; John Foster, D.D. "The Christian Origins of the Taiping Rebellion," The International Review of Missions XL.158 (April 1951), 156-67.

2

The Story of the Rebellion

An adequate comprehensive history of the Taiping Rebellion in any language has yet to be written. This account, of chapter length, cannot pretend to do more than sketch the main chronological events of the movement and indicate the nature of its leadership and reform program. This much, though, is done to provide a main narrative which must be kept in mind when detailed examination of the ideology is attempted. Such a narrative is particularly necessary when one tries, as I have, to speculate upon the relationship between the rebel use of Christian elements in their ideology and the final outcome of the Rebellion.

The Taiping Rebellion grew out of a situation compounded of dynastic decline, agrarian distress, overpopulation, foreign penetration, failure to provide an adequate officialdom, and Chinese resentment against the misrule of alien Manchu overlords.[1] The rulers who succeeded the Ch'ienlung Emperor (1736-96) displayed far less competence than he in performing the normal duties which were exacting even for an outstanding emperor.[2] It was the fate of China to have these men as rulers when Western contacts culminated in the first Anglo-Chinese War (1839-42), a situation unlike China's previous experience with "barbarians" that called for imagination and courage to experiment with new ways of government. A situation productive of revolt was thus created by two sets of failures, failure to care for the normal, recurrent problems of a Chinese dynasty and failure to meet the determined efforts of Westerners to obtain improved terms of trade and diplomatic relationships of a Western type. Of course failures at meeting one set of difficulties made those of the other set worse.

The failure of the Ch'ing government during the first half of the 19th century had far more ramifications than I can indicate below.

But to illustrate, Yung-yen, the Chia-ch'ing Emperor (1796-1820), had to deal with three major rebellions and disastrous floods that cut down the national income and exhausted the surplus funds of the imperial treasury. His successor Min-ning, the Tao-kuang Emperor (1821-51), [3] was short of funds to use in suppressing continued civil disturbance and in fighting the British. He was therefore compelled to raise the land tax continually [4] and to carry to excess a practice known as "contribution for appointment to public office" whereby degrees usually acquired by competitive examination, and offices, merits, grades, promotions, and favorable positions on lists of expectant officials connected with the civil service were sold to provide government funds. [5] The increased taxes levied in the later years of the Ch'ing period, when the forces making for inequity had had full opportunity to make themselves felt, fell upon the classes least able to bear them, and were particularly heavy in the provinces south of the Yangtze River. [6] To pay his land taxes the farmer had to change his copper cash into silver, a medium increasingly dear because foreigners required it of the Chinese when the balance of trade became unfavorable in paying for imports from abroad, particularly opium and raw cotton, as well as for war indemnities. The sale of degrees and offices multiplied the number of candidates for office and discouraged the efforts of those attempting to pass the official examinations, thus creating a reservoir of discontent. [7]

The Tao-kuang Emperor faced the British in 1839 with a military establishment characterized by decentralization and divided responsibility and designed more to minimize the chances of armed rebellion [8] than to meet an outsider, especially one equipped with modern weapons. The failure of these sorry forces against the British in the years 1839-42 destroyed the military reputation of the Manchus.[9] It may also have caused native Chinese to work to establish a regime that would make a better showing against the foreigner.

The failure to use force skilfully, one of the surest signs of the regime that invites revolt, of course made more conspicuous the other failures, but, more than this, it brought to prominence the racial issue. To insure domination of their far more numerous Chinese subjects the Manchus of the ruling house had installed a disproportionate number of Manchus in prominent positions in the central government and in the provinces. Thus, in the central government, the proportion of Chinese to Manchus was about one to two, in the provinces not quite as high. Each important Chinese official had a Manchu to assist (or to watch) him. [10] At the same time, the founders of the Manchu rule, to prevent cultural engulfment and preserve Manchu identity, had established separate government examinations for members of their own race, [11] had prohibited intermarriage between Chinese and Manchus, had continued the banner military organization, and had commanded Chinese to wear the queue as a sign of difference and subservience. These were the most prominent of many measures planned to maintain segregation. So long as the Ch'ing dynasty ruled well, the racial bases for Chinese resentment present in such preferential arrangements were not developed, but when failure in the first Anglo-Chinese War highlighted all the other failures, the superior political and social position of the Manchus was provocative of revolt.

By the time of what is known as the first treaty settlement (1842-4), all of the factors set forth above were in full play. [12] In the south, particularly, government officials were confronted with the growing activities of an anti-dynastic secret society called the T'ien-t'i-hui 天地會, the San-ho-hui 三合會, or the Hung-men 洪門, usually translated as the Triad Society. In the 1830's the Triad Society began to make its influence felt from Formosa to Hunan and from Kiangsi to Kwangtung and Kwangsi, with Fukien the center of its greatest activity. The disorders in which the Society participated grew until in 1850 the Triads were in open rebellion in various parts of Kwangtung and Kwangsi. [13]

Meanwhile, local disorders in Yünnan, Hunan, and Kwangsi grew to the point where it was impossible for the local officials to maintain order. Local communities were encouraged to set up their own defense groups against banditry. In 1850, as the troubles in the south were building up to a climax, Min-ning died. His successor and fourth son I-chu, the Hsien-feng Emperor (1851-61), inherited from him the humiliating limitations of the first treaty settlement, an exhausted treasury, and an unhappy empire seething with rebellion. In 1851 in an area north of Hsün-chou, Kwangsi province, the local disorder set in motion a movement that became the great Taiping Rebellion. The scope of the great rebellion was widened through the fact that anti-dynastic groups like the Nien-fei in Shantung and the Triads in the south and along the coast profited from the dynasty's embarrassment. The story of the Rebellion is the record of much of China in the years indicated.

The movement which shook the dynasty to its foundations was led from start to finish by as eccentric a figure as appears in modern Chinese history.

Hung Hsiu-ch'üan, the titular head of the Rebellion, was born in 1814 in the district of Hua-hsien about 30 miles from Canton. [14] His family were members of a self-reliant

Hakka community.[15] Hsiu-ch'üan was the fourth child in a
family of five children, his father Hung Ching-yang being
a farmer. He grew up in extremely simple surroundings devoid of exposure to foreign influences. Hsiu-ch'üan attended school in the village of Kuan-lu-pu in Hua-hsien;
there he showed sufficient promise as a scholar to call
forth the combined efforts of his family to keep him in
school. As with other Chinese boys of his generation,
Hung's ambition was to win an official position through the
government civil service examinations. At the age of thirteen Hung qualified in sub-prefectural (hsien) tests given
for admission to the prefectural examinations. At the age
of sixteen he took the prefectural examinations and failed.
Candidates who failed at the prefectural level were allowed to try the circuit (tao) examinations. Hung appeared for the circuit examinations at Canton in 1833 or 1834,
in 1837, and in 1843, the last time when he was thirty-one,
but was uniformly unsuccessful.[16] In between competitions
he earned his living as a teacher. There was apparently
little chance of his obtaining the government scholarship
and the designation hsiu-ts'ai (talented) that went with
the lowest recognized grade in the official system. Repeated failure at the only process that led to an official
career probably did much toward making Hung a revolutionary.

The form which Hung's revolutionary efforts were to take
was determined by an episode that occurred after his third
failure. During the examinations at Canton in 1833 or
1834 Hsiu-ch'üan heard a foreign Christian evangelist preach
and was given a set of nine Christian tracts written by
Liang A-fa (1789-1855), a Chinese evangelist and a convert
of William Milne, apparently the first ordained Chinese
Protestant minister. At this time, so his cousin reported
years later, Hung simply glanced at the books and put them
away. His failure the following year brought on what seems
to have been a nervous collapse and it was reported that he
was confined to his bed for forty days. Hung later declared that during this illness he had been carried to
heaven and brought before a venerable old man who represented himself to Hung as the Creator of mankind. The old
man complained to Hung that the human race had forgotten
and forsaken him and was worshipping demons or "perverted
spirits" instead. On another occasion Hsiu-ch'üan heard
the venerable old man summon Confucius and reprove him for
having neglected to expound clearly the true doctrine.[17]
Confucius seemed much ashamed and confessed his guilt. The
Heavenly Father, for so the ancient called himself, then
gave Hung a sword with which to exterminate demons and a
seal whereby he could overcome the evil spirits. During

similar sessions he met a middle-aged man whom he heard
called the Elder Brother and identified as Jesus Christ.
The latter instructed him how to kill demons. During the
illness his family remembered hearing Hung shout, "Slay the
demons! Slay the demons!"
When Hung recovered, he displayed added seriousness,
self-control, and dignity. Yet he told his visions to listeners with perfect earnestness, leaving no doubt that he
regarded himself as the recipient of a divine commission.
Hsiu-ch'üan's childhood name was Huo-hsiu 火秀   Jen-k'un
仁坤 was the name given him when he came of age. But after
his visions Hung insisted on being called Hsiu-ch'üan 秀全
(Accomplished and Perfect), a name which he said was conferred upon him by the Heavenly Father.[18] For six years after his illness Hsiu-ch'üan continued to teach in village
schools, moving to his wife's village, Chiu-kuan, about
ten li (one li is about one-third of an English mile) from
Kuan-lu-pu.
In 1843 a cousin of Hung surnamed Li borrowed the Christian tracts that had been given Hsiu-ch'üan in 1836.[19] These
nine tracts bearing the title Ch'üan-shih liang-yen "Good
Words to Admonish the Age" contained translations or summaries of chapters of the Bible and a number of sermons on
texts from Scripture. [20] When he returned the books, Li
called Hung's attention to their unusual contents and impelled him to read the tracts carefully for the first time.
Upon reading the books, Hung came to the conclusion that
the venerable old man of his visions was God the Heavenly
Father and was confirmed in his belief that the man of middle age who had instructed him and assisted him in exterminating demons was Jesus, the Saviour of the World. [21]
The visions were interpreted to mean that Hsiu-ch'üan himself was recognized as the second son of God commissioned
to destroy demons and idols and to bring China back to the
worship of the true God. Hung also learned the rite of
baptism from the tracts. He and his cousin baptized each
other.
At this point Hsiu-ch'üan began to preach his new belief
to members of his family, his friends, and all others who
would listen. Two of the earliest converts were Hung Jen-kan (1822-64), a cousin and Hamberg's informant, and Feng
Yün-shan (1822 ? -52), a distant relative, schoolmate, and
like Hung an unsuccessful scholar-candidate. Soon a number
of the relatives of the three were converts.
A prominent feature of the new faith was its iconoclasm.
Converts threw out the ancestor tablets in their homes,
gave up Buddhist ceremonies at funerals, and took part in
idol-breaking expeditions. Hung lost his teaching position
because he destroyed Confucian tablets and was unable to
live in his native village.

Troubled by native resistance to the destruction of idols in their own village, Hung and Feng became convinced that Hua-hsien was not the place in which to spread their faith. It is likely that even at this early date Hung had secret plans of overturning the Ch'ing dynasty and of founding a new state. Accordingly, in 1844 Feng, Hung, and two others set out to set out to preach in Kwangsi, centering their activities in Tz'u-ku village, Kuei-hsien, in Kuei-p'ing prefecture, where a cousin of Hung surnamed Wang 王 resided. Hung returned to Hua-hsien in the fall of 1844. For the next two years (1845-6) he taught school and wrote a number of religious discourses and poems, some of which were to be incorporated in the canonical literature of the Taiping movement. Meanwhile Feng centered his preaching activities in the area of Tzu-ching-shan or Thistle Mountain, about fifty li north of Kuei-p'ing, Kwangsi. During the next two years he made several thousand converts among the Hakka inhabitants and natives there, and formed a religious society called the God-Worshippers or Pai Shang-ti Hui 拜上帝會

Back in Kwangtung, Hung heard of a foreigner preaching a doctrine in Canton similar to his. Much excited, in February 1847 he made his way to Canton with Jen-kan his cousin There he met an American Southern Baptist missionary, Issachar J. Roberts, who was in charge of a small mission. Roberts listened to Hung's story and accepted him as a prospective Christian. After two months of instruction Hung was unable to support himself in Canton longer and left for home without receiving formal baptism. Thus, the Taiping leader's personal instruction in Christian doctrine was limited to these two months with Roberts. [22]

In June 1847 Hsiu-ch'üan set out for Kwangsi a second time. Upon arriving in the Thistle Mountain area he was overjoyed to find how successful his friend Feng had been in developing the God-Worshippers into a strong movement numbering more than three thousand converts. Its members, however, began to get into trouble with the local gentry over the results of several idol-breaking expeditions and the spread of what the learned class called unorthodox (i.e. anti-Confucian) teaching. Reports were made by the gentry to local officials denouncing the God-Worshippers as Hui-fei 會匪 or members of secret societies banded together for seditious purposes. Feng himself and Lu Liu, one of his followers, were under arrest for a time. Lu died in captivity before trial; Feng was tried and banished to Kwangtung, but on the way to banishment converted his guards and succeeded in returning to Thistle Mountain, there to continue his work in secret. The imprisonment of Feng and Lu was a unifying experience for the God-Worshippers,

hardening their hate of the dynasty and inclining them
toward positive political action. Meanwhile Hung in the
early part of 1848 sought vainly in Kwangtung for help in
getting his friend released. Returning for the third
time to Kwangsi, he discovered that Feng had been freed;
the two then went back to Hua-hsien to preach and carry on
organizing activity. It is significant that when Hung
Ching-yang, the father of Hsiu-ch'üan, died in 1848, none
of the usual Buddhist rites or ceremonies dictated by popular superstition were performed. The funeral service consisted of the God-Worshippers' version of Christian ceremonies and a prayer. 23

In May of 1849 Hung and Feng returned together to
Kwangsi, the fourth and last time for the two of them. Up
to this point the God-Worshippers had been primarily a
religious group with Hsiu-ch'üan as the oracle and titular
leader and Feng Yün-shan as the organizer. But due to the
oppression of poverty-stricken peasants by landlords and
tax collectors, and on account of great famines in south
China in 1847 and 1849, numbers of bandits appeared, especially in the mountainous province of Kwangsi. Presently
it was impossible for the local officials to maintain order.
Accordingly, local groups organized their own militia. The
God-Worshippers were primarily a religious group but organized themselves to give protection to give protection
to their own members. The superior security their organization afforded was attractive to outsiders, especially
to persecuted Hakkas. There was accordingly a steady
growth in the numbers of the God-Worshippers. The organization first attracted official attention when its aims were
still primarily religious because its persistent iconoclasm
brought its members into conflict with the authorities.
But when it began to evidence political aims as well, then
Chinese were attracted to it who were interested in rebellion against the government for reasons of thwarted ambition, agrarian discontent, or deep-seated hatred of the
Manchus. Before long some members of the secret anti-Manchu Triad Society, a group which aimed to restore the
Ming dynasty, asked to join.

It is probable that as early as 1844 Hung and Feng felt
that it was necessary to overthrow the Ch'ing dynasty in
order to carry out the Heavenly Father's instructions.
Their first public efforts followed religious lines. But
when disorder in Kwangsi grew and official opposition developed, the movement began to take on military and political aspects too. Leaders of each religious congregation
--men with education, military ability, or property--were
formed into a directing nucleus for that community. They
in turn were directed by one of five other chiefs who with

Hung constituted the guiding leadership of the Rebellion. The master plan for the revolt to come was drawn up by Hsiu-ch'uan in concert with these five: Feng Yün-shan, already referred to; Yang Hsiu-ch'ing (d. 1856), a community leader among the charcoal burners of the Thistle Mount area with unusual ability as a military commander; Hsiao Ch'ao-kuei (d. 1852), brother-in-law of Hung, a wood-cutter and native of Wu-hsüan; Wei Ch'ang-hui (d. 1856), an educated Hakka (actually a tsui-li or petty official) and a native of Chin-t'ien, the village where the Rebellion started; and Shih Ta-k'ai (1821 or 1831-1863), a rich Hakka farmer from Kuei-p'ing-hsien. All except Feng came from Kwangsi. Shih Ta-k'ai and Wei Ch'ang-hui were landowners; indeed two of the lesser Taiping leaders, Wu K'o-i and Hu I-kuang, were quite wealthy.

The six principal leaders set about the organizing and equipping of an army. A table of organization was introduced employing military titles of the Chou-li (Rites of Chou), a Confucian classic. A system of military law was established prescribing regular religious observances and a stern moral code, most infractions of which were punishable by death. God-Worshippers were required to dispose of all of their property, the proceeds of which were put at the disposal of a separate department of the headquarters called the Sacred Treasury or Sheng-k'u 聖库. Tools and farm implements were made into arms. Money that was collected was used to buy iron which was smelted with charcoal from Thistle Mountain. Gunpowder was made near the charcoal ovens. The arms-making went on in earnest after the release from prison of Feng Yün-shan.[24] Flags, insignia, and provisions were all collected or prepared in secret. Chin-t'ien in the Thistle Mountain area was designated as the general headquarters.

Two methods of improving the morale of the God-Worshipper assigned to military duties deserve mention. First, soldiers who risked death were told that all who died in battle would go to heaven.[25] Then, liberal use came to be made of the "descent" from heaven, a practice that did not originate in the visions of Hung and that was not part of the quasi-Christianity taught by Feng to the original congregations of God-Worshippers.[26] The practice began in 1848 when Yang Hsiu-ch'ing and Hsiao Ch'ao-kuei claimed to have been the mouthpieces for communications from God the Heavenly Father and the Heavenly Elder Brother Jesus. The descents of God and Jesus continued to occur during the years that followed whenever the military situation became critical. Hung himself admitted the validity of the descents. The record of divine pronouncements on these occasions was made one of the official books of the rebels, the "T'ien-ming chao-chih-shu"(Book of Heavenly Decrees and Imperial Edicts).

The Story of the Rebellion 17

In the summer of 1850 people of all types began to come to Chin-t'ien, the designated headquarters, to enrol in the movement, to be taught the religion of the God-Worshippers, and then to be drilled and receive military instruction. Orders were sent out for the assembly of all the believers and their families at Chin-t'ien in June of 1850. Each family of God-Worshippers was then obligated to dispose of its real and movable property and make its way to Chin-t'ien, a process necessarily slow. The assembling of the insurgents went on till the winter of 1850. After considerable argument Yang was appointed over Feng as the military commander-in-chief and second in authority to Hung himself. As the God-Worshippers arrived at Chin-t'ien, they were organized into military units and received flags, clothing, and food. Women were formed into groups like the men and strict separation of the sexes became the rule. Members of the insurgent groups were ordered to let their hair grow and to bind and cover it with a red cloth. In this practice lay the origin of the government's name for the rebels, Ch'ang-mao-tsei 長毛賊 or "Long-haired Bandits." Not less than ten thousand armed and organized God-Worshippers are believed to have been assembled at Chin-t'ien at this time.

Repressive measures on the part of the authorities against general lawlessness in Kwangsi began while the God-Worshippers were assembling. Though the Ch'ing court had the reports of the provincial governor on the gathering, it did not know the character of the insurgents nor their plans. Its initial aims were only to put down banditry and combat the activities of organized secret societies. So Hsiang Jung and Chang Pi-lu, the provincial commanders-in-chief of Hunan and Yünnan (Chang commanded Kweichow troops), were ordered to assist Min Cheng-feng, the commander-in-chief of Kwangsi, who by July 1850 was unable to restore order in his own province. Lin Tse-hsü was made high commissioner in over-all command and ordered to Kwangsi from Fukien, but died en route in November.

Given the circumstances, incidents between Ch'ing soldiery and armed groups of God-Worshippers were bound to occur and occur they did, the first in October 1850. These incidents were followed by an imperialist attempt to cut off a number of God-Worshippers who were trying to reach Chin-t'ien from Hua-chou in P'ing-nan hsien where Hung, Feng, and other leaders were in hiding. This move unintentionally placed the lives of Hung and Feng in jeopardy. It provoked a successful rescue expedition, celebrated by the Taipings as the fu-chu 扶主 (rescue the leader) incident. The Manchu soldiers retaliated with a direct attack against the whole Taiping host the latter part of December

1850. The rebels were completely victorious in repelling this assault. On the following January 11, 1851, the victory was celebrated in a public ceremony of prayer and thanksgiving. On this occasion Hung formally proclaimed himself the T'ien-wang 天王 or Heavenly King, calling his new state the T'ai-p'ing t'ien-kuo 太平天國 or Heavenly Kingdom of Great Peace. The other five chiefs were given the title of chu-chiang 主將 or commanding general. Yang Hsiu-ch'ing became the Commander-in-chief and Commanding General of the Central Army, Hsiao Ch'ao-kuei the Second Commander-in-chief and Commanding General of the Advance Army, Feng Yün-shan the Deputy Commander-in-chief and Commanding General of the Rear Army, Wei Ch'ang-hui Second Deputy Commander-in-chief and Commanding General of the Army of the Left, and finally Shih Ta-k'ai simply Commanding General of the Army of the Right. Later other chiefs were named ministers, supervisors, commanders, and so on in a regularly constituted military hierarchy. 27

After the ceremony the Taiping host moved out of Chint'ien to seize Chiang-k'ou-hsü, an important market town. The initial victories of the rebels now began to attract leaders of secret societies, who came to Chiang-k'ou-hsü with their followers. Though anxious for reinforcements and willing to enrol any who would help them, Taiping leaders soon learned to suspect the reliability of allies coming from the secret societies. It was decided that members of the Triad Society would not be allowed to join unless they agreed to obey the T'ien-wang, to follow Taiping military regulations, and to subscribe to the religion of the God-Worshippers. Such conditions were too strict for all but a few of the secret society leaders. Two of them, however, found Taiping discipline attractive and joined the insurgents with their followers. One of these was a woman Su San-niang who remained with the movement and acquired the title "Heroine of the Heavenly Dynasty." The other was Lo Ta-kang (d. 1856), a pirate and native of Chieh-yang, Kwangtung; Lo rose to the rank of minister and was at one time Taiping commander at Chinkiang. Nevertheless, collaboration between the Triads and the Taipings as separate entities was impossible. Basic differences in attitudes toward morals, polytheistic practices, and the restoration of the Ming dynasty could not be overcome. Hung intended, of course, to found a new dynasty, not to restore the Ming rulers.

The subsequent course of the Rebellion must be told in much more shortened form.

From the seizure of Chiang-k'ou-hsü at the end of 1850 till March 19, 1853, when occurred the spectacular capture

The Story of the Rebellion 19

of Nanking, the rebel army, steadily growing in size,
fought its way northward into and through Hunan to the
Yangtze and then proceeded by water and by land eastward.
The Ch'ing leaders developed very early a tactic that was
followed during much of the Rebellion, particularly when
the government troops lacked the unified direction, morale,
and sheer fighting ability of their opponents. Once the
rebels had taken a city, they were encircled bit by bit,
the imperialists avoiding battle and fortifying as they
went. When encirclement was complete, a regular siege commenced in which the besieged were greatly outnumbered.
When the Taiping army ran out of supplies, it usually
staged a successful sortie, and then moved out to try its
luck in a new locality. The same process was then repeated, sometimes as a siege of besiegers when the Taipings found a walled city they could not take. The government tactic was referred to as "sitting warfare 坐戰之法."
Until the importation of Mongol tribesmen to defend the
capital and the development of provincial Chinese militia
later in the Rebellion, it was probably the only effective
military effort that government troops were able to make.
 The first walled town to fall to the insurgents was
Yung-an in Kwangsi, which was taken September 25, 1851. The
rebels were besieged in Yung-an for over half a year. Here
a rearrangement of Taiping organization and ranks took place
and the official calendar was promulgated making the year
1851 the first year of the new dynasty. At this time the
title wang 王 (prince, king) was given to each of the five
principal military leaders previously mentioned. Thus,
Yang became the Eastern King, Hsiao the Western King, Feng
the Southern King, Wei the Northern King, and Shih the
Assistant King. Government accounts say that a rebel leader called Hung Ta-ch'üan, a co-sovereign with the Heavenly
King under the title King of Heavenly Virtue 天德王 , was
captured at Yung-an and executed in Peking after inditing a
"confession." In the light of recent evidence it is likely
that the so-called King of Heavenly Virtue was a Triad
chieftain from Hunan named Chiao Liang, who was in Yung-an
at the time of the Taiping sortie from the city. 28 In his
confession Chiao, possibly to exalt his own position and
deflect blame, told the government leaders that he was a
Taiping.
 The Taipings suffered the loss of two of the original six
wangs before they reached the Yangtze. Feng Yün-shan lost
his life when the rebels ran into an ambush set for them by
Hunanese militia at So-i ford several miles northeast of
Ch'üan-chou, Kwangsi province. This occurred in June 1852.
In October of the same year Hsiao Ch'ao-kuei died of wounds
received before Changsha. The first loss was the more serious because Feng, the preacher and original organizer, was
perhaps the most level-headed of the wangs.

The rebel capture of Nanking March 19, 1853 was followed by the decision to make that city the Taiping capital, possibly because of its situation on the main water artery of China and its past role as a capital. The following month expeditions were launched to the north and to the west. At the same time, the imperialists in characteristic fashion established the great camps of Chiang-nan and Chiang-pei near Nanking to harass its occupants and hamper the free movement of trade.

The rebel conquest of the Yangtze valley occurred at a time when British and American officials were becoming exasperated by the conduct of Manchu officials who sought to evade observance of the treaties of 1842-4, particularly as they applied to the opening of trade. Favorable reports that reached Shanghai of the vigor and discipline of the insurgents and of the Christian character of their religious beliefs indicated that more cooperation might be expected from them than from Ch'ing officials. The French, less trustful of the rebels than the English or the Americans, were anxious to make arrangements for the protection of Catholics who were in rebel-occupied territory. Consequently, some four official visits to Nanking occurred between April 1853 and July 1854; two were English, one French, and one American.[29] The American Commissioner McLane was even prepared to grant recognition to the new government. The reception accorded the representatives of the foreign governments showed that the Taiping leaders expected of foreigners the same sort of subservient behavior insisted upon by the Manchus in the days before the first Anglo-Chinese War. There was complete failure to appreciate the strategic possibilities inherent in collaboration with the foreigner. The official missions, none of which saw Hung Hsiu-ch'üan, were told that they were expected to show respect to the Heavenly King and their allegiance to the Taiping religion was demanded. The hoped-for trade privileges were not secured. The opportunity thus missed did not reoccur. During the rest of a decade that saw stubborn imperial resistance to the fulfillment of the treaties at Canton and the second Anglo-Chinese War, the foreigners gave no direct help to the Taipings who were fighting the same opponents.

From 1853 to 1856 the insurgents with their headquarters at Nanking continued to be led by the wangs that had participated in the original activities of the God-Worshippers.[30] There was, however, the growth about each such leader of a court and a personal retinue that eventuated in bitter rivalry. A faction led by Yang Hsiu-ch'ing opposed another faction headed by Hung Hsiu-ch'üan. Yang became the victim

The Story of the Rebellion   21

of inflated pretensions to the point where he dared to reproach the Heavenly King for moral laxity.

The Taiping leaders, though determining to make Nanking their capital, lost no time in organizing an expedition to take Peking itself. E.C.Bridgman was told in 1854 at the time of the visit of the "Susquehannah" that this "Northern Expedition" was the northern arm of a pincers movement intended for the eventual capture of Szechwan.[31] Led by two of the best Kwangsi veterans, Li K'ai-fang and Lin Feng-hsiang, this "Northern Expedition" found itself blocked by imperialist troops from proceeding directly to the north through Shantung, but eventually reached the province in which the capital was located by crossing the Yellow River somewhat west of K'ai-feng and entering Chihli from the southwest via Shansi. By October Lin and Li were at Shen-chou, only 200 miles south of Peking. The Manchu court summoned for its defence the redoubtable Mongol Seng-ko-lin-ch'in, Sheng-pao, and others who blocked rebel progress directly northward. Nevertheless, the Taiping generals were in the suburbs of Tientsin by the end of October 1853. The frightened Manchu emperor made preparations to move from Peking to Jehol and ordered that provincial tribute be sent to him there.[32] This was the high water mark of the Rebellion. The small numbers of the insurgents (who when they crossed the Yellow River numbered no more than 20,000), the growing skill and superior numbers of their opponents, the failure of reinforcements to reach them, and, as southerners, the severe North China climate, were factors that could not be overcome. A contributory cause for their defeat was the Taiping lack of trained cavalry, a necessity for success against the Mongolian horsemen of the Ch'ing emperors on the plains of North China. Lin and Li held out with separated and small forces till their capture the first part of 1855 in Shantung. But the rebels were never again a military threat to Peking.

While the "Northern Expedition" was under way, a second expedition, perhaps the southern arm of the pincers, was despatched to the west to secure important cities along the Yangtze, some of which had been retaken by the imperialists after the Taiping passage through them to the siege of Nanking. This expedition was successful in taking possession of Yangtze cities like Anking and Kiukiang and in recapturing Wuchang. The Taipings defeated their greatest opponent Tseng Kuo-fan at Yo-chou in Hunan and were for a short time in possession of Hsiangtan, one of the main cities for overland trade with Canton. Nanchang, the capital of Kiangsi province, was besieged without success nor did the rebels ever take Changsha, capital of Hunan. Hanyang, Hankow, and Wuchang were the object of repeated capture and recapture, for the rebels here as elsewhere seemed wanting in ability to garrison or in other respects to retain the cities they seized. Beginning with 1854, the Taipings found themselves up against a new type of provincial militia from Hunan led by the scholar-official Tseng Kuo-fan. The latter had some success with a flotilla only to have his vessels bottled up and then destroyed on Poyang Lake. During the years 1853-56 rebel activity of the kind described was incessant in the Yangtze provinces west of Nanking, with the Assistant King, Shih Ta-k'ai, playing a prominent role.

A struggle for power, connected with the pretensions of Yang Hsiu-ch'ing and his rivalry with Wei Ch'ang-hui and Shih Ta-k'ai, threw the Taiping capital into confusion during September 1856 and proved to be a turning point in the course of the Rebellion. Alarmed at Yang's attempts to usurp his position, Hung Hsiu-ch'üan, the Heavenly King, ordered the other two wangs to assassinate Yang. When Yang was dead, Wei attempted to murder Shih and in turn acquired such pretensions that he too had to be killed by Hung's order. At this point Hung decided to reserve positions of importance in the government for his near relatives. Shih Ta-k'ai was shorn of his military powers, and, as a consequence, left the court with a large following to lead his own anti-Manchu movement through eight of the provinces of southern and western China until his final apprehension and execution in 1863.

After 1856 the main Taiping body felt the effect not only of this internal discord and the withdrawal of the gifted Shih Ta-k'ai, but also of the advancement of the elder brothers and cousins of Hung who took the place of the original wangs. Of these the best educated was Hung Jen-kan. Jen-kan had not gone to Chin-t'ien in 1850 and was separated from the rebels until 1859, spending much of the intervening time in Hongkong and Shanghai in the employ of Western missionaries. When Jen-kan rejoined his cousin Hsiuch'üan in 1859, the Nanking nepotism was in operation. He was given at once the title Kan Wang or Shield King and was quickly made prime minister, so quickly in fact as to earn the resentment of the military leaders. Later, he was minister of foreign affairs and in the last weeks of the Nanking resistance regent. [33] Jen-kan suggested religious and political reforms of a Western type and made efforts to improve relations with the treaty powers, but he was not strong enough to prevail upon Hung Hsiu-ch'üan.

Hung Hsiu-ch'üan himself never assumed the active direction of affairs, even in times when Nanking was seriously threatened. He remained the abstracted spiritual and titular leader, preferring the life of palace and harem to any other—a situation far different from the universally

The Story of the Rebellion

observed segregation of the sexes during the first years of the Rebellion. Military affairs were assigned to the direction of the able commanders Ch'en Yü-ch'eng and Li Hsiu-ch'eng. Li eventually became commander-in-chief. The years following the disruptive events of 1856 saw the elevation of hundreds of new wangs; Ch'en became the Brave King and Li the Loyal King.

Taiping military activities after 1856 were mainly defensive and took on increasingly an air of desperation. The expansive force of the movement had spent itself. The rebels fought bravely, knowing that they could expect no quarter, but the rise to leadership of Tseng Kuo-fan, his brother Kuo-ch'üan, Li Hung-chang, and Tso Tsung-t'ang and the growing effectiveness of provincial militia steadily constricted them. Li and Ch'en continued to win victories and capture cities, but their prowess could not compensate for Hung's failure to provide a productive economic base for the regime.

The years 1856 to 1860 saw imperialist armies pressing in toward Nanking. In December 1857 the Taipings lost the key cities of Kuo-chou and Chinkiang in northern Kiangsu to the east of Nanking and then in the spring of 1858 the imperialists who had been forced to retire from Nanking in August 1856 were able to re-establish their Great Camp and attack the Taiping capital again. Meanwhile, in May 1858 Tseng Kuo-fan's forces recovered Kiukiang (on the Yangtze west of Nanking near the entrance to Poyang Lake). These successes called forth the utmost efforts at diversion on the part of Li Hsiu-ch'eng and Ch'en Yü-ch'eng. The Taiping tactic accomplished the desired result in the conclusive defeat of the main body of Nanking's besiegers in May 1860. Nanking was freed from imperial besiegers until the appearance of Tseng Kuo-ch'üan.

Li was then free to turn his attention to the coastal areas of southern Kiangsu and northern Chekiang where rich possibilities for constructing an economic base for the Taiping regime were believed to exist. So, following the relief of Nanking, Li's troops proceeded to seize Changchow (May 1860) and Soochow (June 1860), and to threaten Shanghai itself. In attempting to capture Shanghai, Li had counted on the cooperation of its Western residents. The Western powers were at this time attempting to secure ratification of the Treaties of Tientsin. An Anglo-French attempt to force the forts at Taku had been repulsed and forces were being gathered that were in August to overcome Chinese resistance and occupy Tientsin and Peking. Nevertheless, Western representatives at Shanghai, fearful for their trade, decided to resist the Taipings. An imperialist force aided by a group of adventurers under the leadership of the American Frederick T. Ward, and in the pay of the local government of Shanghai, repulsed the rebels.[34] Li withdrew westward from the Soochow-Shanghai area, probably to enroll a large number of volunteers who were awaiting him in Kiangsi and Hupeh.

Li's armies campaigned in Kiangsi, Hupeh, and southern Anhwei for better than a year until fear of being bottled up led their commander to withdraw into Chekiang. Here he seized a number of cities, among them Hangchow and Ningpo (both December 1861), and then proceeded to devote his attention to the conquest of Shanghai and cities in its neighborhood. As on a similar occasion two years before, Westerners had cooperated with imperialists in repelling the Taiping assault, but this time imperialist forces and Ward's "Ever Victorious Army" were aided by British and French troops, some of which had seen duty against the Manchus in the Tientsin area. What amounted to international action on the part of the British was sanctioned by orders to protect an area within a radius of thirty miles from Shanghai.[35] The allied forces battled the rebels during the first five months of 1862 for the possession of cities in the vicinity of Shanghai. By June 1862 Li had the better of the fighting and was on the point of taking Sungchiang, south of Shanghai, when urgent messages from Hung Hsiu-ch'üan recalled him to the relief of Nanking, again beleaguered.

This time the Taiping capital was besieged by Tseng Kuo-ch'üan, who encamped before its walls at the end of May 1862. Kuo-ch'üan had succeeded after a prolonged struggle in overthrowing Anking (Sept. 5, 1861), the important capital of Anhwei province. In this reverse the Taipings also lost one of their best generals Ch'en Yü-ch'eng, who was pursued and died the following year. The fall of Anking led directly to the investment of Nanking.

When Li returned to the Nanking area, fifty-six days of furious attacks failed to dislodge the determined imperialists and the Taiping commander-in-chief again resorted to diversionary tactics. But now the imperialist forces were formidable, the countryside would not support Li's troops, nor could Tseng Kuo-ch'üan be lured away from Nanking. Efforts to reduce the imperialist bases of Anking and Yangchow failed and it was necessary for Li to come back to Nanking in 1863 to succor Hung and his followers within the walls. Meanwhile, the other two bases of Taiping activity, Soochow and Hangchow, were menaced by Li Hung-chang and Tso Tsung-t'ang. The latter part of 1863 Li Hsiu-ch'eng did his best to persuade Hung Hsiu-ch'üan to lead the Taipings in a general withdrawal from the Nanking area, but the latter, invoking Divine Providence, refused to leave the Heavenly Capital or to lay in adequate supplies. In the fall of the

The Story of the Rebellion 25

same year Li left Nanking to relieve Soochow, then besieged by forces under Li Hung-chang and by the "Ever-Victorious Army." In March 1863 the latter came under the command of Charles George Gordon, a British officer loaned to the imperialists.[36] Li had to retire to Nanking without raising the siege. In March 1864 Hangchow was taken by the imperialist Tso Tsung-t'ang with French help.[37] This meant a concentration upon Nanking, the remaining Taiping base. The rebel defenders were under constant attack and were finally starved out. The end came July 19, 1864 after Tseng's troops had undermined the city walls and the Heavenly King had died. Although thousands of the rebels were then slaughtered by Tseng's troops, none surrendered. Li Hsiu-ch'eng, Hung Jen-kan, and Hung Hsiu-ch'üan's fifteen year old son escaped but were soon captured and executed. Taiping remnants made their way to Kwangtung where they were overcome by February of 1866. Thus ended the Rebellion.

The role played by the various foreign powers in the suppression of the Rebellion has been both magnified and minimized. Probably foreign action would not have occurred had the rebels not menaced the coastal ports. It is evident that the rebel forces in the Shanghai area could not withstand accurate rifle and musket fire or shell-fire from foreign artillery and naval vessels.[38] Whether it was Ward's irregulars, the British regulars within a thirty mile radius of Shanghai, or the Franco-Chinese force that captured Hangchow, the possession of Western arms and training meant victory for the bombarding or assaulting force. Without the foreign determination to defend the treaty ports in the years 1860-63 it seems clear that the Taipings could have had all of Kiangsu south of the Yangtze River. Its resources and control of the mouth of the Yangtze could have prolonged the Rebellion, but it is doubtful that the final outcome could have been different.

In a very real sense the British decision to defend Shanghai was an outcome of the bankruptcy of the Taiping policy and methods. Despite a much more considerate rebel attitude than had characterized rebel-British contacts in 1853 and 1854, British leaders in China were convinced as early as the spring of 1861 that trade was utterly ruined wherever the Taipings gained control.[39] The rebels were permitted to hold Ningpo from December 1861 until May 1862, an experiment that strengthened this conviction. The British came to the conclusion that an area around each foreign settlement had to be made free from Taiping disturbance to provide food for the treaty ports and to absorb Western goods. Also, British leaders realized by the 1860's that the rebels were not winning the support of the Chinese people, that they had the opposition of the scholar-gentry, the traditional leader class, and that they could never operate a civil government. From this conclusion grew a second conviction, that the sooner the Manchu government could master its corruption, train up a new generation of civil servants, and build an army on the Western model, the better for China and for Western trade. In this view, the insurgents were hardly more than a symptom of Manchu weakness. The French cooperated with naval and land contingents. The Americans were sympathetic, but could not offer more material support because their armed forces had been withdrawn for the American Civil War.

British leaders strove to achieve their aim by permitting their regular forces to clear an area about Shanghai, and then by lending officers like Gordon to train and command Chinese who were armed with Western weapons. These Western-led Chinese who made up the mass of the "Ever Victorious Army" cooperated with the imperialist forces. The British tried consciously to serve Manchu purposes as little as they could help and to return to a neutral position as soon as possible. [40] For example, permission for Gordon and others to continue to serve the imperialist cause was withdrawn several months before the fall of Nanking. [41] The "Ever Victorious Army" itself was mustered out in May 1864 and did not participate in the siege of Nanking. Foreign action in the 1860's was thus a step which might have been reversed had the Taiping performance in civil affairs equalled its military record.

Considering the limited education of the Taiping leaders, the political and economic system they planned to establish showed a great deal of creative ingenuity. [42]

The Taiping government was designed to be a theocracy with the Heavenly King as both a spiritual and a temporal ruler. The original five wangs and a hierarchy of officials beneath them had both civil and military duties. The Taiping military organization was used for political and social purposes as well. Soldiers were expected to be farmers.

The smallest social unit was the family. The lowest social group over which officials took responsibility was a unit of twenty-five families. All affairs, judicial, military, social, or religious, occurring within this larger unit were managed by an officer called <u>liang-ssu-ma</u>. The <u>liang-ssu-ma</u> could refer troublesome decisions to a hierarchy of officials ending in the Heavenly King himself. Officers such as the <u>liang-ssu-ma</u> were recruited by civil service examinations given every year. The Taiping examination essays we have do not show a high standard of performance.

The Taiping leaders planned to divide land under their control into nine grades and to distribute this equitably among the people with no distinction made between men and women. The effort was made to give each family an equal amount of desirable and undesirable land. Individuals under fifteen received half of the allotment for adults. Each person in addition to farming was required to pursue a special occupation such as raising poultry or making clothing. Products of farming or of these side-lines left over after basic personal needs were satisfied had to be turned into the public treasury. The contents of the public treasury were for the people of the whole empire. In time of famine the surplus from areas where there was a good harvest would support famine areas. The rebel land system may well have been influenced by agrarian conditions in South China when the Rebellion began.

The evidence available seems to show that the political organization of the Taipings was carried out, but that only a beginning was made at putting the land system into operation. It is suggested, with reason, that the warfare which featured every year of the Rebellion made impossible the taking of a land census and the undisturbed and impartial distribution of land. There was never the opportunity to establish a civilian state.

The Taiping leaders enforced rigidly certain rules for the maintenance of commerce, but they shared the usual Chinese low opinion of the merchant and made no plans for adding to their wealth through trade. Though their capital was on the Yangtze, the greatest waterway of China, and though foreign firms were eager to buy the tea and silk from areas which the rebels sometimes held, the Taiping leaders, despite an urgent need for foreign arms, were unaware of trade possibilities or unable to exploit them.

Taiping discipline and their equalitarian treatment of women were unusual. Women could hold equal civil and military positions with men. Foot-binding was forbidden. Marriage was a matter for arrangement by the individuals concerned. But at the same time the sexes were segregated. The higher evaluation of female personality (and also the segregation of the sexes) may have reflected the treatment accorded women worshippers by Roberts and by missionaries whom Hung Jen-kan saw in Hongkong. The Taipings enforced rules against idols, and against the use of opium, alcohol, and even tobacco into the last years of the regime. The internal discipline, particularly of the veteran rebels, persisted until the last.

Writers on the Rebellion have accounted for its _failure_ in a number of ways. [43] _It is believed that the rebels lost their great chance for success in 1853 when they did not concentrate their full power upon taking Peking._ Foreign intervention could have been avoided by not attacking Shanghai. The promised social reforms were not carried out. A serious source of failure was the corruption which developed among the wangs at the top. Hung and Yang set bad examples, eventuating, as has been shown, in the disastrous murders of 1856. After this the leaders lost their revolutionary character and succumbed to nepotism and sectionalism. From the first the movement suffered from a lack of educated trained leaders, a lack made worse by the events of 1856. Education and training were the monopoly of the Chinese gentry class whom the Taipings were seeking to overturn and who from the earliest idol-breakings on were their sworn enemies. Though it possessed many improvements, the Taiping program could not be carried through with the leadership obtainable.

In this study I expect to show how the nature of the Christian borrowing reveals the ingenuity of the rebels but at the same time their failure at leadership.

Footnotes.

1. General contemporary accounts in English either center attention on the first years of the Rebellion or upon the period after 1860 when Frederick Townsend Ward and Charles George Gordon aided in its suppression. Useful books on the earlier period have been the following: J.C. Callery and M. Yuan, History of the Insurrection in China, translated by John Oxenford (London, 1854); Thomas Taylor Meadows, The Chinese and their Rebellions (London, 1856); W.H.Medhurst, The Chinese Insurgents at Nanking; to Which Is Added a History of the Kwangse Rebellion (Shanghai, 1853); John Scarth, Twelve Years in China: The People, the Rebels, the Mandarins (Edinburgh, 1860); Henry Vizetelly, The Chinese Revolution: the Causes Which Led to it, etc. (London, 1853). Short summaries of the whole Rebellion by present-day scholars, based on contemporary works, may be found as follows: K.S.Latourette, The Chinese Their History and Culture (New York: MacMillan, 1947), 354-62; H.F.MacNair, Modern Chinese History: Selected Readings (Shanghai, 1923), 328-76. Special mention is reserved for W.J.Hail, Tseng Kuo-fan and the Taiping Rebellion (New Haven: Yale University Press, 1927) and for the biographies of Taiping and government leaders of the period by Teng Ssu-yü in Arthur W. Hummel, ed., Eminent Chinese of the Ch'ing Period (Washington: U.S.Govt. Printing Office, 1943-4). Chinese interest over the last two decades has produced a number of general surveys, the titles of which appear in the bibliographical appendix.

2. Hsieh Pao-chao, The Government of China (1644-1911) (Baltimore: Johns Hopkins Press, 1925), 31-4; J.K.Fairbank and S.Y.Teng, "On the Types and Uses of Ch'ing Documents," Harvard Journal of Asiatic Studies, 5.1 (Jan., 1940), 33-4.

The Story of the Rebellion   29

  3. For biographies of these two rulers see Hummel, Eminent Chinese, II, 965-9; I, 574-6.
  4. Wang Yü-ch'üan, "The Rise of Land Tax and the Fall of Dynasties in Chinese History," Pacific Affairs, IX.2 (June, 1936), 201-20. Hsieh, The Government of China, 195-6.
  5. Hsieh, 105-13. See also Meadows, The Chinese and Their Rebellions, Chap. X, and Hail, Tseng Kuo-fan, Chap. 1. On Nov. 12, 1852 a deliberately sponsored plan was announced for selling offices to raise money for defeating the Taiping rebels. Vizetelly, The Chinese Revolution, 41-3.
  6. ". . . in 1850 there was all over China, but especially in Kwangtung, Kwangsi, Hunan, and other provinces south of the Yangtze River a large population which had everything to gain and nothing to lose by any political disturbance. Nor was it an accident that these provinces, Kwangtung, Kwangsi, Kweichow, and Hupei, which had the highest maximum rates for silver tax on people's land should have been the scene of rebellion." G.E.Taylor, op. cit., XVI.4 (Jan. 1933), 575.
  7. ". . . very many are rejected, in every respect equal to those selected. Where the examiners can see no real difference, they are necessarily guided by fancy or chance . . . ." Meadows, op. cit., 75. Hsieh, 145-83 takes up the system in illuminating detail.
  8. Hsieh, 253-62. Hail, op.cit., Chap. 1.
  9. Chien Yu-wen, T'ai-p'ing chün kuang-hsi shou-i-shih (History of the uprising of the Taiping army in Kwangsi) (Chungking: Commercial Press, 1944), 90-5.
  10. Hsieh, 81, 385.
  11. Karl A. Wittfogel and Feng Chia-sheng, "History of Chinese Society, Liao (907-1125)," Transactions of the American Philosophical Society, 36 (1947), 13.
  12. Meadows, op. cit., 30-3, 121 has an apt summary from the viewpoint of a contemporary.
  13. William Stanton, The Triad Society or Heaven and Earth Association (Shanghai: Kelly and Walsh, 1900), 11.
  14. For the story and chronology of the Rebellion up to the time Taiping armies left Kwangsi, I have relied mainly upon Chien, T'ai-p'ing chün kuang-hsi shou-i-shih, to date the most exhaustive study of the early part of the movement. The source for all accounts of Hung's early experiences and the early history of the Rebellion is the written record of what was told orally by Hung Jen-kan, a distant cousin of the Heavenly King and a fugitive in Hongkong from the Ch'ing soldiery, to the Rev. Theodore Hamberg. See Theodore Hamberg, The Visions of Hung-Siu-Tshuen and Origin of the Kwang-si Insurrection (Hongkong, 1854), translated into Chin-

ese by Chien Yu-wen under the title T'ai-p'ing t'ien-kuo ch'i-i chi; both Chinese and English texts were published together by the Yenching University Library in 1935.
15. The Hakkas or "guest-settlers" were migrants to South China from other provinces to the north. See the paragraph on the Hakkas and the citations given in Teng, New Light, 50-1, 115.
16. Chien, Shou-i-shih, 67, 68, 70, 83. The date for the first of the three circuit examinations that Hung took was earlier than 1836, the date given in the Visions. Basing his conclusions upon a report of the London Missionary Society, Foster believes that the most likely date was August 1834.   John Foster, D.D., "The Christian Origins of the Taiping Rebellion," op. cit., 158.
17. Hung's later recitals of what happened in the course of his visions are more elaborate and mention episodes not included in earlier reports. For example, the "T'ai-p'ing t'ien-jih," published in 1863, relates that God ordered the flogging of Confucius, an episode not mentioned by Hamberg. "T'ai-p'ing t'ien-kuo kuan-shu shih-chung (Ten official documents of the T'ai-p'ing t'ien-kuo)," Kuang-tung ts'ung-shu ti-san chi (Third Kwangtung collectanea) (Canton, 1949), vol. 4, p. 10, 1.7-8 under "T'ai-p'ing t'ien-jih."
18. Chien, op. cit., 96-7.
19. Hamberg, Visions, 14-9.
20. A more meaningful alternative translation is "Wholesome Advice to Persuade the World."
21. I have a suspicion, which I believe is shared by Mr. Teng Ssu-yü, that this part of the story was manufactured. It is more probable that Hung's prior perusal of the pamphlets was more thorough than he would admit and that their reading inspired the visions.
22. For Hung's teacher's version of the episode see I.J.Roberts, untitled article in The Chinese and Missionary Gleaner, October, 1852; Issachar J. Roberts, "Tai Ping Wang," Putnam's Magazine, VIII.xlvi (Oct., 1856), 380-3.
23. Chien, 148.
24. The Wei family from which one of the six leaders came participated prominently in the making of arms. Afraid that the noise of the manufacture of arms would alarm the village population, the Wei family arranged to have some of the families making arms buy and keep geese so as to cover up the sounds of the making of weapons. When finished, the arms were thrown for concealment into a pond outside the village. When they were needed, the arms were recovered from the pond and the story was spread that God had provided them. Chien Yu-wen, Chin-t'ien chih yu chi ch'i t'a (A journey to Chin-t'ien and other articles) (Chungking: Commercial Press, 1944), 45,8 to 46,11.

The Story of the Rebellion					31

25. See S.L. 1.10b, 1 under the title "T'ien-ming chao-chih-shu." For this and other abbreviations of titles of document collections see footnote 1, Chap. 3.
26. Chien, Shou-i-shih, 169. See also Chien, Chin-t'ien chih yu chi ch'i t'a, 30.5-11.
27. See the Taiping army list 太平軍目 in T.S. 2.
28. Teng, New Light, 24, 103.
29. British Parliamentary Papers (hereafter abbreviated P.P.): Sessional Papers Printed by Order of the House of Lords, 1852-3, Papers Respecting the Civil War in China, XXI, 431. These contain the official correspondence and reports relating to the voyage of the "Hermes" to Nanking. A full supplementary account by the commander of the "Hermes" is E.G.Fishbourne, Impressions of China and the Present Revolution, its Progress and Prospects (London, 1854). The French mission of Dec. 1853 is reported in R.P.Mercier, Campagne du "Cassini" dans les Mers de Chine 1851-1854 (Paris, 1889). A record of the visit of the American ship "Susquehannah" to Nanking is contained in 35th Congress, 2d session, Senate executive documents, No. 22, part 1, "Commissioners to China," vol. I, 47-92. Marcy's instructions to McLane to recognize the rebels if he saw fit are in 36th Congress, 1st session, Senate executive documents, no. 39, 3. A report of the visit to Nanking in 1854 of the British ships "Rattler " and "Styx" is in the North-China Herald, 206 (July 8, 1854).
30. For the following summary of events from 1853 to 1864 I have placed main reliance upon the biographies in Hummel of prominent rebel and imperialist leaders by Teng Ssu-yü and upon Teng, New Light, especially pp. 60-70. I have occasionally consulted Kuo T'ing-i, T'ai-p'ing t'ien-kuo shih-shih jih-chih (Day to day records of historical events of the Heavenly Kingdom of Great Peace) (Shanghai: Commercial Press, 1946-47), 2 vols., an indispensable reference work.
31. ". . . (The rebels) said . . . they had four armies in the field. . . . Two of these had gone northward, one along the Grand Canal and one farther westward; they were designed to cooperate, and, after storming and destroying Peking, to turn westward and march through Shansi, Shensi, Kansuh, into Sz'chuen, where they are expected to meet their other two armies, which from Kiangsi and the Lake provinces are to move up the Great River and along through the regions on its southern bank." Letter by E.C.Bridgman, dated July 4, 1854. North-China Herald 208 (July 22, 1854).
32. The period of the "Northern Expedition" saw the Emperor and the court in straitened circumstances. Grain shipments to Peking via the Grand Canal came to an end due

to a shift in the lower course of the Yellow River; thereafter the grain tribute came by sea or was commuted into silver. Harold C. Hinton, "Grain Transport Via the Grand Canal," Papers on China from the Regional Studies Seminars (mimeographed), IV (Harvard University, 1950), 36.

33. So Kwan-wai and Eugene P. Boardman, Hung Jen-kan, Taiping Prime Minister, 1859-64 (unpublished manuscript, University of Wisconsin, 1950), 12-4.

34. For a description of the Taiping attack on Shanghai August 1860 and the total inability of the rebels to stand up to Western arms see P.P. 1861, 66 (2754), Encl. 6 in No. 72, pp. 145-9.

35. The development of the British 30 mile radius policy may be traced in the following: P.P. 1861, 66 (2754), Bruce to Lord John Russell, May 30, 1860, pp. 60, 62; P.P. 1861, 66 (2840), Hope to the Secretary of the Admiralty, April 6, 1861, Encl. 1 in No. 6, pp. 10-11. P.P. 1862, 63 (3058), Correspondence between Vice Admiral Hope and Mr. Bruce, Encl. 1 & 2 in no. 6, pp. 10-11. P.P. 1862, 63 (3058), Bruce to Stavely, April 23, 1862, pp. 24-25.

36. The loaning of British regular officers to the Chinese Emperor to instruct and command mixed forces outside the 30 mile limit became possible through an arrangement whereby the officer concerned was detached from his regiment and received half-pay. His service with the Chinese did not count for promotion. If wounded in such service he was not entitled to a pension or if he was killed, his widow would not receive more than the ordinary pension given to the widow of an officer dying while on half-pay. Regular officers who retained their regimental rank had to keep within the 30 mile limit. P.P. 1862 (3057), "Notice to Officers Volunteering for Service under the Chinese Government," Admiralty, July 12, 1862, p. 5; P.P. 1862, 63 (3057), Paget to Hammond, June 25, 1862, p. 2. Orders in Council allowing British to serve in the Chinese forces are found as follows: British State Papers 52, p. 482; 53, p. 312.

37. W.L.Bales, Tso Tsungt'ang, Soldier and Statesman of Old China (Shanghai: Kelly & Walsh, 1937), 161.

38. See footnote 34.

39. P.P. 1862, 63 (2992), Encl. 8 in No. 2, March 18, 1862, pp. 8-9 describes the danger to imperialist trade in Taiping activities near Shanghai.

40. P.P. 1862, 63 (2976), Encl. 4 in No. 41, p. 117.

41. P.P. 1864, 63 (3408), Encl. in No. 5, De Grey and Ripon to Brown, April 26, 1864, p. 18.

42. Teng, New Light, 82-92 has in convenient form the principal features of the Taiping political and economic system.

43. See ibid., 70-4 for a handy summary of reasons for the failure of the Rebellion.

3

The Taiping Appeal to China

To be successful, a revolutionary movement must persuade as well as overthrow. In common with other historic uprisings the Taiping Rebellion had its case to make to the Chinese people. [1]

The Taiping appeal was put in writing that took several forms. Some of the writings were religious tracts and instructional materials intended for the use of initiates and neophytes but suitable for making converts. Other writings were intended to attract the notice of the outside and are of a non-religious character. These are commonly marked Chao-shu 詔書 (proclamations) or Yü 諭 (edicts). The proclamations and edicts, unlike the religious tracts, were usually not the work of Hung Hsiu-ch'üan but of his subordinate wangs or the military leaders under them. In their more exalted form, edicts were published for a specific occasion by one or more of the principal leaders with Hung's formal approval. For example, the subordinate wangs petitioned Hung, the T'ien-wang, for permission to compose and issue the calendar for each new year. Permission was duly granted and the new calendar was published in the form of a memorial bearing official approval. Yü of more than momentary value seem to have been collected and preserved under the name of Chao-shu. Yü were used by the Taipings to reassure localities after they had been occupied by Taiping troops. They were also employed by the Triads, but in advance of occupation, performing somewhat the modern role of leaflets dropped to a civilian population before an invasion. [2] We have the text of a number of yü of both types, copied from originals and brought to Western missionaries in the treaty ports. [3] The most notable of the Taiping edicts published during the first three years of the Taiping regime were issued in the name of Yang Hsiu-ch'ing, the Eastern King, and his colleague Hsiao, the Western King. These compositions display a quickened and practical spirit bent on turning Hung's theories and visions to immediate ends.

The appeal made to the Chinese can be divided into two elements, the non-religious and the religious. These are usually entwined, no matter what the purpose of a given document. The religious portion of the rebel ideology will be examined at length later. The non-religious part of the Taiping case is in a sense inseparable from the religious element so that a brief discussion of it is necessary to provide the background against which to present the religious element.

The non-religious portion of the Taiping case attacked the Manchu regime on the ground that it was un-Chinese. The Manchu rulers were called usurpers who had seized land and property rightfully belonging to Chinese. They had taken advantage of internal confusion to deprive the Chinese of their empire. 4 Once installed, the foreign dynasty had instituted customs that revealed its unnatural and barbarian nature. Chinese were commanded to shave their heads and wear "a long tail behind, thus causing the Chinese to become animals." 5 The Manchus had forced their Chinese subjects to discard the proper robes and headdress of Chinese dynasties for foreign and outlandish clothing. Chinese laws were changed into un-Chinese enactments and the Chinese spoken language corrupted by the Manchu speech. Thousands of Chinese girls, it was stated, had been forced into defiling intermarriage with their Manchu masters. The Taiping writers summoned patriotic Chinese to assert their manhood and expel their alien rulers.

Taiping leaders had a strong case to submit against the Manchu government on the ground that it was inefficient and corrupt. Allusions were made to conditions that were matters of common knowledge. The government sold shamelessly its scholarly titles and honors. The student without private means, unable to buy the wherewithal for official position, came to feel that study was useless and scholarly offices and titles meaningless. When the rewards of study could be purchased, the position of literature was degraded, they said, and the study of Confucius and Mencius dishonored. Manchu government officials were notorious for avarice and rapacity. Bribes were the price of office, money the price of pardons. There was little hope for the advancement of poor men of talent. Taxes were exorbitant. Through government monopoly, salt, a daily necessity, had risen to one hundred cash per pound. At the same time the government was not doing what it was paid to do. The Manchus could not keep order. They failed to fulfil the traditional responsibilities of governments of China to control floods and provide for famine. Their treatment of Chinese was inequitable. Manchu police and soldiers got double pay, but in battles Manchus were placed in the rear while Chinese were posted in front. There was favoritism in the dispensation of justice.

The Chinese were summoned by the Taipings to support, in place of the alien Manchus, a regime that was led by Chinese and would behave in a Chinese manner--a government which promised to be efficient and to reward merit.

The writers of Taiping tracts made manifest attempts to appear as Chinese in form and in ideas as they could. For example, the third part of one of the principal religious compositions is devoted to amplification of the five relationships mentioned by Mencius. This is done by alluding to the fraternal concern of Christ for his earthly brothers and sisters and at the same time praising the obligations connected with the five relationships as worthy of emulation for their own sake. The writer of this part of the tract makes Christ appear acceptable because he acted in a Chinese manner. [6] In counseling against gambling and avarice Hung Hsiu-ch'üan admonishes his followers to content themselves with what Heaven has sent them. They are to emulate Confucius and Yen who "were happy with a vegetable and water (contained) in gourds and baskets." [7] Another part of the same composition is entitled Songs on the Hundred Instances of Correct Conduct. This abounds in allusions to Chinese historical figures all the way from early Chou to T'ang times. [8] The ideal of correctness which it extols is in entire keeping with Chinese ethical standards. The third part of the "T'ai-p'ing chao-shu," called "Yüan-tao hsing-shih hsün"(Instruction on rousing the world with the basic doctrine), is a discourse on tolerance and international brotherhood. This mentions Confucius and Mencius. It quotes at length from Confucius on the characteristics of an ideal society. [9] In the fourth and last composition of the "T'ai-p'ing chao-shu," the "Yüan-tao chüeh-shih hsün"(Instruction on awakening the world with the basic doctrine), the author quotes from the Book of Songs and Book of History. Extensive use is made of Chinese history to support Taiping arguments against idolatry. [10]

The foregoing are illustrations of the Taiping attempt to anchor in Chinese tradition as many of the new theological and revolutionary ideas as was possible. The Taipings used pre-Confucian tradition and historical references from Ch'in through T'ang times freely, but they appear less certain in their treatment of Confucian teaching. When the Taiping movement started, it was plainly directed against Confucian practices as part of three heretical teachings, Confucianism, Buddhism, and Taoism. Yet there is evidence in the presence of varying texts of the same composition of an attempt to modify an earlier anti-Confucian position. [11]

The writers both of religious tracts and edicts never

tired of pointing out how the Manchus were an alien race. Thi[s]
negative criticism is consistently accompanied by positive
evidences of the rebel possession of Chinese cultural orthodoxy as noted above.

In addition to demonstrating their right to be considered
genuinely Chinese, the Taiping leaders promised their com-
patriots that they would sternly sweep away every vestige of
Manchu influence and punish the Manchus. Then a number of
points were made in connection with an implied promise to improve the government. Taiping troops on the march were subject to standing orders enjoining the considerate treatment
of the Chinese population. The four statements that follow
are from their "Rules for the March":

> "5. Let no officers or soldiers, male or female,
> enter the villages to prepare rice, or take food;
> do not let any injure the dwellings of the people
> or steal property or ransack the apothecary shops
> in the offices of officials in the prefectures and
> districts.
> 6. Let no one impress the outside menials who
> sell tea, water, or rice as coolies . . . .
> 8. Let no one burn the dwellings of the people
> or defecate in the roads or in people's houses.
> 9. Do not wickedly put to death aged and infirm
> coolies." [12]

Prohibitions against the destruction of property failed
significantly to refer to public buildings used for worship.
Taiping leaders promised order to those who were obedient,
asking that at the approach of the rebel armies each person g[o]
about his usual vocation. [13] Further, the pledge was made tha[t]
as soon as Nanking was taken, Yang Hsiu-ch'ing would reform
the literary examinations and select scholars according to
merit. At the same time, property possessed by Buddhist and
Taoist priests and by brothels and gambling houses would be
seized and distributed among the poor people of the vill-
ages. [14] Rules for the redistribution of land as well as
for the new administrative system were set forth in a separate official publication. [15]

The secular part of the Taiping appeal shows considerable
applicability to the situation in which China found herself
in the mid-nineteenth century, but it is evident that insufficient attention was paid to the positive program which
the Heavenly Kingdom of Great Peace was to introduce. Nothing like the processes of discussion and debate before the
great French Revolution, nothing like the talents of Montesquieu or Quesnay, went into the preparation of the Taiping
program. There is conspicuous failure to take account of

the formidable Ch'ing problems and to prepare a program to meet them. The very paucity of rebel speculation about reform foretold an absence of statesmanship and was a portent of failure.

Representative elements of the secular portion of the ideology have been referred to. In addition there are important evidences of Buddhist and Taoist as well as of basic Confucian influences in the religious part of the ideology. To examine these beyond the point reached by Chinese and Western authors requires separate treatment.[16] The same may be said for traces of secret society practices and for Chinese elements antecedent to Confucius.

With the non-Western strains of influence indicated, the main task of this study, an examination of Christian influence upon the ideology of the Rebellion, may now be begun.

Footnotes.

1. Beginning with Chapter 2 frequent references are made to the existing published compilations of Taiping documents. Full entries for these will be found in Chapter 8, but for brevity's sake a glossary of authors and titles, each preceded by an abbreviation, is given below. References to documents in these compilations will give the abbreviation for the title of the compilation, the number of the ts'e or stitched volume, and then the page or pages and line or lines. With all citations the first or right-hand face of a leaf will be indicated by a number only; the letter b will denote the second or left-hand face. For example, S.W.C.1.19b, 9-10 refers the reader to lines 9 and 10 on the second face of leaf 19 in the first volume of the compilation indicated.

Abbreviations for Titles of Published Compilations.

S.L. Ch'eng Yen-sheng, T'ai-p'ing t'ien-kuo shih-liao ti-i chi (First collection of historical materials of the T'ai-p'ing t'ien-kuo).

S.W.C. Lo Yung and Shen Tsu-chi, T'ai-p'ing t'ien-kuo shih wen ch'ao (Anthology of the poetry and prose of the T'ai-p'ing t'ien-kuo).

T.S. Hsiao I-shan, T'ai-p'ing t'ien-kuo ts'ung-shu ti-i chi (First collection of books of the T'ai-p'ing t'ien-kuo).

Y.S. Ling Shan-ch'ing, T'ai-p'ing t'ien-kuo yeh-shih (Non-official history of the T'ai-p'ing t'ien-kuo).

As a further aide to brevity, abbreviations have been devised for the commoner titles of official religious documents. Full entries for the latter will be found in Chapter 8. The abbreviations given below bear no periods to distinguish them from the abbreviations for the titles of published compilations listed above.

Abbreviations for Titles of Taiping Religious Documents.

STC	San-tzu-ching.
TMCCS	T'ien-ming chao-chih-shu.
TPCS	T'ai-p'ing chao-shu.
TPCSK	T'ai-p'ing chiu-shih ko.
TPTJ	T'ai-p'ing t'ien-jih.
TTS	T'ien-t'iao-shu.
YHS	Yu-hsüeh-shih.

2. Mr. Chien Yu-wen is my authority for this statement.

3. The texts of a number of proclamations and edicts exist in English for which there is no Chinese text. Particularly is this true of documents originating during the last years of the Rebellion quoted in A.F.Lindley, Ti-Ping Tien Kwoh--the History of the Ti-Ping Revolution (London, 1866). Lindley's work was translated into Chinese in 1915 under the title Meng Hsien-ch'eng 孟憲承, T'ai-p'ing t'ien-kuo wai-chi 太平天國外紀 (Taiping foreign relations). Excerpts from this are reproduced rather uncritically in the S.W.C. To eliminate the more dubious evidence, in this chapter documents for which there is no Chinese original are disregarded, whether there be a subsequent Chinese translation or not. The titles and sources of these excluded documents are listed for further reference in Chapter 8.

4. A reference to the invitation of Wu San-kuei to the Manchu regent Dorgon to give aid against the rebel Li Tzu-ch'eng. The Manchus used their victory over Li in 1644 to establish the Ch'ing dynasty with Peking as the capital. Hummel, 877-8.

5. A reference to the queue. From "Feng-t'ien t'ao-hu hsi pu ssu-fang yü" 奉天討胡檄布四方諭 (Edict received from heaven to punish the Tatars and publish the order everywhere S.W.C. 1.33.1 and S.L. 1.4b,9 under this title. The entire document is reproduced in Chapter 8.

6. "(God) repeatedly sent his own son down into this world. He swept away and destroyed the fiends . . . he saved all (his) brothers and sisters. (Therefore) sincerity and filial feeling should be displayed." T.S. 4.9,4 ff. under the title "Chiu-shih ko."

The Taiping Appeal

7. S.L. 2.3,12, under the title TPCS from the composition "Yüan-tao chiu-shih-ko." Yen refers to Yen Hui, favorite disciple of Confucius.

8. This part contains conspicuous reference to Confucius, who "converted 3000 and then used correct doctrines to transform the incorrect." S.W.C. 1.12,12. The entire ode appears in S.W.C. 1.12, 8-8b and S.L. 2.4,3-4b,4. T.S. 1 reproduces other parts of the TPCS but fails to include the "Pai-cheng ko."

9. S.L. 2.5b,1-4 under TPCS; S.W.C. 1.13b, 8-12. T.S. 1.5b,4-7,8 reproduces this document but all references to Confucius are deleted.

10. S.W.C. 1.14b, 1-19,1; S.L. 2.6,5-10b,4 under TPCS. T.S. 1.7,9-14,2 reproduces a document with the same title except that the last character is chao 詔 instead of hsün 訓. In this, references to the devil and evil spirits replace allusions to the Book of Songs and Book of History.

11. See footnotes 6,7, and 8 above. The relationship between the Taiping ideology and the Confucian tradition deserves separate investigation.

12. T.S. 2.4,1-4b,1; 4b,9-5,2 under the title "T'ai-p'ing t'iao-kuei." See also S.W.C. 2.131b,9-132,2.

13. See "Proclamation by the Insurgent Chiefs," an English translation of an original so far unobtainable, appearing in the North-China Herald no. 151, 182 (June 18, 1853). We learn from another document that inhabitants of towns where the Taipings were expected were told they had nothing to fear if they put up the character shun 順 (obedient) over their doors. "Kao chiang-nan shih min yü" 告江南士民諭 (Edict to scholars and people of Kiangnan), S.W.C. 1.39,7-8.

14. Ibid., S.W.C. 1.39,9-10.

15. "T'ien-ch'ao t'ien-mou chih-tu" 天朝田畝制度 (Land system of the heavenly dynasty), T.S. 4; S.W.C. 2.135b,12-137,10.

16. C.C.Stelle, "Ideologies of the T'ai-p'ing Insurrection," Chinese Social and Political Science Review XX.1 (April, 1936), 140-49 refers to the influence of Buddhist and Taoist ceremonies. Teng Ssu-yü in his comments upon a paper presented by the author before the December 1948 meeting of the American Historical Association said that in his opinion Taiping leaders were actually more influenced by Taoism than by Christianity. "The Sixty-third Annual Meeting," American Historical Review LIV.3 (April, 1949), 727. The influence of the secret societies is described briefly in Hsieh Hsing-yao, T'ai-p'ing t'ien-kuo ti she-hui cheng-chih ssu-hsiang (Social and political theories of the T'ai-p'ing

t'ien-kuo) (Shanghai: Commercial Press, 1935). A recent full treatment of the entire ideology with elaborate footnoting is P'eng Tse-i, <u>T'ai-p'ing t'ien-kuo ko-ming ssu-ch'ao</u> (The dynamic thought of the Taiping revolution) (Shanghai: Commercial Press, 1946).

4

The Christian Component
What Was Available to the Taipings

A. Points of Contact with Christian Doctrine

An examination of the Christian origins of Taiping ideas should address itself first to a consideration of those Christian influences both written and spoken to which rebel leaders may have been exposed and to the associated question of those to which it is certain they were exposed.

To judge from the nature of the terms that the Taipings borrowed [1] and from their iconoclastic attitude toward the use of images it seems certain that the Taipings took their so-called Christianity not from Catholic sources but from the first generation of Protestant Christian missionaries to reach China. [2]

For the first thirty years the labors of these missionary pioneers were of necessity chiefly linguistic and literary. The job of preparing acceptable translations and explanations of the Bible was arduous and time-consuming. The acquirement of a sufficient knowledge of literary Chinese was in itself no light task, particularly before teaching aids for Westerners were developed. To preach in Chinese effectively involved learning a vernacular different in its choice of terms from those used or considered proper for written speech. In the Near East in the nineteenth century missionaries had to decide whether to preach in colloquial or classical Arabic. This amounted to a choice of whether to be understood or respected. Before the usual audience neither speech could accomplish both. Something of this was present in China. The language difficulties involved in beginning the Christian missionary enterprise must have caused dismay.

Furthermore, before 1842 the Chinese Empire forbade the residence of foreigners in China except under extremely restricted conditions such as prevailed in the factories at Canton. The gospel could be preached in the interior of

China by Chinese converts only. This prohibition caused the parent missionary societies to establish stations among emigrant Chinese outside the empire, notably at Malacca, Singapore, Batavia, and Penang. The first Western missionaries had to devote themselves at these stations to translation and the instruction of overseas Chinese.

Language difficulties and the hostility of the Chinese government had an encouraging rather than a discouraging effect upon the activity of the missionary societies. The London Missionary Society was the first to enter the field and became the leader in supporting the early work. This began in 1807 with the arrival in China of Robert Morrison (1782-1834), the first translator of the Scriptures into Chinese. Joshua Marshman (1768-1837), translator of an early version of the Bible, William Milne (1785-1822), author of many tracts in current use, Walter H. Medhurst (1796-1857), veteran missionary, sinologue, and translator of Taiping documents, and Dr. William Lockhart (dates unknown), founder of medical missions to China, were all representatives of the London Missionary Society. From the first the British and Foreign Bible Society gave liberal support to the translation, printing, and dissemination of the Bible. Malacca and Singapore were the centers for the printing of missionary materials until the opening of treaty ports. The American Bible Society soon began to aid the work that was presently to bring the Bible to the Taipings.[3] In 1829 the American Board of Commissioners for Foreign Missions sent its first two missionaries to Canton; one of these, E. C. Bridgman (1801-61), was on board the "Susquehannah" when she visited Nanking in 1854. By 1840 seven missionary societies were supporting a missionary body of over a score of workers [4] with something under one hundred baptized Chinese Christians. [5]

The literary activities of Robert Morrison and William Milne were transmitted to the Chinese through the evangelical activity of two early converts, Liang A-fa, already mentioned, and his compatriot Kew A-gang (dates and characters unknown). Both of these Chinese were very active.

"Kew A-gang, a convert of Liang Ah-fa, in 1830, in company with Liang Ah-fa, itinerated 250 miles into the interior of China, following in the train of one of the public examiners. They thus had free access to the young literati at every examination center and distributed upwards of 7,000 tracts on the most important subjects. This is specially noteworthy as the earliest attempt to reach the literati."

One of these tracts, written by Liang A-fah, was "Good Words to Admonish the Age." [7] A copy of this is known to have reached Hung Hsiu-ch'uan when he came to Canton in 183 or 1834 to take the civil service examinations the second time. This work, a nine-pamphlet publication that made extensive use of the Morrison translation of the Bible, was the first Christian print to be seen by the titular head of the Taiping movement and his preacher-relative Feng Yün-shan.

The most versatile and prolific disseminator of Christianity during the years when the Bible was being prepared and taken to the Chinese was a German, Karl Friedrich August Gützlaff (1803-51), who was first sent to the Far East in 1827 by the Netherlands Missionary Society. [8] Gützlaff participated strenuously in translation activities, in dissemination, and in arousing interest in Chinese missions in Europe and in the United States. [9] In December 1834 Gützlaff became Chinese secretary and interpreter to the British consular authorities. The regular salary from this official work helped to support these evangelistic activities.

Of particular pertinence to the present topic was the existence of a body of converted Chinese called the Chinese Union, organized in 1844 and trained under Gützlaff's direction at Hongkong. Members of this group undertook to travel throughout China distributing copies of the Old and New Testaments and other religious publications. The British and Foreign Bible Society gave substantial assistance. [10] Down to the autumn of 1846 the work of the Union was concentrated in Kwangtung and had a membership then of 300, 50 of whom were preachers. The work was subsequently greatly expanded. There is no direct mention in primary sources of contact between the first God-Worshippers and the Chinese Union; it is possible, however, that the Bible reached them through the services of Chinese belonging to that organization. The Bible could easily have been in the hands of the insurgents by 1851, when their movement had begun to leave the Kwangsi hills. The earliest portion of the Bible printed by the Taiping rebels, a virtual reprint of a translation by Gützlaff, bears the date 1853. The earliest Taiping tracts are dated 1852. The presence of certain terms in these tracts indicates rebel knowledge of the Gützlaff Bible. This Bible may have come to the rebels through the Union. A contemporary Western author suggests without substantiation that among the rebel leaders were many members of the Union. [11]

It is far more likely, however, that copies of the Bible which the Taipings used were given to Hung Hsiu-ch'üan by Roberts during the two months of 1847 when Hung was Roberts' catechumen.[12] There is no record of Hung's having seen the Bible itself in Chinese before 1847 when he went to Canton for Christian instruction with the latter. On the other hand, definite mention is made in a composition by Hung

Hsiu-ch'üan written in 1848 that he saw both testaments of the Bible when with Roberts. [13] Which translation of the Bible did Roberts give him to look at?

Issachar Jacox Roberts (1802-71), an American Baptist, came to China originally as a result of the mission propaganda of Charles Gützlaff. [14] He served as Gützlaff's assistant in Hongkong from the time of his arrival in 1838 until 1844 when he was assigned to work in Canton. By this time the Medhurst-Gützlaff translation of the Bible had been in print for at least six years. It is probable that Roberts was using this translation. It was better than the earlier Morrison-Milne translation which while understandable to Chinese was awkward in style and contained mistakes incident to first translations. As Gützlaff's disciple, Roberts might easily have preferred his mentor's translation.

Hung Hsiu-ch'üan and his cousin Hung Jen-kan presented themselves to Roberts, professing the desire to be taught the Christian religion. Hung Jen-kan left Canton shortly afterward, but Hsiu-ch'üan stayed and studied with Roberts for about two months. He then applied for baptism, requesting that after baptism an arrangement be made for his support. The advice to put forth such a request may well have been a trick on the part of fellow-countrymen in Roberts' establishment who were envious of Hung's ability and zeal and desirous of eliminating a competitor. At any rate, Hung's early request for baptism threw doubt on his motives and displeased the missionary preacher so much that he postponed the baptism. Hsiu-ch'üan, without means of further support, returned to Kwangsi. [15] Thus, the only personal instruction in Christianity that the early Taipings received was given to their leader in Canton during two months of 1847.

In addition to "Good Words to Admonish the Age," the copies of the Bible which may have reached the insurgents either through the Chinese Union or through Roberts, and the personal instruction which the two Hungs received in Canton a further source of Biblical influence remains to be explored. This is the evangelistic literature disseminated by Protestant missionaries in China after 1844.

In the 1830's before the first Anglo-Chinese War, efforts were made to distribute Christian literature not only through the use of Chinese colporteurs but by distribution from ships along the coast. Gützlaff's three voyages, for example, were the means of giving out an immense amount of printed matter. Indeed, the trading firm of Talbot, Olyphant and Company purchased a brig in New York "principally for the purpose of aiding missionaries in circulating religious

Available Christian Influences   45

books on the coasts of China and the neighboring countries."
This vessel, the "Himmaleh," reached China August 1836.
But all of these earlier methods had to struggle with a discouraging official attitude toward the entrance of foreigners and foreign doctrines.

The settlements concluding the first Anglo-Chinese War (1839-42) were a marked improvement, for they permitted residence in the ports. Prior to the negotiation of the first treaties, resident missionary work was out of the question except at the Portuguese station of Macao and at Canton, where there were British and American factories; even there Chinese interference was likely. The treaties between China and the various Western nations following the first Anglo-Chinese War permitted foreigners to reside in the five treaty ports of Canton, Amoy, Foochow, Ningpo, and Shanghai; to construct churches, and to do what had previously been done unlawfully--hire native assistance in learning Chinese. Foreigners were liable to arrest if they traveled outside the treaty ports. As a result of French interest in having Catholic missions made legitimate, the Emperor in 1844 proclaimed official toleration for the religion of the "Lord of Heaven." [17] After differences in the Christian religion had been explained, this permission was broadened the following year to include the Protestant sects. Chinese could now lawfully become Christians anywhere in China, but they could not receive Christian instruction from foreigners outside of the treaty ports. This limited relaxation of former prohibitions brought a quick expansion of previous Protestant missionary activity. In the ten years 1843-53 the number of missionary societies in the field rose from twenty odd to 165. [18] There was a corresponding spurt in Christian literary activity in Chinese, already well under way by 1842.

The production of Christian tracts in Chinese deserves elaboration. One way of measuring the output of such literature is to count the titles and the names of authors of tracts appearing in the standard contemporary catalogue that could have been carried to the Taipings in time to influence their ideas. [19] It is doubtful whether a composition published later than the year 1851 so qualifies. If 1851 be set as the last allowable year of publication, the Protestant literary effort to the end of that year amounted to 266 Chinese titles exclusive of new editions or reprints. Less than half of the total number were produced in the thirty years preceding 1842, the date of the first treaty settlement at Nanking. By the end of 1850, 39 of the 148 Protestant workers who had gone out to the China station had published Christian materials in Chinese, some like Gützlaff (54 titles) and Medhurst (40 titles) voluminously. There was a tendency to favor works in literary Chinese over those in dialect. Only after a mission had been established for a time did attention turn to publications in dialect. Accordingly, 253 of the 266 titles are in literary Chinese, the rest in Cantonese, Shanghai dialect, or colloquial Mandarin.

Leaving out of account the Medhurst-Gützlaff version of the Bible and "Good Words to Admonish the Age," how many of these tracts reached the Taipings? One of the titles listed by Wylie did reach the insurgents and was reprinted by them. This was a composition by W. H. Medhurst originally printed at Batavia in 1833 under the title Discourse on Theology 神理總論. A revision of its first volume was printed at Shanghai in 1844 with the title"T'ien-li yao-lun"(The Essentials of Heaven's Principles). The Taipings used the same title and the same text in their edition, dated 1854. The "T'en-li yao-lun" may have been given to Hung by Roberts. On the other hand, it may have reached the Taipings no earlier than 1853 when Sir George Bonham of the "Hermes" exchanged several tracts for Taiping publications at Nanking.

Wylie also lists four compositions by Roberts, composed by 1840. [20] On the supposition that a teacher will use his own compositions with students where possible, Hung may have been shown and given any of these during his two months with Roberts. Medhurst's review of the books of the insurgents mentions a tract of Roberts, issued in 1840 at Canton, that contains wordings of the Ten Commandments similar to those of the Taipings. Medhurst also cites an edition of the Ten Commandments printed by the American Presbyterian Mission at Macao in 1844. Any of the foregoing may have been used during Hung's brief period of instruction, but the only fragments available for the present study are Medhurst's actual quotations [21] and a revised version of the Medhurst New Testament.

How many of the 266 titles mentioned by Wylie as having been in print by 1851 reached the Taipings cannot be determined definitively until a representative number of the originals in Chinese can be secured for textual comparison.[2] It is likely that the works of Gützlaff, at least, appeared in Kwangsi. A successful tract such as William Milne, Chang Yüan liang yu hsiang-lun 張遠兩友相論 (Dialogue between two friends, Chang and Yüan), may well have been added to Gützlaff's own pamphlets for circulation by colporteurs of the Chinese Union. Nevertheless, the part played by Christian tracts in the formation of Taiping ideology, with the exceptions noted above, is still obscure.

In summarizing what Christian literature was available to the Taipings in Chinese during the formative period of the Rebellion, one notes three points of contact with Christian

Available Christian Influences   47

literature. In descending order of probability they are as
follows.
    1. "Good Words to Admonish the Age," given to Hung
Hsiu-ch'üan by Liang A-fa in 1833 or 1834 at Canton. An
established contact.
    2. Chinese Bibles and Christian tracts shown to Hung
during his short stay with Issachar Roberts at Canton in
1847. A probable contact.
    3. Chinese Bibles and Christian tracts taken into the
interior by members of the China Union. A possible contact.

    B. <u>Materials Available for Comparison.</u>

    Of the Christian literature that reached the Taipings
through these contacts the following are available for the
present comparison: "Good Words to Admonish the Age," quotations from Christian material in Medhurst's "Critical Review of the Books of the Insurgents," and several early
Protestant translations of the Bible.
    Four translations of the Bible into Chinese were in print
by 1854, all four in literary Chinese. One of the two earliest, the Lassar-Marshman version, was prepared at Serampore
and finally published in 1823 at Malacca. Although used in
some of the early Baptist missions, it was never widely circulated and possibly never got to China. This was not the
case with the Morrison-Milne version, published at Malacca
in 1823, the same year. Liang A-fa made extensive use of
this translation in the composition of his tracts. It is
not known whether the Morrison-Milne Bible as such ever
reached the Kwangsi rebels. If it did, it made no impression
upon their religious literature. Of sufficient influence
upon the Taipings to cause them to reprint it in 1853 was
the Medhurst-Gützlaff revision, begun by a committee composed of W.H.Medhurst, E.C.Bridgman, J.R.Morrison, and Gutzlaff. The resulting New Testament was first printed in 1835
and the corresponding Old Testament, mostly the work of
Gützlaff, in 1838. The whole Bible of the revision, repeatedly edited by Gützlaff and reprinted, was the one distributed throughout China by the China Union. The latest and
best of these four early translations was the Delegates'
Version (New Testament, 1853; Bible, 1854, Shanghai), translated by a committee chosen in 1843 by all the Protestant
missionaries in China. This version exhibits a decided
change in style and in terms. As will be seen, it is improbable that it ever influenced the Taipings. [24]
    The copies of "Good Words to Admonish the Age" and of
the Bible in Chinese actually used in the present comparison
are listed briefly below and described at length in Chapter
8. As with the published compilations of Taiping documents,

an abbreviation which includes the date of publication is
assigned to each title and precedes the title.

Materials available for comparison.

1. <u>Mor. 1823</u>. <u>Shen t'ien sheng shu</u> 神天聖書 (Holy Bible),
21 vols. or <u>ts'e</u>. Malacca, 1823. The so-called Morrison
Bible or what I have termed the Morrison-Milne version.
2. <u>G. 1847</u>. The Gützlaff Bible, 1847. Evidently one of
the earlier revisions of the original Medhurst-Gützlaff
translation. For convenience I call this the "Gützlaff Bible"
to distinguish it from a later revision.
3. <u>G. 1855</u>. The Modified Gützlaff Bible, 1855. A revision by William Lobschied published four years after Gützlaff's death.
4. <u>D. 1852</u>. <u>Hsin-yüeh ch'üan shu</u> 新約全書 (Complete New
Testament). Shanghai: London Missionary Society, 1852. This
is commonly known as the "Delegates' Version."
5. <u>T.P. 1853</u>. The Taiping Bible, first officially published by the Taipings in 1853 as separate books of the Old
and New Testaments. No Chinese title for the Bible as a
whole. The parts which I have seen convince me that it was
printed character for character from a Gützlaff Bible of
the kind circulated in China during the 1840's.
6. <u>C.S.L.Y. 1832</u>. Liang A-fa, <u>Ch'üan shih liang yen</u>
("Good Words to Admonish the Age"), Canton, 1832.

The materials available to me of what the Taipings used
or may have used in constructing their ideology constitute a
sufficient basis, I believe, for attempting a comparison between Taiping tracts and Western Christian literature.

Footnotes.

1. Jesuits in China during the Ming dynasty approved
the term <u>Shang-ti</u> (occurring frequently in the Chinese
Classics) as a synonym for Yahweh on the ground that it denoted a personal entity who ruled over all things. Their
opponents the Dominicans asserted that the term <u>Shang-ti</u> 上帝
referred to one among four classes of spirits who were agent
of the <u>T'ai chi</u> (Supreme Ultimate) or one final cause behind
the universe and could not therefore be equivalent to the
Christian term for God. The issue, part of the famous Rites
controversy, was settled in March 1715 when Clement XI forbade the use of the terms <u>Shang-ti</u> and <u>T'ien</u> 天 (Heaven) for
God. Arnold H. Rowbotham, <u>Missionary and Mandarin--The
Jesuits at the Court of China</u> (Berkeley: University of California Press, 1942), 128-29, 165. Hence the Catholic term
for God was T'ien-chu 天主 (Lord of Heaven), a created term

Available Christian Influences   49

without Chinese antecedents. The Taipings consistently used Huang-shang-ti (Great Supreme Ruler), a term evolved by Protestants of the 1830's as equivalent to God. The three characters Huang-shang-ti recalled to Chinese the ancient Shang-ti and, as will be seen, suited Taiping theology very well. In this study the term Shang-ti will be rendered as "Supreme Ruler (or Lord)," the closest translation of the Chinese, or as "God," the concept for which it was adopted, depending on the context. Before much was known of them the first Taipings were officially reported simply as "God-Worshippers."

2. Three general accounts are followed here. They are: William Dean, The China Mission (New York, 1859); D. MacGillivray, A Century of Protestant Missions in China (1807-1907), Being the Centenary Conference Historical Volume (Shanghai, 1907); and K.S. Latourette, A History of Christian Missions in China (New York: MacMillan, 1929).

3. "In the 20 years beginning with 1833, it (the American Bible Society) expended $ 101,351.65 in preparing, printing, and circulating the Scriptures in China, By far the greater part was used in translation and revision work." MacGillivray, A Century of Protestant Missions in China, 577.

4. Latourette, 223-30.

5. Dean, The China Mission, 164.

6. MacGillivray, 3.

7. Liang A-fa, Ch'üan-shih-liang yen (Original English title: Good Words to Admonish the Age) (Canton: Religious Tract Society, 1832). The author prefers the translation "Wholesome Advice to Persuade the World."

8. See Herman Schlyter, Karl Gützlaff als Missionar in China (Lund, Sweden: C.W.K. Gleerup, 1946), which is the best work to date on Gützlaff based on letters, archives of mission societies, and a wide range of printed matter. Gützlaff emerges as the prototype of the independent missionary in China and the "grandfather of the China Inland Mission." Gützlaff felt that the Chinese should be converted to Christianity by a process of rapid evangelization carried on by itinerant preachers. Chinese should be trained as quickly as possible to spread the gospel and assume tasks of Christian leadership. Every province should be evangelized by men from that province.

9. Gützlaff's own records of his voyages are found in Charles Gützlaff, Journal of Three Voyages along the Coast of China in 1831, 1832, and 1833 (London: 2d ed., 1834). He covered ports from Canton to Tientsin, gaining favorable attention by ministering particularly to skin and eye diseases. The published reports of these voyages aroused great interest among Americans and British. In 1835 Medhurst and

Edwin (?) Stevens covered a similar itinerary in the brig "Huron."

10. W. Canton, History of the British and Foreign Bible Society, II, 402. 1085 pounds sterling are recorded as going to the Chinese Union and Gützlaff.

11. Vizetelly, The Chinese Revolution, 164.

12. Hamberg gives 1846 for this date but I have preferred to follow Chien Yu-wen and Kuo T'ing-i who say it was during the spring of 1847.

13. "T'ai-p'ing t'ien-jih," I-ching 16 (Oct. 20, 1936), 18, lower page, 1.7. The pamphlet reprinted here was the source of Hamberg's Visions of Hung. Kuo T'ing-i says that Hung examined the Bible in detail at this time, but authority for this is not cited. The same pamphlet may be found in the Kuang-tung ts'ung-shu ti-san chi, vol. 4, under the title "T'ai-p'ing t'ien-kuo kuan-shu shih-chung."

14. Schlyter, Gützlaff, 122, 129-30, 151 211.

15. The account of the incident from Hung's point of view occurs in Hamberg, Visions of Hung, (English text), 30-2; (Chinese text) 14b,1 to 15b,8. Roberts' report is contained in an untitled article by I.J. Roberts in The Chinese and Missionary Gleaner (October, 1852); and Roberts, "Tae Ping Wang," Putnam's Magazine VIII.xlvi (October, 1856), 380-3. At the invitation of the rebels, Roberts lived with them in Nanking from October 1860 until January 1862. He finally left, shocked at the conduct of Hung Jen-kan, who killed Roberts' servant, and bitterly disappointed with the insurgent perversion of Christianity. Enclosure 6 in No. 44, Letter from Roberts, Papers relating to the rebellion in China and trade in the Yang-tze-kiang river -- presented to the House of Commons (London, 1862), 142-3.

16. S. Wells Williams, The Middle Kingdom (New York: Charles Scribners' Sons, revised ed., 1913), II, 330.

17. Ibid., II, 355-7.

18. Dean, The China Mission, 160-64. The Morrison Educational Society is not included, since its aims were not primarily evangelistic.

19. Alexander Wylie, Memorials of Protestant Missionarie to the Chinese (Shanghai: American Presbyterian Mission Press, 1867). Wylie gives the publication dates where they are obtainable; otherwise they have to be inferred from his biographical notes. For example, Dyer Ball did not date any of his ten titles, probably composed in the 1840's.

20. English titles of Roberts' compositions: New Testament with Notes by Roberts; The Holy Book of Jesus, a series of four small tracts; The Teaching of Truth, Catechism in (Macao) Dialect. For further details see Chap. 8.

21. W.H. Medhurst, "Critical Review of the Books of the Insurgents," North-China Herald, 162 (Sept. 3, 1853), 19.

Available Christian Influences   51

The quotations occur in the review of the TTS ("Book of
Religious Precepts of the T'ai-p'ing Dynasty"), in Chap.
8 changed to "Book of the Laws of Heaven."
   22. Six of these originals, including the Dialogue
between Two Friends, are in the collection of the American
Board of Commissioners for Foreign Missions, which in 1940
was on deposit with the Library of the Harvard Divinity
School. The writer is informed that the collection has
since been divided between the Andover-Newton Theological
Seminary, the Houghton Library at Harvard, and the Harvard
College Library.
   23. Hamberg (English text), 8-9, 14-20.
   24. Full discussions of translation activities occur in
Latourette, MacGillivray, Canton, and Wylie. Handy summaries of the entire course of Bible translation into Chinese
are John R. Hykes, Translations of the Scriptures into the
Languages of China and Her Dependencies, American Bible
Society Centennial Pamphlet #22 (New York, 1916) and Eric
M. North (ed.), The Book of a Thousand Tongues (New York,
1938), 87-97. Alexander Wylie, "The Bible in China," Chinese Researches (Shanghai, 1897), 81-109 has interesting
supplementary material.

5

The Christian Component
What the Taipings Took

My method for discovering what the Taipings took of what was offered them has been to search the principal religious writings of the insurgents for terms and ideas at all suggestive of Biblical or Christian origin. Wherever the allusion is sufficiently definite, I have compared it with the characters of the presumed source as they appear in Chinese tracts and translations of the Bible. The result has been to establish a series of textual proofs for the content of insurgent borrowing. The comparisons are made both for terms and concepts.

It should be remembered that Protestant missionaries in China in the first half of the 19th century were much more what may be termed fundamentalist in their beliefs than are many such missionaries in the 20th century. The tendency in the 19th century was to consider the Mosaic law as revealed and absolute rather than simply the distilled "wisdom" of the Hebrews. When Hung heard Roberts expounding the Scriptures, he was exposed to the belief of an American Southern Baptist, a belief that considered other religions pagan and probably heathen. Christian tracts of the period represent the working ideas of missionaries like Roberts. From the tracts I have seen in the American Board collection and the titles given in Wylie's <u>Memorials of Protestant Missionaries to the Chinese</u>, it would seem that missionaries such as he had to center their attention upon combatting native idolatry and transmitting basic doctrine.[1] Hence, the ideal comparison would be between Taiping tracts illustrating the rebel use of doctrine and Christian tracts and letters reflecting the current type of Christianity. Unfortunately a representative number of these early tracts and letters was not available. In using the Bible without the tracts it is necessary therefore to be conscious of the absolute and authoritative position it occupied in the minds of the first Protestant missionaries to the Chinese. Their view of the Bible, transmitted to Chinese believers, would

What the Taipings Took 53

sharpen intolerance and call for obedience far more than could be the case later when the Bible came to be viewed as the "wisdom" of the Hebrews or as one among many worthy scriptures.

It is difficult to separate what the Taipings took or failed to take from a discussion of the reasons for selection or omission. Perhaps such separation is undesirable, for speculation regarding the reasons for their choices and omissions may be a helpful preliminary to describing what their ideology finally became. For the sake of clarity, however, I shall state the content both textual and conceptual of each borrowed item, present appropriate evidence, and then consider possible grounds for its selection. For example, take a borrowed idea like the Biblical conception of God. I shall describe in order the terms involved, the elements of the Hebrew idea of God that seemed to pass over into the Taiping consciousness, evidence for the presence of these elements, and finally possible reasons why this feature of Christian belief is present.

It seems to me that in order to gain inclusion in the religious writings of the rebels, a given item had to meet three conditions. It had to be available, it had to be understood, at least according to rebel lights, and it had to be acceptable. The first condition obviously always had to be met. As far as the second and third conditions are concerned, many items were accepted that were not adequately understood. I am certain, as will appear in Chapter 6, that many items which were adequately understood were not acceptable.

A student of the Bible knowing the wealth of principle and illustration available to readers of Scripture will be impressed at first with the scantiness of what was taken. It is my belief that this scantiness is first a reflection of the small portion of the Bible which the Taiping Chinese could really understand. The element of choice was also in operation, as will be shown, and it probably limited still further the number of borrowed items. In any case, what was taken was confined to the parts of the Scriptures that 19th century Chinese, previously unexposed to Western influences, could understand in at least elementary fashion.

The matter of understanding deserves elaboration. Ideally speaking, full comprehension of the meaning of a translated text depends first upon the skill with which the translation is made and then upon the presence in the reader's mind of a stock of images akin to the subject matter of the text--images the result of previous experience or, if experience is wanting, of reading and a lively imagination. [2] It should not be easy for an Anglo-Saxon, for example, to grasp the whole meaning of a gospel founded on the experiences of the

Jewish people living centuries ago in another part of the world. Indeed it is not easy for Western Christians today, provided though they be with teachers, the best Bible that generations of scientific scholarship can produce, and whatever traditions of a Christian civilization may be helpful. For one thing, the parables of Jesus abound in figures of speech which derive their vividness from the climate, topography, and life of Palestine.[3] Problems of understanding difficult for the Anglo-Saxon missionary must have been considerably magnified when encountered by Chinese of still a third heritage through the medium of an early (and necessarily imperfect) translation and, but for Hung's few months with Roberts, without the benefit of personal instruction.

Further, Chinese readers are accustomed to a wealth of prefaces, commentaries, and editorial notes. So foreign a book to the Chinese as the Bible properly calls for particularly copious notes on manners, customs, geography, and unfamiliar names. Yet early editions of the Bible and "Good Words to Admonish the Age" were supplied to the Chinese totally without such explanatory comment. They thus failed to satisfy either the normal expectations of the Chinese readers or the peculiar needs of Biblical subject matter.

Most of what the Taipings borrowed came from the first five books of the Old Testament. This material has been arranged under four headings, namely: the early Hebrew idea of God, illustrative stories of the Pentateuch, the Ten Commandments, and Old Testament Hebrew attitudes toward the worship of idols and rival gods. Items from the New Testament fall into these categories: the idea of God in the New Testament, the basic facts of Christ's life, Christ's teachings, and Christian rites and doctrines. Mention of Satan and of evil spirits occurs in both parts of the Bible beginning with the story of the serpent in the garden of Eden. Ideas of heaven and hell, like those of Satan and evil spirits, have their origin in the Old Testament but experience most of their development in the New. Accordingly, Taiping references to these matters are contained in separate sections.

A. <u>The Early Hebrew Idea of God.</u>

In their religious writings the insurgents taught that there is only one God, that He alone is the Creator and Supreme Author, and that His name should be used carefully and always with reverence.[4] When Taiping compositions appeared in print, the names of God and Jesus were honored in a special way. Whenever the name of either occurred, a new line was begun at that point, whether the previous line had reached the bottom of the page or not. The first character of references to God or His attributes began four spaces above the level of the text, that of the word Jesus, three spaces. 5 In elevating certain characters to honor what they represented the Taipings were employing a time-honored Chinese device.

Like the Hebrews of the Old Testament, the Taipings thought it was proper to make sacrifices to God. Appropriate offerings were prescribed for a variety of occasions. Presentations to God of animals, wine, tea, and rice were to be made when the following occurred: birthday celebrations, funerals, occasions of thanksgiving, contracting marriage, constructing a hearth, building a house, opening up ground, and even piling up stones. The method of presentation is not described but the absence of exact specifications indicates that the Hebrew custom of building an altar and offering a burnt sacrifice was not followed. In any case the verbal form used when the sacrifice was presented was something like the following: "I _____, Thine unworthy son or daughter, celebrating this birthday, or the coming of a baby, presenting this thanksgiving, or arranging for a wedding, reverently prepare as a sacrifice animals, wine, tea, and rice, and reverently offer them up to Thee, the great God (our) Heavenly Father . . . . " 6

The passages indicated in the footnotes show that the Taipings referred to God as Shang-ti 上帝 (Supreme Ruler), Huang-shang-ti 皇上帝 (Great Supreme Ruler), and T'ien-fu shang-ti 天父上帝 (Heavenly Father and Supreme Ruler). 7 That this is a direct borrowing from Gutzlaff's revision of the Medhurst-Gutzlaff translation can be demonstrated by a comparison of renderings into Chinese of two Bible verses selected at random. The English of the quotations is from the American Revised version, 1901. All romanizations referring to God or Yahweh are underlined.

1. Genesis 2.4: "...in the day that Jehovah God made earth and heaven."

Mor. 1823: Chi Shen-chu 神主 ch'uang ti yü t'ien chih jih shih.

G. 1847: Tang jih Shang-chu Huang-shang-ti 上主皇上帝 ch'uang-tsao t'ien ti.

G. 1855: Tang jih Yeh-ho-hua 耶和華 Shang-ti ch'uang-tsao t'ien ti.

2. Exodus 6.2: "And God spake unto Moses, and said unto him, I am Jehovah."

G. 1847: Shang-ti i wei Mo-hsi yun wo nai Huang-shang-ti.
T.P. 1853: * * * * * * * * * * * *
G. 1855: * * * * * * * * * Yeh-ho-hua.

The Taiping Bible and the earlier Gutzlaff revision confine their appellations for the Deity to Shang-ti or Huang-shang-ti. Gützlaff uses Shang-chu 上主 (Supreme Lord) or Huang-shang-ti for Yahweh instead of attempting to reproduce the sound of the word as in Lobschied's Yeh-ho-hua 耶和華 and the Yeh-huo-hua 耶火華 of the Marshman Bible. For the phrase "Jehovah God" Morrison chose Shen-chu 神主 (God Lord), a term completely neglected by the Taipings. The rebels, if they ever saw Morrison's translation, seem never to have borrowed his terms. It is significant that the Taiping Bible follows G. 1847 here character for character.

Repeatedly the authors of the Taiping religious compositions declare that there is only one God, the Creator. Worshippers are to make the proper sacrifices to Him and are warned against using God's name improperly. In addition, the God of the Taipings was very intolerant of the worship of images, as intolerant as Yahweh toward the cult of Baal. As a result the Taipings were fiercely iconoclastic, the first characteristic to attract the attention of the Manchu government. Although not referred to as often, other attributes of the God of the early Hebrews are present in the deity as conceived by the Taipings.

Huang-shang-ti is represented as a deity who shows mercy and forgiveness. The Taipings conceive of this side of God's nature in a manner close to that expressed in Exodus 34.6-7 and Numbers 14.18 as well as in the New Testament (see Mark 11.25). [8] The possibility of forgiveness is alluded to·in much of their religious literature. [9] God's compassion for mankind is generally mentioned in connection with his decision to send Jesus down to earth for the redemption of the sins of the world. [10]

A reader of the first part of the Old Testament cannot fail to be impressed with the tribal or, in a sense, the national character of Yahweh. God is not interested in all mankind but is concerned with one people, a chosen group. Further, his relationship with them is according to a covenant, sponsorship and protection to be given in return for reverence and obedience. The original promise is made to the father of the Jewish people and reaffirmed to his descendants. [11] Later the promise assumes the form of a covenant agreed to by the Hebrews as a whole at the time of the giving of the Ten Commandments. [12] The covenant is renewed at Shechem just before the death of Joshua. [13]

The Shang-ti of the Taipings is neither a tribal god nor a party to a covenant with a chosen people. Instead, he is regarded as the God of all men.[14] His special attachment to the rebels is not an association over a long period of time, as was that of Yahweh with the Hebrews, but rather a temporary affiliation for the purpose of bringing back the Chinese people to their original relationship with him.[15] Hung Hsiu-ch'üan, the titular head of the rebels and the self-styled younger brother of Jesus, was in fact the instrument chosen to carry out his purpose.[16] It is worthy of note that until the production of the Delegates' Version the term "testament" (which Webster defines as "Bib. A solemn covenant") was not translated by the Chinese character yüeh 約, meaning "agreement" or "compact." Since the appearance of the Delegates' Version, the standard translation of the title of the Old and New Testaments in Chinese has been Chiu/hsin yüeh 舊新約 (Old/New Covenant).[17] Reference to the Chinese title of the Gützlaff revision of 1847, i.e. <u>Chiu/ hsin i-chao sheng-shu</u>, shows that the term "testament" was then translated with the characters i-chao 遺詔 with the meaning of "decrees left for posterity." Hence, the title of the Bible they received failed to convey to the Taipings the idea of a covenant. Moreover, the conception of a solemn agreement between God and his people as covenantors evidently failed to be sufficiently impressive when read in the text of the Old Testament to warrant adoption.

It was the practice of Yahweh to communicate frequently and directly with leaders of the children of Israel. In earlier times a relationship of this nature existed between God and the patriarchs; later he spoke with leaders of Jews like Moses and Joshua and still later with the Jewish kings. Finally, prophets like Elijah and Micah became his mouthpiece. The Taipings conceived of their God as establishing a personal relationship with Hung Hsiu-ch'üan and with the Eastern and Western Kings who were next in authority to him. Yang Hsiu-ch'ing, claimed to have received directly from the Heavenly Father a religious title, Ho-nai 未乃 (no ascertainable meaning, possibly a breakdown of hsiu 秀), and the civil title of Eastern King.[18] The original five wangs[19] are represented as having personally received the commands of God to go down into the world and assist the King of Heaven.[20] But nothing resembling the close and long-continued relationship between Moses and Yahweh, for example, seems to have existed between these Taiping leaders and their God.

Only in two matters does the Taiping <u>Shang-ti</u> approach the activity of Yahweh on behalf of the Hebrews. He is their god of battles and he intervenes personally at crucial moments.

From the time of the Passover onward the God of Israel is more than a deity to whom prayers are addressed. He is at once a rallying point and an active helper. Rules of warfare form part of his law. [21] He outlines the tactics followed in the overthrow of Jericho. [22] On another occasion a hailstorm from heaven becomes an effective military weapon and at the same time permission is given to Joshua to halt the passage of time in order that a victory over the Amorites can be exploited fully. [23] Yahweh gives Gideon detailed directions for selection of the force that eventually defeats the Midianites. [24] A major act of intervention occurs when the Assyrian army besieging Jerusalem is stricken and routed. [25] After the fall of Jericho, Yahweh holds up further proceedings until an Israelite who has done some private looting is found out and put to death. [26]

The God of the Taipings operates less directly than Yahweh and usually through mediums, but he fills an analagous role. Indeed he is given credit by the Taipings for the success of their victorious campaign northward. [27] The Book of Heavenly Decrees and Imperial Edicts records seven occasions between April 1848 and January 1852 when the Heavenly Father appeared on earth. [28] The first appearance was evidently an introductory visit when God displayed proofs of his power and ability to perform miracles. In the course of the second visit he gave directions to the rebels concerning procedure for a certain ceremony of divination. The third, fourth, and fifth descents were for the purpose of enforcing discipline and backing up the authority of the Heavenly King. God's elder son Jesus made an introductory descent and two subsequent appearances before the Taipings for the same purpose. [29] Upon his sixth appearance the Heavenly Father put to death a certain Huang I-chen 黄以鎮 for disobedience in ordering a retreat. His announcement at the time of the last descent at Yung-an, January 8, 1852, suggests that Shang-ti of the Taipings like his Western counterpart had a difficult people to deal with. [30] An entire document, the "Book of Declarations Made During the Heavenly Father's Descent to Earth," [31] is devoted to God's personal conduct of the exposure of an imperialist plot against the rebels. A certain Chou Hsi-neng 周錫能 had been granted permission to go to Po-pai, a district in Kwangsi, to gather and bring back a number of volunteers. The volunteers were taken instead to a camp of the Emperor's forces and only Chou and two accomplices returned. Their intention, it developed, was to organize within the ranks of the Taipings a revolt the outbreak of which should coincide with an imperialist attack. His accomplices were to help in the work of causing disaffection and to act as assassins. In the course of some four descents the Heavenly Father brought Chou Hsi-neng to the point of a public confession. Chou, his wife, and a number of others implicated were condemned to death. Before the execution the chief traitor in the manner of Soviet confessions of the

1930's made public apology and acknowledgment of his guilt. At the same time two Taiping functionaries were interviewed by the Heavenly Father and ordered punished by whipping for failing to report conversations the traitors had with them. The earlier part of God's interrogations of the chief conspirator is made to sound like a catechism. [32] The entire incident becomes an opportunity for demonstrating to the Taiping host the power and goodness of God and his concern for them. [33]

Although similar in the ways noted above, the God-concept of the Taipings fails to share in the development of the character of Yahweh apparent in the later books of the Old Testament. The philosophical problem posed by the Book of Job as to why the righteous should suffer seems beyond the interest of these Chinese, though they would have concurred quickly in the solution reached. In the Books of the Prophets, Yahweh is weary of offerings, [34] particularly if they mean no change of heart. In fact, by that time offerings in themselves are considered unnecessary. [35] No progress toward this point can be made out in the development of Taiping theology. Nor is there naturally any Messianic prophecy. The T'ien-wang was their Messiah.

Practically all of what the Taipings borrowed of the Hebrew idea of God comes from the early part of the Old Testament. This may be the consequence of the failure of its later books to appeal to them. It may also arise from their inability to understand the later books of the Old Testament. There is room, however, for a third presumption, that the later part of this section of the Bible never reached the rebels. The dramatic stories of Daniel and Jonah should certainly have been understandable and appealing to Chinese who were capable of borrowing the entire account of the Passover.

No matter what the degree of resemblance to its Old Testament prototype, the concept of one supreme God was the important borrowing, for monotheism became the keystone of the whole ideological structure. It may have been no more than coincidence that made available to the Taipings the Hebrew concept of God under the Chinese characters Shang-ti or Huang-shang-ti. Compared with the Catholic T'ien-chu 天主 (Lord of Heaven), a coined term with no Chinese antecedents; with a strange-sounding transliteration for Yahweh, e.g. Yeh-huo-hua; or simply with the term Shen 神 (divinity) used by Morrison and one version of the Delegates' Bible, it was understandable and useful. The term Shang-ti recalled a traditional belief of the Shang and early Chou periods before the age of philosophers like Confucius. [36] It antedated by a thousand years the introduction into China of emanations of the Buddha. It was easy to surround this notion of God with historical allusion so that it overshadowed all the current polytheisms. Furthermore, Shang-ti was a Chinese term, safe against the imputation of a foreign origin. If one grants that the Taiping ideology resulted in part from a conscious choice of favorable elements, the term Shang-ti with its Chinese connotations was a desirable symbol of unity for use with a band of outlaws. Those who rallied to the standard of Shang-ti could explain away the foreign origin of the Bible and call the emperor of the Manchu dynasty a foreigner. Accordingly, it may have been no accident that Gützlaff's terms for God were followed exactly in the Taiping Bible and tracts. 37 There was every reason for doing so. Liang A-fa's "Good Words to Admonish the Age" is the one Christian tract which it is certain that Hung Hsiuch'üan saw, yet his preferred term for God, Shen-t'ien shang-ti 神天上帝, was entirely neglected by the insurgents. According to Medhurst's account Liang A-fa used the Gützlaff-Medhurst term Shang-ti by itself only twice.

B. Illustrative Stories of the Pentateuch.

With a wealth of illustration at their disposal the Taipings chose for their religious documents only three stories of the Pentateuch: the Biblical account of creation, Noah and the Flood, and the story of the delivery from Egypt.

The Biblical account of creation is mentioned in a large number of documents, but only to say simply that God created the world in six days and rested on the seventh. 38 To judge from the number of times it occurs, the Hebrew story of creation became a definite part of Taiping dogma.

The Bible story of the deluge is referred to less often. In one instance the flood is mentioned as proof that rain really comes from Heaven rather than from the dragon of the eastern sea, as alleged in popular mythology. 39 In another place the flood is cited as an example of the Heavenly Father's ability to display anger. 40 The characters No-ya 柳亞 for the name of the master of the Ark follow G. 1847 and are in contrast with the No-ya 挼亞 chosen by Morrison.

The story of the Israelites in Egypt and their adventures from the time of their release until the giving of the Law are reproduced in some detail in the Three Character Classic. 41 The account, in meter, three characters to the line, begins with the removal of the twelve tribes to Egypt. 42 The plagues of Egypt are all enumerated, though the order of their occurrence is confused. The flight of the Israelites is described together with the dramatic crossing of the Red Sea. The narrative elaborates upon how the people were fed in the Wilderness and concludes with the giving of the Law on Mount Sinai. The Taipings neglect to include the original

What the Taipings Took

feast of the Passover and Unleavened Bread, a ceremony of interest ostensibly only to the Jews. Two other references occur. One mentions the receipt of the commandments on Mount Sinai in order to stress Yahweh's injunction against the making of idols. [43] Another alludes to Yahweh's descent to save Israel as a second example of the Heavenly Father's capacity to display anger. [44]

Taiping approximations in Chinese of Biblical terms are of particular interest. For example, the children of I-se-lieh 以色列 (Israel) in Mai-hsi 麥西 (Egypt) were represented before Pharaoh by their leaders Mo-hsi 摩西 (Moses) and Ya-lun 亞倫 (Aaron). [45] When the king refused to let the Israelites go, Huang-shang-ti sent down meng-shih 猛虱 (lice), t'ang-lang 螳螂 (grasshoppers), and ch'an-ch'u 蟾蜍 (striped toads). But "the king hardened his heart and would not let them go." [46] "When finally they were not released, He slew their firstborn." [47] While they were on the march the Great Supreme Ruler rode by day in a cloud and by night in a pillar of fire accompanying them. [48] At the critical point in the flight "He caused the Red Sea with its waters to divide; to stand up as a wall, that they might pass between. The Israelites proceeded on foot as though on dry ground and saved their lives." [49] The terms and their sequence follow exactly Exodus 14.29 in G. 1847. When the Children of Israel faced starvation, the Supreme Ruler sent down shun 鶉 (quail), ku 鴿 (doves), and t'ien lu 甜露 (sweet dew). [50] The "sweet dew" was measured out with a sheng 升 (pint) [51] or with a shang 觴 (goblet). [52]

The accounts of Israel in Egypt and in the Wilderness presented more than one likeness to the oppression, hardship, and wanderings which the early bands of insurgents endured. Just as God's aid was forthcoming in the flight from Egypt, just so according to the "T'ien-ming chao-chih-shu" did the Heavenly Father, the Supreme Ruler, descend at critical times in the march northward from Kwangsi. The Taipings may well have fancied the parallel between the law-giving activities at Mount Sinai and their own efforts at organizing an itinerant host.

C. The Ten Commandments.

To the Taipings the most important portion of the Old Testament was the giving of the Ten Commandments to Moses. [53] The insurgents incorporated the Hebrew Ten Commandments into their ordinances. Knowledge of them and obedience to them became compulsory. Because of their importance to Taiping discipline and because of the light which a comparative table may throw upon the Taiping technique of utilizing the Bible, I include the following set of comparisons. The appropriate verse of the English Bible is followed by the translation into Chinese given in three early Bibles. The version in Exodus of the Taiping Bible, 1853, then appears. The entry for a particular commandment is concluded by appropriate reference in the "T'ien-t'iao-shu." The Chinese of this composition often differs in phraseology and content from that of the Scriptural translation. My own English translation is given in such cases. The reader will contrast the similarity between T.P. 1853 and G. 1847 with the differences introduced in the "T'ien-t'iao-shu." The latter represented what the Chinese assimilated. It was presumably intended for wider circulation than the Scriptures themselves and can therefore be counted upon to give an authoritative view of the use to which Taiping leaders put the heritage they were transmitting. Each of the Taiping commandments is accompanied in the original by a commentary and a hymn, the contents of which will be occasionally quoted or paraphrased. The Bible verses in English are from the American Revised Version (1901) of the King James Bible.

A Comparison of Missionary Translations into Chinese of the Ten Commandments with the Version in the Taiping Exodus, 1853, and in the "T'ien-t'iao-shu."

I. Exodus 20.3: "Thou shalt have no other gods before me.

Mor. 1823: 爾不可有別神也
G. 1847: 毋在本面崇異神馬
G. 1855: ＊＊我＊＊＊上帝馬
T.P. 1853: ＊＊＊本＊＊＊神＊
TTS: "First law of Heaven: 54 'Worship the Great Supreme Ruler' 第一大條崇拜皇上帝 ."

The commentary remarks that this commandment springs from the gratitude which every human should feel toward the "universal Father of all men." The hymn holds out the promise of heaven to all worshippers. The Taiping expression is much weaker than that in their own or in the missionary scriptures, but the lack of severity here is compensated for in the other ordinances.

II. Exodus 20.4: "Thou shalt not make unto thee a graven image, nor any likeness of anything that is in heaven above, or that is in the earth beneath," etc.

Mor. 1823: 爾不可為自而造何雕刻的像
G. 1847: 毋自作偶塑與凡偶像彷彿天上或地下
G. 1855: Same.
T.P. 1853: Same.
TTS: "Do not worship perverted gods"55 不好拜邪神 .

Commentary: "God said: '(Thou) shalt have no other gods beside me'" 除我外不可有別神也 . The hymn threatens consignment to hell for all who disobey.

The commentary seems to belong properly with the first commandment. The Taipings enforced the second commandment with conspicuous rigor and ruthlessness.

III. Exodus 20.7: "Thou shalt not take the name of Jehovah thy God in vain; for Jehovah will not hold him guiltless that taketh his name in vain."

Mor. 1823: 爾不可徒然而用神主爾神之名
G. 1847: 毋瀆稱汝上主皇上帝 之名夫皇上帝無不罪妄稱其名者
G. 1855: ＊＊＊＊上帝耶和華＊＊＊耶和華＊＊＊＊＊＊＊＊
T.P. 1853: Same as G. 1847.
TTS: "Do not take the name of the Great Supreme Ruler in vain" 不好妄題皇上帝之名 .

Commentary: "The great God's own name is Jehovah. Men should not take it in vain" 皇上帝本名耶大華世人不可妄題 . Apparently the Taipings intended this to cover blasphemy more than common cursing.

IV. Exodus 20.8: "Remember the sabbath day, to keep it holy."

Mor. 1823: 記憶撒吧日以守之聖然
G. 1847: 必誌安息日以成聖之
G. 1855: Same.
T.P. 1853: Same.
TTS: "On the seventh day, worship and praise the Great Supreme Ruler (for His) kindness" 七日禮拜頌讚皇上帝恩德

Commentary: "In the beginning, the Great Supreme Ruler made heaven and earth, land and sea, men and things in six days; the seventh day, having finished his work, he called the day of rest" 皇上帝當初六日造成天地山海人物 第七日完工名安息日 .

The hymn adds to the commandment a reminder say grace at meals.

V. Exodus 20.12: "Honor thy father and thy mother, that thy days may be long in the land which Jehovah thy God giveth thee."

Mor. 1823: 敬爾父爾母致爾各日可為長多於神主爾神給爾之地
G. 1847: 孝敬父母則可遐齡在皇上帝爾上主所賜之地矣
G. 1855: ＊＊＊＊＊＊＊＊＊＊耶和華＊＊帝＊＊＊＊＊
T.P. 1853: Same as G. 1847.

TTS: "Be filial and obedient to (thy) father and mother"
孝順父母.
  Commentary: "The Great Supreme Ruler said: 'be filial and obedient to (thy) father and mother that (thou) may enjoy longer life!'" 皇上帝曰孝順父母則可遐齡. This needed little adaptation for members of a society well nourished already on principles of filial piety.

VI. Exodus 20.13: "Thou shalt not kill."

    Mor. 1823: 爾不可殺人
    G. 1847: 勿殺
    G. 1855: Same.
    T.P. 1853: Same.
    TTS: "Do not kill or injure men."
     The hymn bases this appeal upon principles of human brotherhood and mutual tolerance.

VII. Exodus 20.14: "Thou shalt not commit adultery."

    Mor. 1823: 爾不可姦人妻
    G. 1847: 勿姦
    G. 1855: Same.
    T.P. 1853: Same.
    TTS: "do not do evil or lewd things" 不好奸邪淫亂
     This commandment is expanded in the commentary to include strict separation of the sexes, the casting of amorous glances 丟邪眼, the harbouring of lustful thoughts 爾不可殺人, the smoking of foreign tobacco (opium) 吸洋烟, or the singing of libidinous songs 唱邪歌.

VIII. Exodus 20.15: "Thou shalt not steal."

    Mor. 1823: 爾不可偷人物
    G. 1847: 毋偷
    G. 1855: Same.
    G.P. 1853: Same.
    TTS: "Do not steal or rob" 不好偷竊劫搶.
     The hymn enjoins each to be contented with his station in life.

IX. Exodus 20.16: "Thou shalt not bear false witness against thy neighbor."

    Mor. 1823: 爾不可妄證乃爾鄰
    G. 1847: 毋對他人誣證
    G. 1855: Same.
    T.P. 1853: Same.

TTS: "Do not tell lies" 不好講謊話 .
This is expanded in the hymn to embrace scandal-mongering and even garrulousness.

X. Exodus 20.17: "Thou shalt not covet thy neighbor's house, thou shalt not covet thy neighbor's wife, nor his manservant, nor his maidservant, nor his ox, nor his ass, nor anything that is thy neighbor's."

    Mor. 1823: 爾不可貪爾鄰之家 etc.
    G. 1847: 毋貪他人之屋毋貪他人之妻僕婢牛驢與凡他人之所有

    G. 1855: Same.
    T.P. 1853: Same.
    TTS: "Do not conceive a covetous desire" 不好起貪心
    The commentary declares **gambling** an offense against this commandment.

The Ten Commandments as translated into Chinese evidently satisfied the Taiping requirements. They were understandable and, when modified slightly, could be readily made an instrument for the discipline of masses of Chinese.

    D. Old Testament Attitudes toward the Worship of Idols and Rival Gods.

The first and second commandments of the Decalogue were as important to the Taiping religion as they had been to that of the Hebrews, for the pantheon of the Chinese was surely as crowded as that of the neighbor nations of the Hebrews. A type of theism centering in the worship of T'ien (Heaven) or Shang Ti (the Supreme Ruler) had developed in China by the end of the Chou dynasty. This power was regarded as supreme, but was never worshipped to the exclusion of all other spiritual beings. Moreover, the Chinese attitude toward religions has always been characterized by tolerance and eclecticism fortified by a practical desire to subscribe to any faith that might bring good fortune. A deity jealous of the allegiance of his followers found competition well developed in China, for there were in addition to the spirits and divinities recognized by the official Confucian state cult the many divinities of Buddhism and Taoism and numerous humble household and patron gods. Taiping apologists were keenly conscious also of the hosts of kuei 鬼 (evil spirits), mythical creatures, and mystic influences with which the beliefs of Chinese abound. The would-be founders of a monotheism in the first half of the nineteenth century needed all the authority that the Decalogue and records of Hebrew experience in the Old Testament could supply.

The presence of the first and second of the Ten Commandments in Exodus is the first indication in the Old Testament that the worship of other gods and their representations was a problem for the Hebrews. Shortly afterward is related the episode of the Golden Calf. 56 It is evident that the leaders of the Hebrews had to struggle against two tendencies on the part of their people, the impulse to put the object of worship into a tangible form, 57 and, as a natural consequence of cultural exchange, the disposition to borrow the gods of their neighbors. 58 Association with the women of neighboring peoples was especially dangerous on this account. 59 These tendencies persisted and were a problem for the Hebrew prophets. 60

What was the Taiping attitude toward idols and images? The second commandment as modified in the "T'ien-t'iao-shu" does not refer to idols nor does the corresponding hymn and commentary. The matter is not neglected, however, in other portions of Taiping religious documents.

Consider first the correspondence of terms. Gützlaff and the Taiping Bible both use ou-su 偶塑 for "graven image" and ou-hsiang 偶像 for "likeness" (see p. 62). Liang A-fa employs ou-hsiang similarly, but also has a number of phrases all his own. 61 Taiping references to images are almost equally divided between the compound ou-hsiang 偶像 for "image" and p'u-sa 菩薩 for "idol." G. 1847 in rendering into Chinese Leviticus 19.4 ("Turn ye not unto idols, nor make to yourselves molten gods") uses the expression p'u-sa which is also the Chinese abbreviation for Bodhisattva. The Biblical approval of the term p'u-sa was helpful, for the Biblical injunction against idols could thus at the same time specifically mean the destruction of the Bodhisattvas to be found in Buddhist temples everywhere.

The Taipings were undoubtedly happy that the Old Testament took a position similar to the one in which they found themselves on the worship of other gods and images, but they had no occasion to borrow the arguments of Hebrew leaders. The Chinese were not continually breaking an original covenant with Yahweh. Hence, though the Taipings sometimes allude to God's command from Mt. Sinai, 62 the main appeal is to reason. Why, they argue, abandon reason and worship material objects? "(When you) bow down to lumps of clay, to wood and stone, (I) ask when did you lose (your) mind?" 63 Intelligent creatures should not worship mere matter. "But all those images of wood and stone, mud and paper, are matter. Men are more noble than matter, and more intelligent than matter. Why then do they not regard themselves as noble, more noble than matter? Why do they not consider themselves as intelligent, more intelligent than matter?" 64 The worship of images is stupid, for there is a true god whom all should worship. "(You) do not worship (Him), but on the contrary worship a variety of wooden, stone, clay, and paper images which do not know or understand--stupid objects that have mouths and cannot speak, noses and cannot smell, ears and cannot hear, hands and cannot grasp, feet and cannot walk. How much more foolish this is!" [65] Idols could not have been responsible for creation, since they too had to be created. "Then call on God and await assistance. Never praise idols for creation. If creation really was dependent upon idols, it is difficult to understand the arrangement of things before they were set up." [66] In one place the writer is at pains to refute an argument that images are needed to assist God in protecting mankind. [67] The idea is attacked as a deceit of the devil and idols as his embodiment. [68] No worshipper of idols can expect to reach heaven. [69]

The Taipings were as resentful of the use of images as the Hebrews, though for different reasons; however, they failed to borrow much of the Hebrew attitude toward the worship of other gods. This is easily demonstrated by the changes made in the first commandment. The Bible version says: "Thou shalt have no other gods before me." This precept was interpreted in an uncompromising fashion. Not only was God the highest god of the Hebrews; he had to be the only one. The Taiping expression was simply: "Worship the Great Supreme Ruler," (see p. 62), an altered and less absolute requirement.

The reasons for the alteration may be sought in the religious situation in China as the Taipings found it. For one thing, no tradition existed of a covenant between Shang-ti and the ancient Chinese. No breach of faith had occurred, therefore, on account of the worship of the Buddha and the Tao. No ground existed for an appeal to honor, nor could the Chinese be threatened with punishment for breaking a solemn promise. Then, from what is known of the early Chinese religion, Shang-ti was believed to be content with recognition as the highest of all gods. [70] A late representation puts him at the head of an organized kingdom of deities and genii. [71] According to the Taipings, therefore, God's resentment was directed mainly toward the worship not of other gods but of unorthodox or perverted gods, hsieh-shen 邪神. [72] This idea was more their creation than a borrowing from the Bible or early Chinese tradition.

Taiping writers explain how the situation which confronted them arose. Two conditions, they say, caused the Chinese to forget Shang-ti and worship corrupt gods: a clouding of the former clarity of Chinese perception, and a deliberate deception on the part of Taoists, Buddhists, and the Devil himself. The supporting argument [73] is studded with references to well-known figures and incidents of Chinese history.

From the earliest times [74] until the era of the Three Dynasties (Hsia, Shang, and Chou) both princes and people worshipped Shang-ti. During that era the dangerous mistake was made of hiring men to represent the ghosts of the departed at funerals and some began to believe in "perverted gods," but as a whole the Chinese people continued to serve Shang-ti. The Ch'in Dynasty (255-206 B.C.) marked a change in former customs, for respect began to be paid to genii and apparitions (shen-hsien 神仙 ; kuai-shih 怪事); also the people commenced sacrificing to the legendary emperors Shun and Yü. The Han Emperor Wen (179-156 B.C.) and Hsüan (73-48 B.C.) of the Han Dynasty set poor examples, the former by a bargain with the well-known Kitchen God, Tsao Chün 灶君, the latter by sacrifices to Sovereign Earth, Hou-t'u 后土. The Emperor Ming (A.D. 58-76) of the Han Dynasty is blamed for the introduction of Buddhism into China. Reference is made to Emperor Wu (A.D. 502-549) of the Liang Dynasty who on three occasions took the vows to Buddha, entering a monastery as a priest, and to Hsien-tsung (A.D. 806-821), an emperor of the T'ang Dynasty, who went out to greet a cortege bringing one of the Buddha's bones to the capital. The Emperor Huan (A.D. 147-168), a ruler of the Sung Dynasty, gave the designation Shang-ti to the highest deity in the Taoist pantheon, Yü-huang-ta-ti 玉皇大帝, the so-called Jade Emperor. This case is chronologically the last historical example given.

During this time a few individuals possessed a degree of enlightenment. [75] For example, Emperor Wu (A.D. 561-578) of the Northern Chou Dynasty proscribed Buddhism and Taoism, abolishing improper sacrifices. At one point during the T'ang Dynasty 1700 idolatrous temples were burned. In the reign of the above-mentioned Emperor Hsien-tsung, Han Yü, a government official, reproved the emperor for going out to welcome a bone of the Buddha. Nonetheless, the Chinese people continued to sink deeper and deeper into error until the first part of the 19th century, 1837 to be exact.

At this point, " . . . the great God our Heavenly Father and Supreme Lord, angry at the errors of mankind and grieved that the true doctrine was lost, especially sent . . . the celestial elder Brother Jesus down into the world . . . Fearing lest the men of the world should not be speedily converted and altogether revert to the true doctrine, . . . he sent our master the King of Heaven down into the world . . . . " [76] It may be remarked that the mission of the elder Brother Jesus and of the T'ien Wang (Hung Hsiu-ch'üan) was to enlighten, and not to rebuke or chastise as might have been expected had Shang-ti been Yahweh.

As on the subject of image worship, the Taiping appeal

here was to reason supported by threats of hell and promises
of heaven. Instruction on Awakening the World with the
Basic Doctrine (Yüan-tao chüeh-shih-hsün) is the title of
the religious ccomposition that embodies most of the case
against idolatry and shows the emphasis intended. "Wake
up, Chinese," the Taipings said, "realize what the true nature of things is, and refuse to believe in spirits. Cast
out the 'perverse disciples of Buddha and Lao, who, covetous and aiming for gain, delude people in matters of which
they are necessarily ignorant in order to profit by the deception, and induce people to adopt religious ceremonies and
processions in order that they may enrich themselves.'" 77
Unimaginable punishments awaited those who, once enlightened, persisted in error, while those who awoke had the prospect of "a glorious and delightful state of happiness to be
enjoyed forever in heaven." 78 Naturally all converts were
forbidden the use of Buddhist ceremonies at funerals. 79
An additional avenue of appeal for a Chinese was to a standard of correct conduct. 80

From the foregoing one concludes that the Taiping leaders
took the same stand on the worship of images as the writers
of the Old Testament, but used a different set of arguments
in defense of their position. Yahweh's intolerance of all
other gods they did not or could not copy, preferring to
direct prohibitions against the "perverted gods" of certain
cults. The Taiping terms <u>hsieh-shen</u> (perverted gods) and
<u>hsieh-mo</u> 魔 (perverted devils) correspond with expressions
employed by Gützlaff and Liang A-fa in dealing with material
from the New Testament. They will be referred to further in
the section on Satan and evil spirits.

E. The Idea of God in the New Testament.

Several elements of the Taiping concept of God that were
borrowed from the Bible were either not present or not
stressed in the Hebrew Yahweh. One of these was the attribute of fatherhood, another the characteristic of universality, and a third the presence of a mode or function of God
called the Holy Spirit. Still another was the idea of a
personal God, for only occasionally do we find the Yahweh of
the Old Testament worshipped by those who are not priests
or dignitaries.

On the other hand, the Taipings failed to follow the
orthodox Christian belief, based on the New Testament, relative to the divinity of Christ.

One of the significant attributes of God which Christ
stressed in the Gospels was the characterization "Father."
This addition allowed emotions connected with the human male
parent to create a more personal and more meaningful notion

of God. Yahweh inspired fear, respect, or trust, but a God
who was the Father of his children could also inspire love.
Reference to the relationship between a father and his
children has been made effectively by people of all ages,
witness use of the expression "The Father of His Country," 81
but never more so than by Christ in the New Testament, 82
particularly to explain his own position. 83

The Taipings had need of the fatherhood concept for
similar reasons. It enabled them to tap a reservoir of
filial feeling that was peculiarly Chinese and to account
for Hung's authority as the leader of the movement.

The use made by the insurgents of the fatherhood concept
is as close a parallel of its source as any of their borrowings. God is referred to in the forms for public prayer as "the great God the heavenly Father," "the heavenly
Father the great God in heaven," and "God the holy and
heavenly Father." 84 Variants appear thus: "the great God
the heavenly Father and supreme Lord;" 85 "God is originally the venerable parent;" 86 and "the spiritual father"
(see below). On January 29, 1851, Hung Hsiu-ch'üan is supposed to have lectured to the officers and soldiers of the
Taiping host on the nature of their god. On that occasion
he announced that the titles Supreme (shang 上), Lord (ti 帝),
and Father (yeh 爺) were reserved for God alone. "The great
God, the heavenly Father and supreme Lord, is a divine
father and a spiritual father. Formerly WE had ordered you
to call the first and second ministers of state and the army
commanders of the van and rear royal fathers. WE were in-
dulgent in following the corrupt custom of the world. According to the true doctrine this was inconsiderately of-
fending the heavenly Father and heavenly Elder Brother. (God
alone is the father." 87 The Taipings failed to bring out
the gentler implications of the fatherly relation nor is
the relationship between Hung and Shang-ti represented in
the intimate terms of the New Testament. 88

One of the basic distinctions between the Hebrew Yahweh
and God as depicted in the New Testament is the universal
character of the latter. The change from the tribal to the
larger concept was not brought about readily, for, after
all, Christ was a Jew preaching to Jews. Yet Christ wel-
comed Gentile believers. He also healed Gentiles and in
one case used an act of faith on the part of a Roman cen-
turion as an example to the Jews. The God of the Jews de-
finitely became the God of all peoples through the injunction to preach the gospel to all nations. 89 Through the
labors of the apostles Paul and others the Christian church
itself became an embodiment of the principle of universality.

What the Taipings Took

Shang-ti never had to expand his field of concern for the Taipings. For them he had always been universal. Indeed, the universality of Shang-ti was the basis of Taiping theory. One of God's sons had been born to the inhabitants of western Asia 1800 years before; Hung was another son of God, making his appearance in an age and a locality far removed from Bible times.

In reading their documents one has the sense that the Taipings borrowed as much from native Chinese ideas on the subject of universality as from the Bible, though they may have been glad of Biblical support. 90

The authors of the "T'ien-t'iao-shu" were particularly interested in convincing their readers that God is a personal deity to be worshipped by everyone, not by sovereign princes alone. 91 Reference is made to T'ang, the founder of the Shang dynasty (1766?-1122? B.C.) and to Wen, founder of the Chou dynasty (1122?-256 B.C.), both of whom paid homage to God before they became sovereign princes without damage to their later careers. 92 An individual is encouraged to pray for the forgiveness of personal sin, protection against sickness, and the restoration of health. 93 Emphasis is placed upon the thought that God belongs to all. "The great God is the common father of all nations in the universe. All men are created and reared by him; all men are protected by him; thus men should morning and evening honor and worship (Him) with acknowledgments of his goodness." 94 Altogether there is evidence of considerable effort to develop the God to man relationship. In this the Taipings paralleled a Hebrew development shown in the Gospels as well as in the Book of Psalms. 95

As portrayed in the New Testament the entity known as the Holy Spirit was intended to succeed Christ upon the latter's departure. It represented the transcendent aspect of God. The Holy Spirit entered into the lives of humans, carrying on there the activities of the Christ. 96 In Acts 2.1-4 the story is told of how the Holy Spirit descended to the Apostles as a mighty wind fifty days after the resurrection at a time now celebrated as Pentecost. Christ spoke of the Holy Spirit in these words: "But the Comforter, even the Holy Spirit, whom the Father will send in my name, he shall teach you all things, and bring to your remembrance all that I said unto you." Later Peter promised that converts would receive the gift of the Holy Spirit at the time of baptism. Such a man as Stephen was characterized as "full of faith and of the Holy Spirit." 97

Taiping leaders did not use the term Holy Spirit often in their religious documents although they were surely familiar with it. Nor was the concept developed along anything like Christian lines. It is doubtful whether the significance of the Holy Spirit was understood, for the Taipings failed to use a number of opportunities for its effective mention. One of their prescribed prayers for the forgiveness of sins, however, has the phrase, ". . . grant (him) the Holy Spirit to change (his) heart." [98] The only reference to the Holy Spirit and the Trinity together in the text of the religious writings considered occurs in a doxology prescribed for common worship. [99] A late edition of the New Testament, published in 1860 or later but marked with the date 1853, contains annotations by Hung Hsiu-ch'üan himself. [100] In these notes Hung declared the Eastern King, Yang Hsiu-ch'ing, to be the Holy Spirit. [101] Like early Christian theologians, Hung struggled to evoke a separate essence that was yet part of the Godhead. [102] This was a late attempt to add a fourth member to the Christian Trinity. Hung's effort to stretch a tripartite into a quadripartite essence is an example of the direction that ideas borrowed from the Bible later took.

In rendering the phrase Holy Spirit the New Testament used the Greek word pneuma, which meant "wind," "air," or in a derived sense "spirit," reflecting the feeling that there was a connection between life and breath. Translators of the New Testament into Chinese represented pneuma by feng (wind) a character which did not carry the additional meaning of "spirit"; sometimes, to remedy this lack, they added shen, the character for "spirit" or God, thereby, with the prefix sheng, "holy," producing the compound Sheng-shen-feng (lit. Holy Spirit Wind). Thus, in one verse, Acts 5.3, Morrison employed Sheng-feng for Holy Spirit; in another, John 14.26, appeared the three character term Sheng-shen-feng. The rebels employed the second compound Sheng-shen-feng, one of the rare instances of correspondence between Morrison and the rebel scriptures. They used Ch'üan-wei-shih 勸慰師 for the term Comforter. The compound for Comforter in G. 1847, John 14.26, is the same as the Taiping one, whereas G. 1855 gives an-wei-che 安慰者 and Morrison tao-che 導者. Medhurst reproduces a doxology printed by the American Baptist Mission in 1848 which is the closest of all missionary texts to the Taiping doxology contained in the "T'ien-t'iao-shu" except for the appearance of chen-shen 真神 (true God), the term used by the Baptists for God. [103]

In both the American Baptist and Taiping doxologies, Sheng-shen-feng and Sheng-ling, the designations for Holy Spirit and Sacred Spiritual Force, are identical. The early date at which the borrowing of the terms occurred suggests that Hung's ponderings on the nature of the Holy Spirit took place later than the first appearance of the terms in the religious writings of the Taipings. Therefore his speculations were controlled by the term Sheng-shen-feng more than

What the Taipings Took   73

by the nature of the essence he was seeking to describe. In seeking to explain the lack of closer correspondence between the two versions Medhurst suggests the possibility that Roberts gave Hung a copy of the Baptist doxology bearing an earlier date than 1848, when members of that mission used the same term for God, i.e. Shang-ti, as Gützlaff.

F. The Basic Facts of Christ's Life.

The Taiping scriptures supply a few basic facts about the life of Christ. The information they furnish is confined to the reason for his appearance on earth, the region of his birth, the manner of his death, his resurrection and appearance to the disciples, and his ascension. Nothing is said about his early life or ministry.

A catechumen of the Taiping host discovered that God the heavenly Father, upon observing the sins of mankind, decided to send Jesus his first-born son down to earth. The mission of the latter was to rescue the people of the world and deliver them from sin and the penalties of God's violated law.104 The story of the crucifixion, resurrection, and ascension is related in two brief accounts, worded so as to emphasize a few incidents and establish the fact of salvation for virtuous believers. 105

Taiping phraseology for the most part follows that of Medhurst and Gützlaff. "Jesus the Lord and Saviour" is expressed by Chiu-shih-chu Yeh-su 救世主耶穌, the same as both G. 1847 and G. 1855, whereas Mor. 1823 in the title of the New Testament adds the character wo 我 (my, our) before "Lord," thus: Chiu-shih wo-chu Yeh-su. G. 1847, G. 1855, and T.P.1853 all have fu-yin-shu 福音書 for Gospel. The terms for cross, shih-tzu-chia 十字架, and crucify, ting 釘 (nail), employed by the Taiping writers are duplicates of the choices made by both Gützlaff and Morrison. 106 Both Mor. 1823 and G. 1847 (see Luke 24.46, Chinese text) make use of fu-huo 復活 (again living) for the idea of resurrection. The religious writings of the rebels differ here, using either su 甦 (to revive) or fu-chung-sheng 復重生 (to live again). 107 The compound for "ascend to heaven" in both G. 1847 (see Mark 16.19, Chinese text) and in the Taiping writings is sheng-t'ien 升天. The Taipings frequently add the character t'ang (hall) to make a compound t'ien-t'ang 堂 (heavenly hall) for "heaven." 108 They occasionally substitute shang 上 (to go up) for sheng 升. 109

The little that the insurgents borrowed of the life of Christ was on the whole transferred accurately. The idea of God's compassion and its result, the redeeming mission of Jesus, 110 were carried over faithfully with, however, the modification that Jesus was made the first-born rather than the "only-begotten Son" of the Father. Details such as the interval of three days between the crucifixion and resurrection, the forty days on earth after the resurrection, [111] and the darkness at the time of the crucifixion [112] were reproduced correctly. After the resurrection Christ actually did command his disciples to preach the gospel abroad. [113] Except for the reference to baptism, the prediction quoted above regarding believers and unbelievers is a fair paraphrase of Luke 16.16: "He that believeth and is baptized shall be saved; but he that disbelieveth shall be condemned."

From what has been said it is apparent that only a small part of the material available concerning Christ's life was transferred to the religious writings of the rebels. Even if allowance be made for obscurities and imperfections in translation, the percentage of data borrowed is small in comparison with the amount of the text that was understandable and could have been utilized. It is reasonable, therefore, to ascribe to the factor of conscious choice a selection that included only as much of Christ's life as would establish his place in the Taiping hierarchy, furnish an authoritative precedent from another age, and explain the way to salvation. It suited the insurgents to represent an event as important to Christians as the resurrection as an example more of a return to earth than a guarantee of life everlasting. This left the way open for Christ's descent to earth in 1837 and other appearances among men in the years that followed. (See pages 58-9 and 68.)

G. The Teachings of Christ.

Aside from a few phrases and a reference to forgiveness from sin, Hung Hsiu-ch'üan and his companion authors omit mention of the teachings of Christ. [114] The examples which appear below convey the impression of phrases borrowed at random. Two of the three verses quoted are from the Lord's Prayer. The missionary Bible versions of the verses in Chinese are given first, followed by the Taiping equivalent.

1) Matt. 6.10. "Thy will be done, as in heaven, so on earth."

> Mor. 1823: 爾旨成行於地如於天焉
> G. 1847: 聖旨得成在地如在天焉
> G. 1855: Same.
> TTS: "In turn [115] (I) pray the Heavenly Father, the Great God in heaven, that his sacred will may be done on earth as it is in heaven " 轉求天父皇上帝在天聖旨成行在地如在天焉 .

What the Taipings Took 75

2) Matt. 6.13. "And bring us not into temptation but deliver us from the evil one."

Mor. 1823: 勿由我等入誘惑乃救我等出凶惡
G. 1847: ＊＊＊＊＊＊＊＊援＊＊＊＊＊
G. 1855: ＊＊＊＊＊＊＊＊救＊出惡
TTS: ". . . never more allow me to be deceived by malignant demons but perpetually regard me with favor and never let the evil devils injure (me)"

3) Matt. 7.7. "Ask, and it shall be given you, seek and ye shall find, knock and it shall be opened unto you."

Mor. 1823: 爾求而則將得，尋而則遇著拍而則得開門與爾
G. 1847: 求則終爾尋則遇之扣門則開也
G. 1855: ＊＊＊＊＊＊＊＊＊＊＊＊與爾也
D. 1852: ＊＊＊＊＊＊＊＊＊＊＊＊也
"Yüan-tao chüeh-shih hsün:" 117 English equivalent approximately as in Bible verse above. 求則得之尋則遇箸扣門則開

Character for character the Taiping statement in Chinese is closest to the G. 1847 rendering and farthest from the D. 1852 version.

In the New Testament Christ is represented as ever ready to forgive sin. When a man sick with the palsy was let down through the roof before him for healing, in rather spectacular fashion he first announced that the man's sins were forgiven. 118 A woman guilty of adultery was saved from stoning, the usual penalty, and told to go and sin no more. 119 Respectable people complained about the fact that Christ was often in the presence of known sinners. 120 Christ replied that the wayward needed more attention than the upright. Part of the Lord's Prayer is an appeal for forgiveness.

Something of this concern for sin and its forgiveness is present in Taiping writings, principally in two sections of the "T'ien-t'iao-shu." The sections referred to are entitled Chieh-tsui kuei-chü (Form for Removing Sin) and Hui-tsui-chang (Prayer for Repenting of Sin). 121 In the first section the suppliant is told to kneel and pray to God to forgive his sins. He may use his own words or a written form. Afterwards he is directed to wash himself clean with a basin of water, or, better, to bathe himself in the river. When he has thus obtained freedom from sin, the suppliant is admonished to pray morning and evening and before meals, to keep the Sabbath every seventh day, to obey the Ten Commandments, and to refrain from worshipping "perverted gods" or doing evil things. Such a course of conduct will bring divine favor and a life after death in heaven. Hui-tsui tsou-chang is the written form to be used by the penitent. The subject who uses this asks forgiveness and freedom from future transgression. Sin is described as "the transgression of heaven's commands." 122

In these selections "to repent of sin" is hui-tsui 悔罪, "to free from sin" chieh-tsui 解罪, "to pardon former mistakes" she-ch'ien-ch'ien 赦前愆 and "to forgive sin" she-tsui 赦罪. The last term occurs in missionary scriptures which also render "forgive us our debts" literally as mien-chai 免債. 123

There is no discussion in Taiping writings of the deeper aspects of sin or its forgiveness. The omission is in keeping with Taiping interest in the practical uses of religion. It was enough to consider sin simply as disobedience to divine command. Further development of what was, after all, a foreign concept was best left alone.

H. Christian Rites and Doctrines.

There were only two known occasions upon which knowledge of Christian religious observances could have passed by word of mouth to Hung Hsiu-ch'üan: in 1833 or 1834, when he heard an unknown foreign Christian preacher, 124 and during February and March 1847, when he was studying with Issachar Roberts in Canton. So limited an amount of instruction in Christianity accounts for the fact that only two of these practices became a part of the Taiping religion: the rite of baptism and observance of the Sabbath. These were incorporated into their religious documents and were without doubt a part of the insurgents' religious life. Early foreign visitors spread the report that they also observed the Lord's supper, but there is nothing in Taiping writings to show that this sacrament was understood or practiced.

Hung apparently learned the rite of baptism from the foreign preacher and his companion the day he heard them preaching and received his copy of Ch'üan-shih liang-yen. This is indicated by the fact that in 1843, after his fourth unsuccessful try at the provincial examinations but four years before he saw Roberts, he is reported to have baptized his first converts, Feng Yün-shan and Hung Jen-kan, by sprinkling. 125 The three then went outside their village to a certain Shih-chiao pool where they practiced immersion. One of Hung's early poems, Kan-wu hui-tsui shih (To Awake a Repent of Sin), is believed to have been composed as an accompaniment to baptism. Thus began in the first stage of the movement the belief that baptism was the act by which one was admitted to a religious group and obtained freedom from sin as well. 126 All converts made during 1844 and 1845 in

Hung's home district in Kwangtung and in the Thistle Mount area in Kwangsi received baptism. The rite of baptism was from the beginning prominent among ceremonies performed by the God-Worshippers.

An additional stipulation was possibly the outcome of Hung's experience with Roberts in Canton during February and March 1847. It will be recalled that while there he acted upon malicious advice and asked Roberts for baptism prematurely. Roberts was led to suspect that his pupil sought church membership primarily as a means of support and so refused. His means exhausted, Hung left Canton, never to return for further instruction. As a consequence he never received formal baptism at the hands of a Western Christian nor did he ever become a church member. It is likely that from this experience came the T'ien-wang's order that neophytes could baptize themselves and did not need to rely on others.[127] Hung told his followers a story regarding his own experience of baptism that was widely believed and undoubtedly added to the authoritative character of his pronouncements. On a certain night he was on his knees performing with a basin of water the rite of self-baptism. This was outdoors near the gate of his courtyard. As soon as the sprinkling was finished, "Heaven suddenly sent down a great rain" which drenched him to the skin. The T'ien-wang took this as a sign that the Heavenly Father himself had performed the ceremony.[128]

By 1852, the time the "T'ien-t'iao-shu" was first printed, it is evident that baptism had become more a ritual form to indicate freedom from sin than a ceremony conferring church membership. In the directions for baptism contained in this document, the suppliant is asked first to kneel and pray to God for forgiveness of his sins. After the prayer is over, the subject is instructed as follows: "You may either take a basin of water and wash yourself clean or it is better still to wash by immersing (yourself) in the river."[129] "To wash clean" was rendered into Chinese as <u>hsi-ching</u> 洗淨, a term the first character of which had been used in two early Chinese Bibles for "to baptize." <u>Hsi-li</u> 禮 (the rite of washing) is the modern term for the usual type of baptism by sprinkling. "To wash by drenching" appeared in the Chinese of the Taipings as <u>chin-hsi</u> 浸洗, the first character meaning "to drench or immerse." Two other early Bibles preferred <u>chin</u> or <u>chin-li</u> 禮 (the <u>chin</u> rite) as the term for baptism. The latter is the modern compound for baptism by immersion.[130]

In the early days of the movement the ceremony was performed as follows. The applicant for baptism was brought before a table on which had been placed two lamps and three cups of tea. "A written confession of sins, containing the names of the different candidates for baptism, was repeated

... and then burnt, whereby the presenting of (the candidate) ... to God was to be expressed." [131] Then the candidate was required to answer satisfactorily the following questions: "Do you agree not to worship corrupt spirits? Do you agree not to commit acts of wickedness? Are you willing to observe the laws of heaven?" Thereupon the penitent neophyte knelt and the man in charge of the ceremony poured over his head a cup of water from a larger basin. The man thus baptized said, "(My) previous sin is washed away. I have put aside the old and am made new." Then the convert got up, drank a cup of clear tea, and washed his breast with water from the basin to show that he had cleansed his heart. Usually he also went to a nearby river to practice immersion, confess his sins, and pray to God to pardon them. Converts who had been baptized were entitled to receive the various standard prayers (contained in the TTS) for use morning and evening and at meals. [132]

The Taipings did not follow Western Christians in the use of the cross as a religious symbol. The title pages of their religious books are decorated not with the cross but with the dragon. There is evidence, however, that they understood and respected the use of the cross by Western Christians. [133]

Aside from the festivals of the twenty-four solar terms, occurring roughly at fifteen day intervals, the Chinese had never had a regular day of rest. The Taiping leaders changed this. In accordance with the Bible they took over the Western Sabbath but retained the Chinese solar term festivals as well. [134] The Genesis account of creation was frequently alluded to as the basis for the introduction of the new observance, unsupported as it was by Chinese historical precedent. As has been observed, the Fourth Commandment was borrowed intact from the Ten Commandments of the Hebrews. The day itself is reported to have coincided with Saturday on the Western calendar. [135]

The insurgents observed the Sabbath in a fashion different from Westerners. According to a contemporary Chinese account the usual practice within the walls of Nanking was as follows. [136] The day before the Sabbath a large flag was set up in the street bearing characters which read: "Tomorrow is the Sabbath. Each should be reverent and worship." At midnight cakes and fruit were made ready and all chanted a doxology to the deafening accompaniment of cymbals and firecrackers. The doxology sung was the one prescribed for common worship in the "T'ien-t'iao-shu." [137]

Taiping borrowings are characterized throughout by a tendency to take over a given precept or body of data to the neglect of the reasoning behind such a precept or body of fact. Such was particularly the case with the New Testament Hung and other Taiping leaders also showed little capacity t theorize. Their consideration of Christian dogma was confined to four topics: the incarnation, the atonement, sin and its forgiveness, and the Trinity.

In its theological sense the term incarnation denotes the embodiment of God in human form in the person of Christ. The Taipings denied the fact of the incarnation, for from the first Hung failed to affirm the divinity of Jesus. Jesus, he said, was the t'ai-tzu 太子 (heir apparent) of God and the Heavenly Elder Brother, but not the only-begotten son; he was the Saviour of the World, but not God. His subordination to the Heavenly Father was indicated in official documents by commencing the characters for his name one space lower than those for T'ien-fu huang-shang-ti. [139] As has been noted, the titles Shang (Supreme) and Ti (Lord) were reserved in a special proclamation for the Heavenly Father alone, though Jesus shared with God the appellation Sheng (Holy). [140] Hung's most explicit remarks on the subject occur in annotations to a late edition of the Taiping New Testament. In a note appended to 3 John, Hung declares, "God alone is most high. Christ is God's first-born." [141] The annotation opposite Mark 12.30 reads: "My Great Elder Brother clearly declares that there is only one supreme Lord; why then did His disciples afterwards mistakenly explain that Christ is God?" [142] Christ's intended place in a celestial family is made certain by reference to his spouse, "the heavenly elder brother's wife, virtuous and very thoughtful, constantly urging the elder brother to be deliberate." [143] His mother is called simply the T'ien mu 天母 (Heavenly Mother). Nowhere in all Taiping literature is there an attempt to transliterate the name Mary.

The fact that the Heavenly Elder Brother was not considered divine had no bearing upon the reality of the atonement. His suffering and death were as efficacious in Taiping dogma as in its Western prototype.

The Biblical idea of sin was conveyed to the Chinese in translation through the use of their character tsui 罪, which meant primarily a crime, offence, or fault. [144] Unprovided with instruction or commentaries, there was nothing in such a translation to convey the deeper connotations of the term as developed by Christian theologians. The "T'ien-t'iao-shu" introduces, however, a working definition of sin with the question: "Who has ever lived in the world without transgressing the laws of heaven?" Several lines later the reader is told that he may avoid sin and go to heaven if he "refrains from the worship of corrupt spirits, does not commit deeds of wickedness, and does not disobey the laws of heaven"; [145] a candidate for baptism must agree to a correct standard of conduct in these three particulars (see p. 78). The nature of man's sin before Christ appeared is not described. Why was it necessary that such sin be atoned for? Exactly what did Christ's suffering and death accomplish? What did the statement "to redeem (men) from sin" mean? [146] The absence of thoughtful answers to these questions suggests that Hung was beyond his depth in borrowing phrases rather than meanings. This much is clear, however; God did not share the act of forgiveness with mankind. [147] Unlike the New Testament in the Taiping writings no charge is laid upon the individual God-Worshipper to forgive the offenses of his neighbors so as to qualify his own offenses for divine forgiveness. [148]

The only mention of the Trinity in the religious writings of the insurgents has been referred to (see footnote 103). The phrase "Praise the three persons (who) united (constitute one true Lord" is not explained in the "T'ien-t'iao-shu" where it appears and is not commented upon in the other religious documents. It was evidently used by the God-Worshippers just as a piece of verbal ritual, much as many Christians today sing hymns. The theological problem of one Lord who could be three or four persons at the same time attracted Hung's serious attention, [149] but apparently was not discussed widely.

I. Biblical Ideas of Satan and Evil Spirits.

Authors of the official papers of the T'ai-p'ing-t'ien-kuo possibly reflected the state of belief in the life about them when they made liberal references both to the devil and to a host of lesser evil spirits. To their way of thinking the forces of evil were exceedingly active. Evil influences beset the path of every Chinese who struggled to revere the Great Supreme Ruler and obey his laws.

The activities ascribed to the devil and his helpers range over a wide field. The minds of people who hold that God can be worshipped only by sovereign princes are deluded by the devil. [150] Men who follow the customs of the world comply with Satan's wishes. [151] Those who accuse the insurgents of following foreigners are the dupes of the devil. [152] A false rumor attributes to the King of Hades, Yen-lo-yao 閻羅妖, the power of determining the length of a man's life. This King of Hades is discovered to be none other than the "old serpent the devil, who transforms himself in a variety of ways to deceive and entrap the souls of men." [153] Jesus is revealed in the role of a champion as well as a Redeemer. "When the impish fiend did strange things in injuring the children of men, (God) repeatedly sent his own son down into the world. (Then) he swept away the impish fiend and the world was at peace." [154] The devil is further identified with

What the Taipings Took   81

the images and idols which the Chinese worship and with the
dragon of the eastern sea. 155
   Satan is believed to have a host of helpers, called var-
iously "corrupt gods," "corrupt devils," "fiends," and
"followers of the fiend." 156 The last-named have fared
poorly. 157 Human beings are easy prey for the legions of
Satan. "Corrupt devils very easily delude the souls of men."
Many are "those who because of their mistaken beliefs end up
in hell," 158 who "have erroneously followed the devil's ways
and allowed themselves to be deceived by the king of Hades." 159
The Eastern King admonishes the people of the world thus:
"Do not worship corrupt gods, do not take the devil's road,
but forsake evil and return to righteousness." 160 A common
phrase at the end of the standard forms for prayers is the
following. "Never allowing (me) to be deceived by impish
fiends, but always caring for (me), never permit the impish
fiends to harm (me)." 161
   So extensive a preoccupation with the devil and his works
developed a sizable repertory of terms. The tabulation below will show the character or characters used in dealing
with infernal influences. For the documents examined it is
complete.

       Tabulation of Taiping Terms for the Devil and Evil
                            Spirits.

	Chinese Characters	Romanization	English Translation
1.	魔鬼	Mo-kuei	The Devil
2.	*	Kuei	The Devil, devil, demon
3.	妖魔	Yao-mo	The Impish Fiend
4.	*	Yao	The Fiend, fiend
5.	閻羅	Yen-lo	The King of Hades (Chinese)
6.	＊＊妖	Yen-lo-yao	Same
7.	老蛇＊鬼	Lao-she Yao-kuei	The Old Serpent and the Fiendish Devil
8.	＊魔	She-mo	The Serpent Devil
9.	邪神	Hsieh-shen	Corrupt gods
10.	＊魔	Hsieh-mo	Corrupt devils
11.	鬼人	Kuei-jen	The devil's men
12.	妖徒	Yao-t'u	Followers of the fiend

   Note that the characters yao and kuei are used to mean
either the devil or one or more of his satellites.

The temptation of Adam and Eve by the serpent [162] and Yahweh's wager with Satan over the behavior of Job [163] in the face of adversity are the principal occasions upon which the devil is mentioned in the Old Testament. In their writings Hung and his followers never refer to the book of Job, but the Genesis portrayal of the devil as a serpent is cited at least once (see footnote 153) and possibly alluded to in the expressions "serpent-devil" and "the old serpent and fiendish devil." The fact of borrowing is evident from the fact that the Chinese have generally excepted the serpent or dragon from a satanic connotation. [164] As more or less of a national symbol the dragon has been for the Chinese a sign of intelligence, beneficence, and power. The Taipings probably felt that they were doing the proper thing in adorning the title pages of official documents with twin dragons. [165]

Allusions to Satan and lesser evil spirits are much more frequent in the New Testament than in the Old, particularly in the case of what are called "familiar" or "unclean" spirit

Satan's temptation of Christ after a forty day fast in the wilderness is a prominent episode, [166] but the important ethical issues developed on this occasion failed to impress the rebels. In the parable of the sower, Satan is said to interfere with transmission of the word. [167] Some of the Jews spread a rumor that Jesus was a demon or had a demon.[168] A conspicuous feature of Christ's ministry is his healing of people believed to have been sufferers from epilepsy and mental disorders. The sick are described as "vexed with a demon," [169] "with an unclean spirit," [170] having "demons," [1? or a "spirit of an unclean demon." [172] Christ's disciples were formally given authority over all demonic influences.[17?] For some reason the personal possession of individuals by demons is not mentioned once in Taiping writings, though the subject should have been congenial to writers obsessed with the activities of evil spirits. Incidents such as Satan's prompting of Ananias [174] run truer to the Taiping formula. Two passages in Revelations are closer to Taiping phraseology than any other references on this subject in the Bible: "And the great dragon was cast down, the old serpent, he that is called the Devil and Satan, the deceiver of the whol world." "And he laid hold on the dragon, the old serpent, which is the Devil and Satan and bound him for a thousand years." [175]

The Chinese terms or compounds employed by early Bibles in phrases describing the devil or evil spirits may be represented by a tabulation of terms and their sources in translations of the Bible.

What the Taipings Took   83

Early Biblical Terms in Chinese for the Devil and Evil Spirits

	Term	Biblical Term Represented	Source
1.	Ti-ya-po-lo 氏亞波羅	The Devil (Diabolo)	Mor.1823, Matt. 4.5
2.	Pi-le-hsi-pu-pai 比勒唏啪啪	Beelzebub	Mor.1823, Matt. 12.24
3.	Pa-le-hsi-pu 巴勒洗布	Same	G.1847. Same
4.	Pieh-hsi-pu 別西卜	Same	G.1855. Same
5.	Hsieh-kuei-wang 邪鬼王	Same	G.1847, Matt. 12.27
6.	Kuei-wang 鬼王	Beelzebub the prince of demons	G.1847, G.1855, Matt. 12.24
7.	Sa-tan-hung ◦撒但哄	Satan	Mor.1823, Rev. 12.9
8.	Sa-tan ◦撒但, 撒但	Same	Mor.1823, D.1852, Acts 5.3
9.	Mo 魔	Same	G.1847, G.1855, Matt. 12.26
10.	Mo-kuei 魔鬼	The Devil	G.1847, Acts 5.3; Rev. 12.9. G.1855, Acts 5.3.
11.	Kuei 鬼	devil or demon	G.1847, G.1855, Matt. 9.32.
12.	O-ti 惡敵	Satan	G.1847, Rev.12.9
13.	Hsieh-kuei 邪鬼	a demon	G.1847, Matt. 12.24
14.	Kuei-feng 鬼風	a devil	Mor.1823, Matt. 9.32
15.	Ta-lung 大龍	The Great Dragon	Mor.1823, G.1847, Rev. 12.9
16.	Lao-she 老蛇	The Old Serpent	Same

A comparison of the tabulation of Biblical terms with that of terms current with the insurgents shows less overlapping than would have been the case had the Chinese had less fertile native sources upon which to draw. Three duplications are noticeable, namely mo-kuei for the Devil, kuei for a devil, and lao-she, the Old Serpent. Of these only the last can be considered because of its un-Chinese nature as an out-and-out borrowing. The clumsy, strange-sounding transliterations invented by Western translators were entirely ignored. Instead, extensive use was made of terms like hsieh-shen, and yao or yao-mo. The assimilation into the new ideology of Yen-lo, the traditional Chinese ruler of the underworld, 176 was to be expected.

To judge from the evidence presented above, Hung Hsiu-ch'üan and his collaborators found the Western Bible an auxiliary but hardly an indispensable source for either terms or ideas with which to describe evil influences. This section of Taiping ideology can be regarded as the counterpart but not the derivative of the corresponding Biblical development.

J. Biblical Ideas of Heaven and Hell.

The concluding section of this presentation of Taiping borrowing from the Scriptures deals with a matter important to the existence of an ideology, a state, or an army, namely the special rewards and punishments prescribed for various courses of action. Seldom are human beings to be controlled by their knowledge alone of the inherent virtue or evil of certain actions. Additional inducements or penalties are necessary. "What hae nae check but human law are to a few restricked." 177

The organizers of the Taiping movement realized the practical importance of an adequate eschatology and set about erecting a formidable system of reward and retribution in the hereafter. As completed the system was used to reinforce a most severe if not cruel enforcement of their own ordinances as well as to inspire the utmost effort during battle. Materials for the construction of such an eschatology were at hand in the Chinese form of Mahayana Buddhism, but so bitter an iconoclast as Hung could scarcely have sanctioned their use, consciously at least. This is the reason, I believe, for the relative scarcity of Buddhist terms throughout the preceding pages, though a few terms like p'u-sa and Yen-lo may have been indispensable in explaining ideas t neophytes. The fact remains that the way was clear for full utilization of the Bible.

The Old Testament was not as well suited to the search for eschatological precedent as it had been to the borrowing of a code of morals.

Aside from the book of Daniel, punishment and reward are treated throughout the Old Testament as matters to be accomplished on earth. A case in point is Deuteronomy 28. The larger part of this chapter is devoted to a recital of the consequences of disobeying God's commandments. This is as ingenious and detailed a portrayal of personal calamity as exists in the Bible; however, the instruments of retribution are enemies, pestilence, and the forces of nature operating on this earth. By the same token, he who keeps the commandments is "blessed" in all his earthly activities. Th Hebrew prophets follow the same line but extend the principl to the behavior of a group. The fall of Babylon, the destruction of Damascus, the captivity of Egypt and Ethiopia, and the ruin of Tyre are predicted by Isaiah in vivid terms;[178] nothing is said regarding mass retribution against the inhabitants of these regions in a hereafter. Jeremiah promises the Jews in Egypt punishment by famine, pestilence, and the sword. The physical destruction of Babylon is depicted in stirring speech. [179] These examples are typical of a pattern of prophetic utterance. [180]

Hebrew concentration upon the relatively immediate consequences of wrongdoing reflects itself in the limited development of Sheol, their term for the underworld. Unlike the Avernus of the Aeneid or the Inferno of the Divine Comedy, Sheol is no more than the abode of the dead. [181] Its inmates seem to be more often the wicked than the righteous, but even they experience no punishment other than oblivion. Figuratively the term is used to connote "deep" or "remote."[182]

Equally remarkable is the virtual absence in the Old Testament of references to heaven. There is no Yahweh"who art in Heaven" to match the first verse of the Lord's Prayer. The righteous receive their reward entirely on earth.

In contrast to the Old, the New Testament was a generous source of example and imagery to the creators of a Chinese eschatology.

Matthew's Gospel, the first book of the New Testament to be printed by the Taipings, offered them an acceptable phrase, "the kingdom of heaven." Heaven was also the abode of God the Father, [183] a concept equally acceptable. The "kingdom of heaven" is a reward, presumably as a residence, for the "poor in spirit," "they that have been persecuted for righteousness' sake," and the victims of calumny in the interests of righteousness. [184] Those who do God's will are similarly rewarded. [185] The simple directness characteristic of childhood is commended; "of such is the kingdom of heaven." [186] The familiar "lay up for yourselves treasures in heaven" [187] is symbolic of the emphasis intended. The nature of the "kingdom of heaven" is illustrated in a number of the parables of Jesus. [188]

In Matthew's Gospel Hell is more than Sheol; it is clearly the scene of punishment for wrongdoing. "The Son of man shall send forth his angels, and they shall gather out of his kingdom all things that cause stumbling, and them that do iniquity, and shall cast them into the furnace of fire; there shall be the weeping and gnashing of teeth." [189] "Thou fool, shall be in danger of the hell of fire." [190] "Ye serpents, ye offspring of vipers, how shall ye escape the judgment of hell?"[191] It is characteristic of Christianity that the torments of hell are reserved also for those who fail to improve opportunities for doing good. [192]

The Gospels of Mark and Luke echo the promises and fulminations of Matthew but mention them less frequently. The phrase "the kingdom of God" [193] is used in place of "the kingdom of heaven," in one instance far less tangibly. [194] John's gospel holds out the promise of "eternal life" [195] to believers instead of the "kingdom of God" or "kingdom of heaven." There is almost no mention of Hell in this gospel; it is seemingly addressed to believers and is more personal than the other three gospels.

The Acts and the Epistles of Paul are not as concerned with the punishments of the hereafter as the Gospels; but the rewards of the hereafter for believers such as "eternal life" are emphasized. [196] The fact of Hell and its punishments is taken for granted except for a passage like the following: ". . . at the revelation of the Lord Jesus from heaven with the angels of his power in flaming fire, rendering vengeance to them that know not God, and to them that obey not the gospel of our Lord Jesus who shall suffer punishment, even eternal destruction from the face of the Lord and from the glory of his might when he shall come to be glorified in his saints . . . ." [197] Revelations, the final book of the New Testament, supplies an extravagance of figure and a profusion of physical detail rivalled in no other book of the New Testament. [198]

In formulating the official Taiping theory of reward and punishment in the hereafter Hung and other leaders of the movement made ready use of the profusion of New Testament models available.

To begin with, Hung adopted the phrase "the kingdom of Heaven" from Matthew as part of the title of the new regime. The phrase is believed to have come to him through a passage in C.S.L.Y.1832 [199] which read 天國降臨 (The Kingdom of Heaven is at hand). T'ien-kuo, which was probably Gützlaff's[20] as well as Morrison's rendering of "the kingdom of Heaven," he evidently took to refer to China. The character for "Heavenly" was then prefaced to names of institutions and personages of the new order, e.g. "Heavenly Dynasty," "Heavenly Army," "Heavenly Elder Brother," and the like.

In Taiping writings heaven is described as the scene of endless bliss. The righteous "ascend to heaven and experience endless bliss." [201] "When you go to heaven you will enjoy happiness without end." [202] Heaven is promised to a wide range of the virtuous. The joys of paradise await believers, those obedient to God's commands, those who trust in God, men who refuse to hold "worldly views," the pious, and finally those who fight for the Taiping cause and refuse to aid the imperialists, commonly referred to as yao (fiends). "Believers will be saved and ascend to heaven." [203] "Honor and disgrace all (come) from (a man's) self. Men should exert themselves to keep the ten commandments and (they) will enjoy bliss in heaven." [204] "Rely on (God) with a true heart. Then you may ascend to heaven." "Throw away all worldly desires. Then you will be able to go to heaven." "Obey heaven's commands, worship the true God, and upon parting (with the present world) it will be easy to ascend to heaven." " . . . seize or decapitate the impish Tatars and come over to submit yourselves to our heavenly dynasty. . . . In the present world you shall have glory and honor without compare and in heaven enjoy happiness without end with eternal dignity and eternal honor. Is not this much better than aiding demons and becoming devils yourselves . . . ?"

Hell is portrayed by the Taipings as a place of punishment and of endless misery, difficult from which to escape, the abode of the utterly lost. The wicked " . . . will certainly be punished (by being) sent down to hell and suffering misery . . . . " [205] Transgressors are warned that God "will condemn (you) to fall into the deepest hell and suffer eternal misery." [206] ". . . (it is) hard to escape from hell." [207] "Afterwards (the wicked) will fall into the perdition of hell." [208] Among the damned are unbelievers, followers of corrupt gods and corrupt devils, the blasphemous, the rebellious, and of course all Chinese who aid the imperialist cause. [209] "Unbelievers will be the first to be condemned." [210] "(If you) mistakenly believe (in corrupt devils), (you) will end up in hell." "Who is the one with the effrontery to call (himself) Ti (designation for God)? But (we) shall see his foolish self-elevation bringing upon (him) the eternal sufferings of hell." "The gates of hell are open to await the rebellious."

In the illustrations above, the Taiping term for heaven is either T'ien 天 or T'ien-t'ang 堂 (Heavenly Hall). The insurgents had two designations for hell, Ti-yü 地獄 or the more elaborate and strictly Chinese Shih-pa-chung ti-yü 十八重 (eighteen-storied hell), a term of Buddhist origin.

The translators of early Christian Bibles employed the same words for "heaven" and "to get to heaven" as the insurgents. Ti-yü is the customary Biblical rendering for "hell," though occasionally the invention of An-fu 暗府 (the Shades) is used. [211]

Footnotes

1. Early Protestant missionaries wrote tracts to supplement and explain the Bible, but these works to judge from their titles had all they could do to expound Christian doctrine and combat native practices. See the list of titles of tracts in Wylie, Memorials of Protestant Missionaries to the Chinese. The following is a sampling of the titles of tracts published up to 1852 with names of authors and the dates of publication where they are known.

T.H. Hudson.	Depravity of Human Nature 邪性記
D.B. McCartie.	Efficacious Prescription for Giving Peace of Mind. 安心解難良方
W.H. Medhurst.	The Lun Yü Newly Modelled 論語新篆 Tract on Idolatry. 1840. 偶像書編
W.M. Lowrie.	Important Discourse on the Sabbath Day. 1847. 禮拜日要論
J.L. Shuck.	Commentary on the Decalogue. 1849. 真神十言
Gützlaff.	Little Faith, Little Happiness. 小信小福

2. A penetrating analysis of the problems of translation arising from the rendering of Chinese (in this case, that of Mencius) into English is I.A. Richards, Mencius on the Mind (New York: Harcourt, Brace, 1932). As Richards notes (pp. 3-4), "Chinese thinking often gives no attention to distinctions which for Western minds are so traditional and so firmly established in thought and language, that we neither question them nor even become aware of them as distinctions. We receive and use them as though they belonged unconditionally to the constitution of things (or of thought). We forget that these distinctions have been made and maintained as part of one tradition of thinking; and that another tradition of thinking might neither find use for them nor (being committed to other courses) be able to admit them." Richards recommends that all logical apparatus and all forms of thought be regarded as tools designed for a particular purpose and that therefore they be employed in translation work in a tentative non-dogmatic manner. A helpful tool for comparative studies would be a series of multiple definitions for terms in common use (see pp. 86-131) that would embrace all meanings possible in both Chinese and English.

3. It is difficult to appreciate the parable of the sower fully until one has seen the poor, rocky soil of Judaea. "A shadow of a great rock in a thirsty land" cannot be vivid to one who has never lived in country like the Syrian desert. References to sheep and the details of a pastoral economy lose force when read by members of an industrialized, urban society. For this reason two generations ago a pilgrimage to Palestine was regarded as a desirable part of a Protestant minister's training; such a clergyman the writer once knew. This man spent three weeks going over the country on horseback. A Lutheran minister described to me recently the quickening effect upon his thought of a visit to the scenes of Luther's life.

4. "The great God says, Thou shalt have no other gods beside me" 皇上帝曰除我外不可有別神也. TTS, S.W.C.2.129, 8. "The true god of heaven is one God" 天上真神一上帝. Ibid. 2.130b,10. "All know that the true god is only one, and you should understand that creative (power) all comes from Heaven

From ancient times on the true god has been God alone" 脊和
真神祇獨一要識造化總由天從古真神惟上帝.. TPCSK, T.S.4.5b, 2-3
under this title. "The true god who created (the universe)
is God alone" 開闢真神惟上帝. TPCS, S.W.C.1.8,5. "At the
beginning, in six days only all things were created, perfect and complete" 當初纔六日萬樣造齊全. YHS, T.S.4.1b,5
to 2,1 under this title. "(Our) exalted heavenly Father is
infinitely honorable; those who disobey him will hardly
escape their (proper) end" 巍巍天父極尊崇犯分干名鮮克終 .
TTS, S.W.C.2,129b, 1.
  5. This left two spaces for honoring references to the
leaders of the Taiping movement, "The Heavenly Dynasty," etc.
See TPCSK, T.S.4.1-5 under this title.
  6. TTS, S.W.C.2.128, 3-4.
  7. The term ti, it is believed, originally referred to a
sacrifice, but later lost this meaning and became the name of
divinities sacrificed to, including deceased rulers. The
term shang-ti may have come from the designation of the first
ancestor of the Shang kings as the Supreme Ruler. Whether a
dead ruler was specifically meant or not, the most important
of many Shang gods was called either ti or shang-ti. When
the Shang was replaced by the Chou dynasty the practice of
applying ti to dead kings was forgotten, but the idea of the
supreme ti was retained and made synonymous with a chief deity
of the Chou people called t'ien or heaven. Herrlee Glessner
Creel, The Birth of China (London: Jonathan Cape, 1936), 181-4,
342-3. In the comparisons that follow asterisks are used as
ditto marks.
  8. "Jehovah, Jehovah, a God merciful and gracious, slow
to anger, and abundant in lovingkindness and truth, keeping
lovingkindness for thousands, forgiving iniquity and transgression and sin . . . ." Compare with "This then is the
extraordinary grace and infinite compassion of the great God"
此乃皇上帝格外恩憐莫大之恩典也 . TTS, S.W.C.2.126b, 9-10.
  9. Ibid.2.125b, 6-8; 126b, 12 ff. In the course of one
of his descents to earth God is described as being unusually
merciful in dealing with an inspector negligent in reporting
treason, a certain Huang Wen-an 黃文安 . "T'ien-fu hsia-fan
chao-shu," S.W.C.2.152b, 10. The first of a series of what
appear to be Taiping examination essays, in justifying a
change in name for Chihli province, speaks of the "unbounded
benevolence" and "fathomless liberality" of God. "Pien yao
hsüeh wei tsui-li lun," S.L.3.2b, 6.
  10. "(Our) Heavenly Father of his great mercy and boundless
goodness, spared not his first-born Son, but sent him down
into the world to give his life for the redemption of all our
sins . . ." 天父鴻恩廣大無邊不惜太子遣降凡間捐命代贖吾儕罪孽
TTS, S.W.C.2.129, 1. See also STC, S.W.C.2.173, 2-3; and
TPCSK, T.S.4.2, 2-6 under this title.
  11. The original promise of sponsorship to Abraham occurs

in Genesis 12. 1-3. It reoccurs in communications with Isaac, Gen. 26. 2-5, 24 and with Jacob, Gen. 28. 13-15, 13. 10-12. In Ex. 3. 15-17 the promise is then made of deliverance from Egypt and eventual possession of a new country.
12. Ex. 24. 3-8.
13. Joshua 24. 15-28.
14. "The great God is the common Father of all nations in the universe" 皇上帝爲天下萬國大共之父 . TTS, S.W.C.2.129,4.
15. "The Chinese in early ages were regarded by God with affection; together with foreign states they walked in one way. From (the time of) Pan-ku down to the Three Dynasties they honored God, as history records . . . . When Ch'in (obtained) the empire, he (the First Emperor of Ch'in) was deceived by the genii and China has (thus) been deluded by the devil for (the last) two thousand years." STC, S.W.C. 2.173, 6-7, 9. The Taipings, of course, were misrepresenting early Chinese religion. See sections on religion and sacrifice in Creel, Birth of China.
16. ". . . Again, he (God) sent our master, the heavenly king, down into the world as a sovereign who has received the Divine decree to exercise authority, that he might exterminate the impish fiends, and awaken the empire, soothing the myriad regions and leading them to the equal enjoyment of real happiness" 復遣我主天王下凡爲真命主誅滅妖魔化醒天下撫綏萬邦同享真福. TPCSK, T.S.4.2, 8-10 under this title.
17. The identical character yaku appears in the names kyūyaku and shin-yakuzenshō, the standard Japanese translations for Old and New Testament.
18. TPCSK, T.S.4.2b, 9; 3, 1.
19. A large number of the Taiping proclamations seem to have been issued jointly by the Eastern and Western Kings. For a sample, see "Chun-pan-hsing chao-shu," S.W.C.1.34b, 2.
20. TPSCK, op.cit. 3b, 9 to 4, 3.
21. Deut. 20.
22. Joshua 6.2-5.
23. Joshua 10. 11-14.
24. Judges 7.2-7.
25. 2 Kings 19.35.
26. Joshua 7.
27. "This was evidently pre-arranged by our Heavenly Father, on which account we proved victorious in every engagement, and successful in every undertaking from Chin-t'ien to Chin-ling (Nanking), a distance of 2,450 (Chinese) miles." TPCSK, T.S.4. 4, 7-9 under this title.
28. The seven appearances may be found in chronological order as follows: TMCCS, S.W.C.1: 1,11-12; 1b, 5-7; 1b, 8-12; 2, 10 to 3, 11; 3, 12 to 3b, 5; 3b, 9 to 4, 8.
29. The three appearances of Jesus in chronological order

are the following: Ibid.1.1,12; 2, 1-7; 2, 9.
30. 千金千喝千睇天千時千話千聞言 "With a thousand inducements a thousand times I have commanded you, yet a thousand times you deceived me. A thousand times I admonished you, and yet a thousand times you have trifled with my word." TMCCS, S.W.C.1.4, 4. The Chinese is extremely condensed; hence the translation is necessarily somewhat free.
31. "T'ien-fu hsia-fan chao-shu," S.W.C.2.145b,2 to 155, 2; S.L.1 (14 pages); Y.S., "Tsung-chiao" section, 3 (summary only).
32. "The Father: 'Now, are you aware that China, in this land of mortals has, for many years past, failed to pay me reverence?'

"Hsi-neng: 'The Chinese, blind to the goodness of the Heavenly Father, have long neglected and ceased to worship Him.'

"The Father: 'Do you know what the measure of the Heavenly Father's (indulgence) is like?'

"Hsi-neng: 'I know that it is as deep as the ocean.'"
"T'ien-fu hsia-fan chao-shu," S.W.C.2.147b, 8 to 148, 1.
33. "Afterwards the whole army rejoiced together at the goodness of the Father; and proceeded to kill pigs and oxen, and offer them up in thanksgiving to the heavenly Father and great God, for his power and mercy in confounding the fiendish schemes of mortal imps and his gracious care over his children." Ibid.2.154b, 11 to 155, 1.
34. Isaiah 1. 11-17.
35. ". . . what doth Jehovah require of thee but to do justly, and to love kindness, and to walk humbly with thy God?" Micah 6.8.
36. K.S. Latourette, The Chinese Their History and Culture, (3d ed. rev.) 68. See also footnote 7 above.
37. See above, pp. 55-6.
38. TTS, S.W.C.2.129b, 3; STC, S.W.C.2. 172, 9-10. In the foregoing the allusion is intended to support Taiping observance of the Sabbath. YHS, S.W.C.2.169, 11; "Yüan-tao chüeh-shih-hsün" from the TPCS, S.W.C.1.16b, 3; TPCSK, T.S.4. 1, 1 to 1b, 2; "Chun-pan-hsing chao-shu," S.W.C.1.31, 12 to 31b, 1; TMCCS, S.W.C.1. 7,5. In these the allusion occurs to enhance the Lord's prestige as a champion.
39. "Yüan-tao chüeh-chih-hsün," S.W.C.1.15, 6-10.
40. "Chun-pan-hsing chao-shu," S.W.C.1.31b, 3-4.
41. STC, S.W.C.2.172, 11 to 173, 1.
42. Ibid.2.172, 11 to 172b, 1.
43. "Yüan-tao chüeh-shih-hsün" from the TPCS, S.W.C.1.16, 11 to 16b, 1.
44. "Chun-pan-hsing chao-shu," S.W.C.1. 31b, 4.
45. A transliteration of the Hebrew designation Misraim.

46. STC, S.W.C.2. 172b, 2.
47. Ibid.2.172b, 4.
48. Ibid.2.172b, 5.
49. Ibid.2.172b, 7-8.
50. T'ien-lu (sweet dew) was considered an appropriate rendering of the Biblical "manna" by both the Taipings and the translators of the Medhurst-Gützlaff Old Testament. See Ex. 16.31, G.1847: "The house of Israel called the name thereof man 蔓 (transcription of Hebrew man), which was the same as heavenly dew." T'ien can be considered a synonym for kan in the well-known Chinese expression kan-lu (sweet dew). The appearance of sweet-tasting dew has been regarded since Han times as a good omen and a manifestation of divine favor. Cf. Tz'u Hai (standard Chinese dictionary) under kan-lu. Kan-lu has been used several times as a nien-hao (era name).
51. S.W.C.2.172b, 10.
52. Y.S. 4.9, 8.
53. "In early ages the Great Supreme Ruler descended to Mount Sinai, himself wrote the ten laws of Heaven on tables of stone, and gave them to Moses." "Yüan-tao chüeh-shih-hsün S.W.C.1.16, 11-12.
54. The phrase "___ law of Heaven" is omitted in subsequent citations.
55. Taiping prohibitions in the "T'ien-t'iao-shu" will be seen to prefer the colloquial pu-hao 不好 to the more literary wu 毋 or pu-ko 不可 of the Scriptures.
56. Exodus 32.4-8, 20.
57. Judges 17 illustrates this with a story of the making of images for a certain Micah, these figures to be used in the worship of Yahweh. ". . . his mother said, I verily dedicate the silver unto Jehovah from my hand for my son to make a graven image and a molten image . . . "
58. Judges 10.6.
59. "Israel abode in Shittim; and the people began to play the harlot with the daughters of Moab, for they called the people unto the sacrifices of their gods; and the people did eat and bowed down to their gods." Numbers 25.1-2.
60. The following are typical examples: I Kings 18.18-40; Isaiah 2.6-8; Jeremiah 11.10; Ezekiel 6.3-6; Hosea 8.4.
61. C.S.L.Y.1832 1.4b, 8. Expressions peculiar to this work alone are 泥塑的像 (idols of mud), ibid.1.5,3; 彫紙畫之形模 (images drawn on paper or carved), ibid.1.7b, 2.
62. "God commanded Moses saying, I am the great God, the supreme God; you men of the world must on no account set up images resembling anything in heaven above or in earth beneath, to bow down and worship." "Yüan-tao chüeh-shih-hsün," S.W.C.1.16, 1 to 16b, 1.
63. TTS, S.W.C.2.130b, 10.
64. "Yüan-tao chüeh-shih-hsün," S.W.C.1.18, 2-3.

65. "Yüan-tao chüeh-shih-hsün," S.W.C.1.17, 9-10. This may reflect the influence of Psalm 115. Parts of the quotation seem a close paraphrase of verses 5-7, Ps. 115.
66. "Yüan-tao chiu-shih-ko," S.W.C.1.8b, 8-9. P'u-sa is here used as the term for idol.
67. Op.cit., S.W.C.1.16, 1 to 17, 4. Ou-hsiang is used for image, p'u-sa for idol.
68. "Who is the devil but the images and idols which you worship and sacrifice to?" "Chun-pan-hsing chao-shu," S.W.C.1.34b, 9. Terms for idols and images are p'u-sa and ou-hsiang.
69. "You are none of you the children of idols. Why do you not then repent and strive to get to heaven?" TTS, S.W.C. 2.130b, 12. P'u-sa is the term for idol.
70. ". . . although Shang-ti is introduced as issuing instructions and orders, he is nowhere pictured as demanding sole recognition as the one and only god. Apparently he is very complacent in recognizing the presence of other deities with a right to be revered." P.E. Kretzmann, The God of the Bible and Other Gods (St. Louis, 1943), 101.
71. E.T.C. Werner, A Dictionary of Chinese Mythology (Shanghai: Kelly and Walsh, 1932), 411.
72. "What, we would ask, was the cause of God's anger? He was angry with men for worshipping perverted gods and performing perverted actions." "Chun-pan-hsing chao-shu," S.W.C.1.31b, 9. Two of the approved forms of prayer carry an injunction against worshipping "corrupt gods." TTS, S.W.C.2. 127,5, 11. See also "Yüan-tao chiu-shih-ko," S.W.C. 1.8b, 11. The meaning of hsieh 邪, the opposite of cheng 正, cannot be properly expressed by one English word. It can mean distorted, irregular, unorthodox, heretical and also corrupt, perverted, wrong, wicked, vicious. The "corrupt" or "perverted" which I use in translating hsieh should be taken as symbolic of the other meanings as well.
73. STC, S.W.C.2.173, 6 to 173b, 2; "Yüan-tao chüeh-shih-hsün," S.W.C.1.15, 2-6; 17, 12 to 17b, 12.
74. "In very ancient times men's minds were still intelligent and before they had lost (sight of) the true origin (of all things) they all knew how to honor and worship the great God, the Heavenly Father and Supreme Lord." TPCSK, T.S. 4.1b, 6-8 under this title.
75. "Yüan-tao chüeh-shih-hsün," S.W.C.1.18, 5-6.
76. TPCSK, T.S.4. 1-4, 8-9.
77. "Yüan-tao chüeh-shih-hsün," S.W.C.1.14b, 11 to 15,1.
78. Ibid., S.W.C.1.18b, 11-12.
79. TTS, S.W.C.2.128b, 2.
80. "Truly correct persons cause perverted devils to go away . . . Hsien-tsung of the T'ang dynasty (referred to

above) threw the empire into confusion because he acted incorrectly in listening to his wife (Yang Kuei-fei). . . . Be correct and you may enjoy the happiness of heaven. Be incorrect and you will fall into the region of hell." "Pai-cheng-ko," S.W.C.1.12, 10; 12b, 4; 12b, 6.

81. For example, the Russian Senate in 1721 conferred this title upon Peter the Great. S.F. Platonov, History of Russia (New York, 1929), 229-30.

82. The following illustrate the personalization that accompanied Christ's use of the term. " . . . and glorify your Father who is in Heaven." Matt.5.16. " . . . your heavenly Father knoweth that you have need of all these things." Matt.6.32. "Are not two sparrows sold for a penny? And not one of them shall fall on the ground without your Father." Matt. 10.29.

83. "This is my beloved Son; hear ye him." Mark 9.7. "But whosoever shall deny me before men, him will I also deny before my Father who is in Heaven." Matt.10.33. "And the Father that sent me he hath borne witness of me." John 5.37.

84. TTS, S.W.C.2: 天父皇上帝, 127, 9; 127b, 1; 上帝...天聖父, 128b, 11.

85. 天父上主皇上帝, TPCSK, T.S.4.1, 2; TMCCS, S.W.C.1.1, 11.

86. 上帝原來是老親, "Yüan-tao hsing-shih hsün," S.W.C.1. 14, 9.

87. For a complete report of the incident see TMCCS, S.W.C 1.6, 10 to 6b, 10; S.L.1.11, 6 to 12b, 6. The quotation is in S.L.1.12, 6. The term yeh of these quotations is meant to express great respect as well as the fact of fatherhood.

88. "This is my beloved Son, in whom I am well pleased . . . . " Matt.17.5.

89. See the case of the Syro-Phoenician woman, Mark 7. 26-30; also Luke 7. 2-10; Matt. 28.19; Mark 13.10; and Acts 9.15

90. ". . . foreign nations, though far removed, are protected and cared for by the great God. The same (is true) for China, so near." "Yüan-tao hsing-shih-hsün," S.W.C.1. 13b, 6-7. "God is the Father of the generals of this army. He is also your Father; moreover, he is the father of all men in every nation under heaven. As the ancients have said, 'All under heaven are one family and all within the four seas brethren.'" "Chiu i-ch'ieh t'ien-sheng t'ien-yang yü," S.W.C 1.34b, 6-7. "God the heavenly Father is shared by all men." "Yüan-tao chiu-shih ko" in TPCS, S.W.C.1.8, 6. "Let the true god, the Great God, be honored and adored by all nations; let all the inhabitants of the world unite in his worship morning and evening." YHS, S.W.C.2.169, 9.

91. TTS, S.W.C.2.126, 1-3.

92. Ibid.2.126, 3-8.

What the Taipings Took   95

   93. Ibid.2.127, 1 to 127b, 6; 127b, 9 to 128, 1.
   94. Ibid.2.129, 4-5.
   95. Psalms 23, 71, and 91 are typical, though unequalled by the Taipings in eloquence.
   96. J.S. Whale, Christian Doctrine (New York: MacMillan, 1941), 113-4.
   97. John 14.16, 26; Acts 2.38; Acts 6.5.
   98. 賜聖神風化心 TTS, S.W.C.2.127, 3; T.S.1.2b, 3 under this title.
   99. The full text of the doxology is given in footnote 103. TTS, T.S.1.6, 6-7; S.W.C.2.128b, 11-12.
   100. With a few exceptions (see T.S.5 under "T'ien-ch'ing tao-li-shu" and T.S.6 under "Yü-chih ch'ien tzu chao"), the Taipings were accustomed to give the date of the earliest edition to all editions of a given title. The last edition of the Old and New Testaments is believed to have appeared in 1860 or later, but the title page still bears the phrase "Published in kuei-hao, the third year of the T'ai-p'ing t'ien-kuo." T.S.1.1, 1-4, 9; 1b, 1-4 in the compiler's colophon under "Chiu-hsin-i chao-sheng-shu." In the title of this edition of the New Testament the character ch'ien 前 (previous) replaced hsin 新 (new) before the compound for Testament. It is difficult to account for this substitution except by the hypothesis that rebel leaders came to regard their canonical literature as the "New" Testament; the New Testament of the Bible had become to them a work of Scripture dependent upon previous and less authoritative inspiration.
   101. "The Eastern King is the beloved Son of God, and he, with (my) Great Elder Brother and me, were all born of the one venerable mother. Before the existence of heaven and earth all three of us were as close as sons of one father . . . Now God came down to earth but that which descended to the Eastern King was the Holy Spirit (sheng-shen 聖神). The King's own function then is to be the wind (feng 風), or the Comforter (ch'üan-wei-shih 勸慰師). The Father knew that in the New Testament there were mistakes. Therefore he descended to the Eastern King and proclaimed that the Holy Spirit was God and the wind was the Eastern King." Ibid.1.2, 5-6, 9-11. This was Hung's explanation of an essence, the Shen-sheng-feng, that included both God and the Eastern King with specialized functions as above. After the capture of Nanking eight of the top leaders acquired titles attributing to each an aspect of the natural environment. Attributions are as follows: Hung Hsiu-ch'üan - the sun, his wife Hung Lai-shih 賴氏 the moon, Yang Hsiu-ch'ing - the wind, Hsiao Ch'ao-kuei - the rain, Wei Ch'ang-hui - the thunder, Shih Ta-k'ai - the lightning, the Yü-wang 豫王 the dew, and the Yen-wang 燕王

the frost. Except for Hung who took jih (sun) as a given name and his wife who was called Yüeh-kung (moon-palace), the titles read "Master of the Wind," etc. Yang's title fitted neatly into his identification with Shen-sheng-feng or Holy Spirit. Kuo T'ing-i, T'ai-p'ing t'ien-kuo shih-shih jih-chih,史事日誌. Letter from W.A.P. Martin dated May 2, 1856. North-China Herald 306 (June 7, 1856).

102. Translations of a number of Hung's annotations, the originals of which were not copied out by Hsiao I-shan and do not appear in T.S.1, are printed in Rev. W.T.A. Barber, "The Rebel Bible," The Chinese Recorder and Missionary Journal, XXII, 7 (July 1891), 305-8. Barber saw the latest editions of the Old and New Testaments listed in Chapter 8 (nos. 1 (3) and 2 (3), p.133) briefly. Hung's original annotations for these later editions of the Bible deserve publication in full.

103. An English translation of the Taiping doxology and the two versions in Chinese matched character for character appear below.

English Translation of Taiping Doxology
Praise God, the holy and heavenly Father.
Praise Jesus, the holy Lord and Saviour of the World.
Praise the Holy Spirit, the sacred Spiritual Force (or Example).
Praise the three persons (who) united (constitute one true Lord.

Taiping and Missionary Versions in Chinese

Taiping Doxology: 讚美上帝爲天聖父， 讚美耶穌爲救世聖主
Doxology of Am.
 Baptist Mission: ＊＊真神是＊＊爺，＊＊＊＊ ＊＊＊＊
Taiping Doxology: 讚美聖神風爲聖靈， 讚美三位爲合一真神
Doxology of Am.
 Baptist Mission:＊＊＊＊＊是＊＊，＊＊＊＊是 ＊聖＊

W.H. Medhurst, "Critical Review of the Books of the Insurgents," North-China Herald, 162 (Sept. 3, 1853), 19. S.W.C. 2 contains an alternate text which substitutes hsien 憲 (pattern, example) for ling 靈 (spiritual force) in the third line of the doxology.

104. "On a third occasion, greatly angered, the Great Supreme Ruler sent down the Saviour of the World, the Lord Jesus, who was born in Judaea and on behalf of mankind suffered to atone for (their) sin." "Tsou-t'ien chu-yao chiu-shih an-min yü," S.W.C.1.31b, 5. Judaea is transliterated as Yu-t'ai-kuo 猶太國. See also the sources cited in footnote 10. "Jesus the first-born son God sent that year. (He)

voluntarily gave up (his) life to atone for sin." YHS, S.W.C.2.169b, 3; T.S.4.2, 4 to 2b, 1 under this title. "The Great Supreme Ruler pitied mankind and sent his first-born down into the world. He was called Jesus, the Lord and Saviour. Truly suffering he redeemed (men) from sin." STC, S.W.C.2.173, 2-3.

    105. "(Upon) a cross (they) nailed his body. (He) shed (his) precious blood to save all men. Three days (after) death (he) again lived. For forty days he discussed heavenly things. On the point of ascending to heaven (he) commanded (his) disciples to communicate the gospel and proclaim (his) mandate. Believers will be saved and ascend up to heaven. Unbelievers will be the first to be condemned." Ibid., S.W.C.2.173, 3-5. The term here used for "gospel," fu-yin 福音 (lit. "happy sounds"), has since become the Christian term for "gospel" (Anglo-Saxon "good tidings"). The term chao-shu 詔書 (mandate) had already been used in the Morrison and Gützlaff Bibles to render Testament in the title "New Testament." The Taipings, however, added the character sheng (holy) before shu (writing). "The cross was difficult to bear. The sorrowing clouds obscured the sun. The esteemed Son, honoured in Heaven, died for you, mankind. After resurrection he again ascended to heaven. Resplendent in glory he wields unlimited authority. We know (we may) rely on (him)." YHS, S.W.C.2.169b, 5-7; T.S.4.2b, 3 to 3, 5 under this title.

    106. For a comparison of terms see Mor.1823, Matt. 27.22; G.1847, Mark 15.26; STC, S.W.C.2.173, 3-5.

    107. See footnote 105. Liang A-fa has the same term. C.S.L.Y.1832.I.6b, 4.

    108. TTS, S.W.C.2.127, 6-7.
    109. Ibid., S.W.C.2. 130b, 8-9.
    110. John 3.16-17.
    111. Acts 1.3.
    112. Matt. 27.45; Mark 15.33.
    113. Matt. 28.19-20; Mark 16.15.
    114. Arthur Evans Moule, Half a Century in China (London, 1911), 30 illustrates a rubbing of the eight Beatitudes, carved on a stone slab measuring eleven by nine feet, which he says once stood before the Taiping palace of Hung Jen-kan in Nanking, but which was destroyed when imperial troops captured the city. Chien Yu-wen, T'ai-p'ing t'ien-kuo tsa-chi 雜記 (Miscellaneous records of the T'ai-p'ing t'ien-kuo) (Shanghai: Commercial Press, 1935), 217-23 reproduces a photograph of the rubbing, now in the British Museum, and gives the text of the Beatitudes as they appeared on the stele. Most of the space on the slab is taken by the huge character fu (blessed), carved from a specimen of Hung Jen-kan's calligraphy. The slab was evidently made at Hung

Jen-kan's direction, for it bears his seal and the date 1860. However, the prominence thus given to the Beatitudes occurs late in the course of the Rebellion as a detached episode. There is no sign of the Beatitudes nor of their influence in the religious publications of the insurgents.

115. This is a stock phrase included in a number of the prescribed prayers. S.W.C.2.127b, 1-2; 127b, 12 to 128, 1; 128, 5-6, 11-12; 128b, 7-8. T.S.1.3, 9-10; 3b, 7-8; 4, 7-8; 4b, 7-8; 5, 8-9 under this title.

116. S.W.C.2.127, 11-12. T.S.1.3, 6-7 under this title. The text in the latter omits the second to the last character of the quotation (ch'in, encroach).

117. S.W.C.1.17, 8-9.

118. Mark 2.5. Luke 5.20.

119. John 8.3-11. Similar treatment was given a woman who showed her gratitude by anointing Christ's feet with an expensive ointment. Luke 7.27-50.

120. Mark 2.15-17.

121. The sections are consecutive. S.W.C.2.127, 1 to 127b, 2; T.S.1.2, 8 to 3b, 1. In T.S.1 the first selection is called Hui-tsui kuei-chü 悔罪規矩 (Form for Repenting of Sin) and contains the same material but with a number of different wordings. The two versions of the second selection are the same except for one phrase.

122. Fan t'ien-t'iao 犯天條.

123. The examples below will illustrate. Chinese romanizations referred to are underlined.

1) Matt.6.12: "And forgive us our debts as we also have forgiven our debtors."

> G.1847: Ch'iu mien-chai ju wu mien jen fu-chai wo yeh.
> G.1855: Erh mien-chai same from here on.

2) Matt.6.14: "For if ye forgive men their trespasses, your heavenly Father will also forgive you."

> G.1847: Fu erh she jen chih tsui chi t'ien-fu i chiang she erh.

3) Matt.6.15: "But if ye forgive not men their trespasses, neither will your Father forgive your trespasses."

> Mor.1823: Tan jo erh pu she jen chih tsui erh fu i pu she erh chih tsui yeh.

124. There is some question as to the identity of the evangelists whom Hung saw and the date of the preaching. Jen-kan reported that Hung Hsiu-ch'üan heard a foreigner

What the Taipings Took   99

speak who was dressed in Ming dynasty costume, who did not
know Chinese, and whose words were interpreted by a Chinese
companion. See Hamberg, Visions, 8; Chien Yu-wen, transl.,
"Ch'i-i chi," in T'ai-p'ing t'ien-kuo tsa-chi, 14, 1.11 to
15, 1.4. Chien believes that Liang A-fa was the Chinese
interpreter mentioned. Chien, T'ai-p'ing chün Kwangsi shou-
i-shih, 68, 1.15. P'eng Tse-i, however, quotes a biography of
Liang A-fa to show that Liang left China in 1834 and worked
in overseas stations such as Singapore and Malacca until
1839. For Liang to have been present the second examination
which the Taiping founder attended could have been no later
than 1834. P'eng, T'ai-p'ing t'ien-kuo ko-ming ssu-ch'ao,
5, which refers to page 93 of a Chinese translation of Geo.
H. McNeus, The First Chinese Protestant Evangeliser Leung
Faot, 1789-1855 (Shanghai, 1931). Wilhelm Oehler, Die
Taiping Bewegung (Gutersloh: C. Bertelsmann, 1923), 234
believes that the foreign preacher was a certain Edwin Stevens (d. 1837) who first came to China in 1834. Hamberg,
Visions, 8 gives 1836 as the date when Hung heard the preaching and received the tracts; in the confession written in
1864 twelve years after he talked with Hamberg Hung Jen-kan
says it happened in 1837. Hsieh Hsing-yao, T'ai-p'ing
t'ien-kuo ts'ung-shu (Collectanea of the T'ai-p'ing t'ien-
kuo) (Peip'ing: Yao-chai ts'ung-k'o, 1938) 2d compilation,
2, 1.3 under the title "Kan-wang Hung Jen-kan k'ou-kung."
Meadows, The Chinese and Their Rebellions, 75-6 thinks that
Hung's contact with the preacher happened in 1833 and that
Liang A-fa was the interpreter. Apparently Liang was in
China in 1833, for in a report to the London Missionary Society Robert Morrison remarks that Liang and two others were
distributing tracts to examination candidates in October
1833 and implies that 1833 was the year for the triennial
examination. On the other hand, a letter from Liang to the
Society translated in its report for 1835 says that 1834
was the year of the triennial examination and that he and
two companions were able to distribute books to the candidates from Aug. 20 to Aug. 23. On Aug. 24 police stopped
these activities, and subsequently arrested the two assist-
ants, and confiscated some of the tracts and wooden blocks
from which they were printed. Liang escaped to carry on his
work with overseas Chinese. I am inclined to the opinion that
Liang was the Chinese interpreter as reported in the Visions,
but that Hung Jen-kan failed to date the second examination
early enough. Either 1833 or 1834 should be given as the
year with the evidence favoring 1834. Cf. Foster, "The
Christian Origins of the Taiping Rebellion," op.cit., 158.
Edwin Stevens could have been the foreign preacher on this
occasion since he arrived in China in 1834. The identity
of the foreign preacher, however, must still be established.

125. Chien, Shou-i-shih, 68, 99.
126. Confession accompanied baptism in the earliest Gospel accounts as well.   Matt.3.6, 11; Mark 1.4-5.
127. Chien, op.cit., 130. Hung did not blame Roberts for the refusal; his respect for his former teacher continued. In 1853 after Nanking had fallen, Hung sent Roberts a letter inviting him to visit the rebel capital. Roberts' tentative request to the American authorities that he be allowed to go to the rebels to "assist that the gospel may be made plain" was refused by Humphrey Marshall, the American commissioner, with the remark that such activity at that point would constitute the most powerful sort of unneutral action. Enclosures 1 and 2, Humphrey Marshall to Marcy, June 21, 1853, Dispatches from United States Ministers to China, Vol. 8, Aug. 5, 1852 - Feb. 22, 1854.
128. Chien, op.cit., 99.
129. TTS, S.W.C.2.126, 2-3; T.S.1.2, 10 to 2b, 1 under this title.
130. A comparative table showing the choice of characters employed in four early Chinese Bibles appears below. Romanizations of the characters for baptism are underlined.

Comparative Table Showing the Choice of Characters Used in Early Chinese Bibles to Convey the Idea of Baptism

Mark 1.4: "(John) . . . baptized in the wilderness."

Mor.1823: tsai yeh shih hsi.
G. 1847: chin-hsi yü yeh.
G. 1855: chin yü yeh.
D. 1852: tsai yeh shih hsi.

131. Hamberg, Visions, 35.
132. Chien, op.cit., 136-7.
133. "Frequently they (foreigners) were requested to make bare their arms and breasts to display the tattooed crucifix often found on sailors, for although no superstitious reverence is paid to the cross by the Taiping men, yet they regard it with respect as the emblem of their purer newly adopted faith." Report of an American deserter from an imperialist warship. "Dr. MacGowan's Contributions to the History of the Insurrection in China XVII (concluded)," North-China Herald 354 (May 9, 1857).
134. "T'ai-p'ing t'ien-kuo kuei-hao san nien hsin li," (New calendar for kuei-hao, the third year of the T'ai-p'ing t'ien-kuo), T.S.3. 1-24 under this title. The official calendar of the regime began Feb. 3, 1851. The above is for the third year of the reign and is the earliest Taiping calendar extant.

135. Taiping dates may be readily compared with those of the Chinese lunar calendar and the Western solar calendar by reference to Cheng Hao-sheng (ed.), Chin-shih chung-hsi shih jih tui-chao piao (Comparative table of dates for recent Chinese and western history) (Shanghai, 1936), 853-80. Cheng states (p. 3) that his comparative table of Taiping and lunar and solar dates is based upon a comparative table prepared by Hsieh Hsing-yao and appearing both in the Yenching University Historical Annual, Vol.2.1 and in Hsieh's T'ai-p'ing t'ien-kuo shih-shih lun-ts'ung (Essays on the history and affairs of the T'ai-p'ing t'ien-kuo) (Shanghai: Commercial Press, 1935), 34-117. A study of the Taiping calendar appearing the year after the publication of Cheng's book presents evidence that the rebels used the combination of characters following that employed by the imperialists in the lunar calendar to denote a given date. Thus, the Taipings used chia-tzu 甲子 for the same day as that designated by imperialists as i-ch'ou 乙丑 and so on. Cheng's tables should be corrected to have the cyclical combinations refer to one day later than they now do. Kuo T'ing-i, T'ai-p'ing t'ien-kuo li-fa k'ao-ting (A study of the calendar of the T'ai-p'ing t'ien-kuo) (Shanghai: Commercial Press, 1937), 14-15.

136. Li Kuei 李圭, Chin-ling ping-shih hui-lüeh 金陵兵事彙畧 (Resumé of military affairs at Nanking) (Date and place of publication not given), Chap. 1, quoted in Hsieh Hsing-yao, T'ai-p'ing t'ien-kuo ti she-hui cheng-chih ssu-hsiang, 24-5.

137. See footnote 103 for an English translation of the first part of this. The complete text is in S.W.C.2.128b, 11 to 129, 2; T.S.1.6, 6 to 6b, 1 under this title. The versions differ slightly.

138. STC, S.W.C.2.169b, 3; 173, 2.

139. TTS, T.S.1.3b, 7-8; 4, 7-8 under this title illustrates this.

140. See p. 79. "In heaven above and earth beneath and among men who surpasses Jesus in greatness? Yet Jesus was not called Ti." "Yüan-tao chiao-shih hsün," S.W.C.1.18b, 5-6.

141. T.S.1.2, 4 in the compiler's colophon under "Chiu-hsin-i chao-sheng-shu."

142. Barber, "The Rebel Bible," op. cit., 305-8.

143. STC, S.W.C.2.173b, 8-9. Hung may have been encouraged to believe that Christ had a wife by the passage in Rev. 19. 6: " . . . for the marriage of the Lamb is come, and his wife hath made herself ready."

144. An experienced missionary's impression of the Chinese reaction to the term tsui is conveyed by Wolferstan, The Catholic Church in China, 75: "Nor had the Chinese any correct idea of sin, . . . one driven into the Jews by object

lessons. Sin with them meant 'offence' ; 'I offend you' ; in a deprecating form 'I beg your pardon' ; and not gathering the true sense the Chinese wondered at the importance we set upon it."
145. TTS, S.W.C.2.125b, 6-7.
146. Shu-tsui 贖罪. YHS, S.W.C.2.169b, 3.
147. She-tsui 赦罪. TTS, S.W.C.2.127, 2.
148. Matt. 6. 14-5.
149. T.S.1.2, 4 to 2b, 5 in the compiler's colophon under "Chiu/hsin-i chao-sheng-shu."
150. TTS, S.W.C.2.126, 1.
151. Ibid., 130b, 5.
152. Ibid., 126b, 10.
153. "Yüan-tao chiao-shih hsün," S.W.C.1.14b, 7. "There was one who looked on enviously, namely the King of Hades; much wrought he uncanny things, this serpent devil." STC, S.W.C.2.173b, 6. "Who is this devilish serpent and envious king of Hades but the old serpent who was created in the beginning when the great God made heaven and earth?" "Chiu-i-ch'ieh t'ien-sheng t'ien-yang," S.W.C.1.34b, 10-11.
154. TPCSK, T.S.4.9, 4-5 under this title.
155. "Chiu-i-ch'ieh t'ien-sheng t'ien-yang," S.W.C.1. 34b 9-11.
156. Romanizations and sources for these terms are as follows: Hsieh-shen, TTS, S.W.C.2.125b, 7; 127, 11. "Yüan-tao chiu-shih-ko," S.W.C.1.8b, 11. Hsieh-mo, "Pai-cheng-ko," S.W.C.1.12, 10. TTS, S.W.C.2.129, 9. "Yuan-tao chüeh-shih-hsün," S.W.C.1.17b, 5. Yao, STC, S.W.C.2.173b, 7. TPCSK, T.S.4. 3,1 under this title. Yao-t'u, "Yüan-tao chüeh-shih-hsün," S.W.C.1. 18b, 9.
157. "The devil's men, having taken the devil with them, finally bring the devil on them." "Yüan-tao chiu-shih ko," S.W.C.1. 11, 2. This recalls the current practice in Kwangtung and other provinces of south China of calling Taoists to rid a household of devils.
158. TTS, S.W.C.2. 129, 10.
159. Ibid., 126b, 7-8.
160. TPCSK, T.S.4.3, 5.
161. TTS, S.W.C.2.127, 11-12.
162. Genesis 3. 1-15.
163. Job 1. 6-12; 2. 1-10.
164. "The dragon in Western mythology is generally pictured as a cruel monster, an evil creature, symbolic of sin. The enemy of God and man, saints and martyrs throughout history engaged him in mortal combat." But the Chinese dragon is a beneficent being who rules the oceans, presides over the eastern quadrant of the heavens, and regulates the rainfall. The dragon dominates "every twelfth hour, day, month

and year of the lunar calendar." He was revered and worshipped. The Emperor's throne was the Dragon Throne, the flag of China the Dragon Flag. The Chinese dragon is similar to the Western dragon only to the extent that both guard or are in association with water. Juliet Bredon and Igor Mitrophanov, The Moon Year--A Record of Chinese Customs and Festivals (Shanghai: Kelly & Walsh, 1927), 335-6. See also Harry T. Morgan, Chinese Symbols and Superstitions (South Pasadena, Calif.: Perkins, 1942), 4-7; L. Newton Hayes, The Chinese Dragon (Shanghai: Commercial Press, 1923), 3, 42; Wolferstan, The Catholic Church in China, 75.

165. Illustrated in all of the nine volumes of T.S.
166. Matt. 4. 1-11. Mark 1. 13.
167. Mark 4. 15.
168. John 8. 52; 10. 20.
169. Matt. 15. 22.
170. Mark 1. 23; 5. 2; 7. 25. Luke 9. 38-42.
171. Luke 4.33.
172. Luke 8. 27-39.
173. Luke 9.1.
174. Acts 5.3.
175. Rev. 12.9; 20.2.
176. Buddhist in origin, the Chinese equivalent of the Sanskrit Yama. As used by Chinese Buddhists it is a twin god, one twin male and the other female; each twin ruled over infernal inhabitants of his own sex. See the Tz'u-yüan and Tz'u-hai dictionaries. For a description of the origin of Yen-lo see William Edward Soothill and Lewis Hodous, A Dictionary of Chinese Buddhist Terms (London: Kegan Paul, 1937), 452.
177. From Robert Burns' "Letter to a Young Friend," Robert Burns, The Complete Writings of Robert Burns (Boston: Houghton Mifflin, 1926), I., 293.
178. Isaiah 13-14; 17-19; 23.
179. Jeremiah 44.12; 51.
180. See also Jonah 3.4; Amos 1.2-13, 2.1-6; Ezekiel 29. 1-16.
181. "The shades of the dead went down into Sheol to linger for a time there in the dust and gloom and then disappear." Edward McNall Burns, Western Civilizations Their History and Their Culture, 3d ed. (New York: W.W. Norton, 1949), 83.
182. The most numerous illustrations of the Biblical use of Sheol are in the book of Psalms. "Our bones are scattered at the mouth of Sheol." Ps. 141.7. "The cords of Sheol were round about me; the snares of death came upon me." Ps. 9.17. "Let the wicked be put to shame, let them be silent in Sheol." Ps. 31.17. ". . . thou hast delivered my soul from the lowest Sheol." Ps. 86.13. "If I make my bed in Sheol, behold thou art there." Sheol is used similarly in

other books of the Bible. Cf. Deut. 32.22; Prov. 1.12; 5.5; 9.18. Is. 38.10, 18. Ezek. 31.15. Jon. 2.2.
183. "Our Father who art in heaven." Matt. 6.9. ". . . him will I also deny before my Father who is in Heaven." Matt. 10.33. See also inter alia Matt. 5.16; 18.10.
184. Matt. 5.3, 10-12.
185. "Not every one that saith unto me, Lord, Lord, shall enter into the kingdom of heaven; but he that doeth the will of my Father who is in heaven." Matt. 7.21.
186. Matt. 19.14.
187. Matt. 6.20.
188. Matt. 13, 31, 33, 44-5; 23. 2-14.
189. Matt. 13. 41-2; also 49-50; 8.12.
190. Matt. 5.22.
191. Matt. 23.33.
192. Matt. 25. 31-45.
193. Mark 4. 26-32; 10.14. Luke 6.20; 8.1; 9.60; 10. 9-11; 13.18-21; 18.24; 21.31.
194. Luke 17.21. ". . . the kingdom of God is within you.
195. John 3.16; 5.24; 6.47, 68; 14.2.
196. Rom. 6.22-3; 8.18. I Cor. 15.24. I John 2.25.
197. II Thess. 1. 7-10.
198. See especially the account of the Last Judgment in Rev. 20.4-15 and the "New Jerusalem," Rev. 21.2-8, 10-27; 22. 1-5. Hell is described as "the lake that burneth with fire and brimstone."
199. Hamberg, Visions, English text, 24. Chien, Shou-i shih, 101.
200. Parts of G. 1847 and Mor. 1823 examined do not include passages of Matthew which would establish this for sure.
201. TTS, S.W.C.2.127b, 1. Also ibid.2.125b, 7-8.
202. TPCSK, T.S.4.8b, 5 under this title.
203. STC, S.W.C.2.173, 5.
204. The sources for this and the following four quotations are as follows: YHS, S.W.C.2.172, 5-6; TTS, T.S.1.9, 2; ibid.1.9, 4; ibid.1. 8b, 5; "Chiu i-ch'ieh t'ien-sheng t'ier yang yü," S.W.C.1.35b, 3-4, 6-7. This quotation is representative of the practical end to which most of Taiping eschatology was devoted.
205. TTS, S.W.C.2.125b, 9. See also ibid.2.125b, 12.
206. "Yüan-tao chüeh-shih hsün," S.W.C.1.18b, 9-10.
207. TTS, T.S.1.8b, 6 under this title.
208. "Chiu i-ch'ieh t'ien-sheng t'ien-yang yü," S.W.C. 1.34b, 12.
209. See the second half of the composition cited at the end of footnote 204.
210. The sources for this and the following three quotations are as follows: STC, S.W.C.2.173, 5. TTS, S.W.C.2.

129, 10. See also "Yüan-tao chüeh-shih hsün," S.W.C.1.18b, 9-10; ibid.1.18b, 6-7; "Yüan-tao chiu-shih-ko," S.W.C.1.11, 3.

211. Illustrations of the terms used in early missionary scriptures can be found as follows:

t'ien: G.1847 and G.1855 - Luke 19.38.
Mor.1823, G.1855, D.1852 - Matt. 11.23.
t'i-yü: G.1847 and G.1855 - Matt. 5.22.
Mor.1823, G.1847, G.1855 - Matt.11.23.
t'ien-t'ang: G.1847 - Matt. 11.23.
an-fu: D.1852 - Matt. 11.23.

6

The Christian Component
What the Taipings Failed to Take

It is appropriate at this point to review the elements of the Bible which the Taipings found suitable and borrowed. If the content of what was taken resembled Christianity in its essentials, the expectations of early missionaries to China were justified and the failure to reach a rapprochement between the insurgents and Westerners may be justifiably deplored. If the Taiping religion contained just those Biblical elements that might contribute to the success of a revolutionary movement, then that fact too should be understood without at the same time disparaging the sincerity of the mass of its believers.

From the Old Testament came the concept of God as the only God, the supreme creator, and its corollary that no images or competing "corrupt gods" could be worshipped. Like Yahweh and also God of the New Testament this god was a personal deity who might be appealed to directly without the intermediary services of a priest. Though characterized in some degree by the attributes of mercy and forgiveness, this god like Yahweh also was their Lord of Battles, intervening personally at critical moments in the military progress of the movement. He was likewise a stern god who had issued a code of commandments the strict observance of which was required. Disobedience to these commands, particularly the ones forbidding idolatry and polytheism, constituted sin.

Certain elements of the Taiping religion either resembled Christianity as depicted in the Gospels or came from it. Their God was the god of all men; not just of Jews or Chinese. He was also their heavenly Father. His son Jesus, the Saviour, had been sent down into the world to suffer for the sins of mankind and to give his life in redemption. Penitent sinners could pray to God in the expectation of having their sins forgiven. Such freedom from sin was symbolized in an approximation to the Christian rite of baptism. Believers and those who obeyed God's laws were assured of residence

What the Taipings Failed to Take

and eternal happiness in heaven. Unbelievers and confirmed transgressors were told to expect as punishment eternal suffering in hell. God's opposite, the Devil, and a host of his satellites were indefatigable and frequently successful in their efforts to lead men astray. Lip-service was paid to a form of God called the Holy Spirit. Every seventh day was observed as a day of rest and worship.

Are the Biblical elements described sufficiently expressive of the genius of Christianity to qualify the Taiping religion as a form of Christianity? The answer to be given will take into account the absence in the Taiping ideology of concepts indispensable to Christian belief as well as the improper use to which elements that were borrowed were put. This chapter is concerned with Christian essentials that Hung and his associates failed to take.

The essentials of the Christian faith were transmitted to the Western world through the labors of the apostle Paul. They are expressed today in numerous statements of faith, in effect tests of church membership, based upon Scripture but embodying doctrines developed in the growth of the Christian church. These statements or creeds differ in their details. It is not my object to discuss the particulars wherein the Taiping religion fails to satisfy the requirements of this or that creed. It is my purpose, rather, to outline a series of general propositions common to Christian belief and based upon the Gospels the complete absence of which no creed can justify.

A distinctive feature of the Christian gospel is the high value set upon the forces of love. It is declared that all the rules for a good life and all the sayings of the prophets are epitomized in two commandments, to love God and to love one's neighbor. [1] God's love for the world is given as the reason for the appearance of Christ. [2] Christians are enjoined to love their enemies [3] and to forgive others to the limit. [4] "This is my commandment, that ye love one another even as I have loved you." [5] Paul has a famous description of this cardinal Christian virtue. [6] Yet the religious writings of the Taipings are conspicuous for their failure to transmit this most Christian of emphases.

Christian rules of conduct are summarized in one statement commonly known as the Golden Rule. [7] This precept is a prominent part of the Christian ethic. It was reprinted in the first volume of "Good Words to Admonish the Age." [8] It is hard to believe that Hung could have failed to have had the Golden Rule explained to him during his two months' stay with Issachar Roberts. Yet nowhere in all of Taiping literature does the Golden Rule appear.

A third characteristic of Christian teaching is the concern expressed for the welfare of others and the use of possessions toward that end. The aspiring Christian is instructed to "love thy neighbor as thyself." [9] To one version of this commandment is appended a vivid answer [10] to the question, "Who is my neighbor?" The essential quality of this characteristic is demonstrated in the story of the rich and virtuous young man who was told to satisfy his one deficiency by selling all his possessions and giving away the proceeds to others. [11] Allusion is made to the difficulty in this connection with which a rich man meets the qualifications for entrance to heaven. [12] The obligation to feed the hungry, clothe the naked, visit the sick, and entertain the stranger is laid upon all who aspire to eternal life. [13] This aspect of the Christian heritage has been referred to in the United States in recent years as the "social gospel" and proclaimed in support of movements for social reform. The Taiping rebels failed to give space in their official writings to the "social gospel." Mention is due them, however, of the fact that from the first days of the organized movement onward all property was held in common. Shortly before the first mobilization in 1850 the early God-Worshippers disposed of their lands and possessions and brought the proceeds to the common Sheng-k'u (Sacred Storehouse). The rule was strictly enforced that no plunder or loot might be kept by an individual. All booty was turned in to the common store. [14] It is curious that so salient a feature of the rebel administration remained unsupported by Biblical precedent.

The phrase "the kingdom of heaven" or its alternate "the kingdom of God" was considered by Hung to refer to his own regime, whereas the sayings of Jesus in the New Testament describe Christ's kingdom as an intangible essence not of the world. Whether as an indwelling ideal, [15] an ideal state, [16] or the regime of a coming Messiah, [17] the "kingdom" was not a terrestrial conception! The rebels failed to understand the unworldly nature of the "kingdom." For them Heaven was the deserved residence of the righteous and "the kingdom of heaven" their own state with no less tangible entity in between.

Humility, the absence of pride and arrogance, is a quality praised in the Gospels. ". . . for everyone that exalteth himself shall be humbled; but he that humbleth himself shall be exalted." [18] The Christian appeal was directed to the lowly and oppressed. For this purpose Christ represented himself as "meek and lowly in heart." [19] The "meek" and "poor in spirit" are called "blessed." [20] Paul asked the inhabitants of Ephesus ". . . to walk . . . with all lowliness and meekness . . . ." [21] Sanction was therefore present for a phenomenon manifesting itself in the early Christian church and more recently in the Christian missionary

What the Taipings Failed to Take

enterprise in India, namely, the tendency of the religion to appeal first to the lowest classes of society. The mass of the Taiping rebels were lowly, uneducated peasants, but the new religion that reached them first through the preaching of Hung and Feng never appealed to the fact of their humble origin. The virtue of Christian humility is not mentioned in the "T'ai-p'ing chao-shu" or the T'ien-t'iao-shu;" never did Hung or his rebel leaders set their followers an example of humility.

To catalogue all the lesser omissions would demonstrate no more than has already been shown; several other matters, however, deserve passing mention. The sacrament of the Eucharist or the Lord's Supper is one of the most generally performed of all the sacraments. The incident upon which it is founded is related in three of the gospels. [22] It is hard to believe that Hung failed to observe the performance of the Lord's Supper or to receive instruction in its meaning during the time he was with Roberts. If the Taipings practiced baptism, why did they neglect the Eucharist, a symbolic ceremony of equal prominence? Hung's neglect of Christ's ministry has been referred to in the section on the teachings of Christ. The parables, illustrations of Christ's handling of ethical issues, and the Sermon on the Mount are left out completely, except for a phrase or two. The expositor of Christian principles usually relies strongly upon these parts of the New Testament. The Taiping religion was characterized by a strong moralist emphasis on obedience to the letter of the rules. It is likely that this proceeded from the stern, uncompromising character of the founder himself. [23] In so stressing the strict observance of the law Hung ran counter to an attitude that Christ was at pains to inculcate, namely, that laws were made for people and not people for laws. [24]

Another way of bringing out what the Taipings did not take and one fairer to them is to examine the nine tracts which were the starting point of Hung's religious revelation. There is no record of Hung's having seen the entire Bible in Chinese until he went to Canton for Christian instruction in 1847. He was probably given a Bible then; it is hard to believe that he was not at least shown one. But this occasion was more than ten years after the time when it is certain that he received "Good Words to Admonish the Age." At this time, according to one account, [25] he merely glanced at the set of nine tracts and put them away; another account says that he read the pamphlets several times on two different days. [26] His celebrated visions occurred at least three years later after a third failure to pass the provincial examinations. In June of 1843, [27] by accident Hung again turned to the pamphlets, this time studying them and recalling his visions of six years before. The first preaching in

Kwangtung and the conversion of the first three thousand God-Worshippers in Kwangsi by Feng Yün-shan were based upon no more than Hung's visions and the ideas contained in "Good Words to Admonish the Age." The same may be said of the four compositions written by Hung himself during the two years 1844-45, later published together under the title "T'ai-p'ing chao-shu."

"Good Words to Admonish the Age" consists of nine small volumes containing an average of twenty-five leaves of fifty pages each. These volumes are a composite of quotations from the Morrison Bible, paraphrases of Scripture, short sermons, and random statements illustrating Bible truths. One-fourth of the whole is taken exactly from the Morrison version. The sixth volume contains among other things Liang A-fa's autobiography and the account of his baptism in 1817 by the Rev. Wm. C. Milne. The style of the compositions is hardly respectably idiomatic Chinese, for its author was influenced far more by foreign examples and expressions than by native Chinese influences.

In quoting from the Bible did Liang choose passages representative of the more important ideas of the Christian faith? It is my belief that he did. [28] I base this upon a tabulation of the portions which he quoted that illustrate the general propositions set forth earlier in this chapter. The Sermon on the Mount (Matt. 5, 6 & 7) and the 13th chapter of First Corinthians are conspicuous inclusions. A number of the Bible verses are followed by lengthy and discursive exegesis. The page references in C.S.L.Y.1832 include exegetical material where present. It is hardly necessary to repeat that the subject matter of the verses below does not appear in Taiping writings.

Essential Christian Bible Verses Emphases	Verses Quoted	Location of Quoted Verses and Accompanying Exegesis in C.S.L.Y.1832
1. The Forces of Love and Forgiveness	Matt. 5. 43-6; 6.12, 14-5	1.18, 7 ff. (Reference is for the entire Sermon on the Mount)
	John 3.16	2.26,1 to 31,6
	Romans 12	5.22b,5 to 24.3
	Romans 13	5.24,3 to 25,2
	Ephesians 5	6.3,2 to 4,4
	I Cor. 13	7.24b,2 to 25,7
	I John 4	7.25,7 to 27,1
	Colossians 3	9.11,5 to 15,5
2. The "Golden Rule"	Matt. 7.12	1.18, 7 ff.

What the Taipings Failed to Take   111

Essential Christian Emphases	Bible Verses Quoted	Location of Quoted Verses and Accompanying Exegesis in C.S.L.Y.1832
3. The Welfare of One's Neighbor and the Use of Possessions to That End	Matt. 19.23-4	2.10, 2 to 17, 5 N.B. The story of the rich young man detailed 2.10, 8 to 11b.
4. The Spiritual Nature of the Kingdom of Heaven	Matt. 5.10, 19-20; 6.10, 33. John 6.27	1. 18, 7 ff.
5. Christian Humility	Matt. 5. 3,5 Colossians 3 (see 3,12)	1. 18, 7 ff. 9. 11, 5 to 15,5

The Taiping neglect of the parables of Jesus and of his ministry as well as of the Lord's Supper may spring from similar treatment on the part of Liang A-fa, who, when quoting Scripture, apparently preferred the Epistles to the Gospels.

Hung's indifference to the essentials of Christian doctrine did not extend to other parts of "Good Words to Admonish the Age." The subject matter of certain other Bible verses and of discourses thereon is reflected in the religious writings of the Taipings. Bible quotations in C.S.L.Y. 1832, subject matter of which may have been borrowed by the insurgents, are tabulated below.

Subject Discussed	Supporting Bible Quotations	Location of Quotations and Exegesis in C.S.L.Y.1832
1. Monotheism	Isaiah 45. 5-21	3.19b,3 to 21b,1
2. Forbidden Worship of Graven or Molten Images	Isaiah 44.9-12, 14-21	1.14b,8 to 15b,6
3. Diatribe Against Familiar Spirits or Wizards	Isaiah 8.9	2.17,6 to 25,8
4. The Atonement and Forgiveness of Sin	I John 1.9	5.56,2 to 7.3
5. Illustrative Stories from the Old Testament	Genesis 1 & 2 (The Creation) Genesis 6 & 7 (The Flood)	3.21b,1 to 24b,2 4.16,2 to 19b,3

Liang's digressive style is such that topics are touched in the explanation of a given verse that bear no relation to the content of that verse. Several discourses are not prefaced by a text. These sections of "Good Words to Admonish the Age" as well as the more strictly exegetical discourses contain a sizable amount of material that could have easily influenced the Taipings: it is highly possible that much of it did.

A major portion of Liang's attention is devoted to the disparagement of the San-chiao 三教 or Three Teachings, those of Buddhism, Confucianism, and Taoism. [29] The worship of idols and false gods and the veneration of superstitions likewise arouse his indignation. [30] The examination system itself, he said, was a kind of fetish; [31] Chinese spent their lives futilely trying for a degree. Resentment was directed against the Western Paradise of the Buddhists, [32] the Taoist Trinity, [33] and every kind of idol and Buddhist image. [34] It is not unreasonable to assume that the iconoclastic practices of the God-Worshippers sprang from the strong impression that these sections of "Good Words to Admonish the Age" made upon Hung Hsiu-ch'üan; even the anti-Confucian passages seemed to have had their effect. [35]

It will be recalled that the insurgents reprinted the Genesis account of creation and the story of the Flood; both of these Liang quoted in full. He tells how the first man was "deceived by the serpent devil;" [36] "the serpent devil is a corrupt god." [37] Both of these terms, particularly the latter found ready employment with the rebels. Hung was particularly fond of one phrase "Behead the demons," later a rallying cry against the imperialists. Hung related in his vision how the Heavenly Father had sent him on a mission to do just that and had given him a sword with the characters Chan-yao-chien 斬妖劍 (Sword for beheading demons) engraved upon it. [38] Yet Chan-yao, the phrase referred to, occurs in the Ch'üan-shih liang yen. [39]

The wording of at least three of the Ten Commandments which the Taipings used follows what Liang used rather than that employed by one of the early Bibles. [40] He, like them, frequently discusses the Atonement, the rewards of heaven, the punishments of hell, and the activities of the Devil and evil spirits. [41]

The third volume of "Good Words to Admonish the Age" has the statement: "Moreover, in the Books of History coming down from antiquity there is a great deal said of a ruler who unites heaven and earth." [42] An accompanying argument brings out the point that God belongs to the Chinese also. This section bears a sufficient likeness to Taiping theology as it evolved to qualify as a source of Hung's theory of Shang-ti.

What the Taipings Failed to Take

It is interesting to compare Liang's account of his baptism by Milne with a common phrase in the prayers of the "T'ien-t'iao-shu" and with the tests for baptism that the Taipings used. The Taiping prayer reads: "And grant him the Holy Spirit to change his heart." 43 Milne said baptism meant "to wash a person clean from the pollution of his sins that by the Holy Spirit his heart may be changed." 44 The Taiping term for Holy Spirit is different but the thought is the same. Mr. Milne told Liang: "If you whole-heartedly repent of sin and change your evil (ways), (if) you believe in following the teachings of Jesus the Saviour and practice them . . . afterwards you cannot worship likenesses of the various kinds of gods and Buddhist idols . . . (If) you further pay reverence to the great ruler of heaven and earth, men and things, having set aside previously committed acts of adultery, depravity, excess, and wickedness, having done with deceitful lies, then upon Sunday, the holy day of rest, you may come to receive baptism." 45 This statement embraces practically all of Taiping thought regarding baptism.

Though lengthy, the preceding examples should serve to prove that enough material was taken from Liang's pamphlets to permit all of the contents being used had the founder of the Taiping regime been so disposed. Despite Liang's curious language and non-Chinese examples based upon an imperfect translation of the Bible, Hung could have taken over more characteristic qualities of Christianity than he did had they appealed to him. On this point Hung's cousin has this revealing quotation: "Siu-tshuen often used to praise the doctrines of Christianity, but, added he, 'Too much patience and humility do not suit our present times, for therewith it would be impossible to manage this perverted generation.'" 46 As a result largely of the character of the founder, the Taipings were not exposed to the more vital parts of the Christian ethic.

Generally speaking, Protestants of the 20th century have stressed the Christian ethic and the "social gospel" far more than did their 19th century forbears. It is easy for a 20th century researcher to say readily that the Taiping ideology cannot be called Christian because of the absence in it of indispensable features of the Christian ethic. 47 It should be remembered, however, that the Taipings were exposed to a 19th century fundamentalist faith that stressed other aspects. Further, it may be remarked that the early Christians looked upon the books of the Old Testament, from which the Taipings borrowed significantly, as their scripture, while later Christians always regarded the Old Testament as authoritative. Also, early Christians shared with the Taipings a respect for the law and a feeling that God is active in history.

These facts place the Taiping religion in truer perspective but they are not enough in themselves to make up for the body of Taiping omissions. The Taiping religion still was not Christianity.

Footnotes

1. Matt. 22.36-40. Luke 10.25-8.
2. John 3.16.
3. Matt. 5.39, 44.
4. Matt. 6.12; 18.21-2.
5. John 15.12.
6. I Cor. 13.
7. "All things therefore whatsoever ye would that men should do unto you, even so do ye also unto them; for this is the law and the prophets." Matt. 7.12. Also Luke 10.27-8.
8. C.S.L.Y.1832.1. 18, 7 ff.
9. Matt. 22.39. Luke 10.27.
10. The parable of the Good Samaritan. Luke 10.30-37.
11. Mark 10.17-22.
12. Matt. 19.23. Mark 10.23-6.
13. Matt. 25. 34-46.
14. Chien, Shou-i shih, 189. Hamberg, 55. See also a proclamation of Hung to the army, dated Oct. 11, 1851. TMCCS, S.W.C.1.5, 9-12.
15. Luke 17.20-21.
16. "But seek ye first his kingdom and his righteousness . . . ." Matt. 6.33. Matt. 13.31-3, 44-5, 47. Matt. 22.1-14. Mark 4.26-9; 30-2.
17. Matt. 24.2-44. Mark 13. Luke 21.6-36.
18. Luke 18.14; also 14.11.
19. Matt. 11.28-30.
20. Matt. 5. 3, 5.
21. Ephesians 4.1-2.
22. Matt.26.26-9. Mark 14.22-5. Luke 22.19-20.
23. Chien, Shou-i shih, 65, 102. Chien remarks that from boyhood on Hung was intolerant of criticism and arbitrary in dealing with others of differing opinions. In his hands the use of authority changed from Wang-tao 王道 (The Kingly Way) to Pa-tao 霸道 (Despotism).
24. The subject Christ most frequently discussed was observance of the Sabbath. Mark 2.27; 3.1-16. Christ's general position on regard for the letter of the law is set forth in Mark 7.1-23.
25. Hamberg, 9.
26. Chien, op. cit., 68. It is difficult to avoid the conclusion that Hung made more than what Jen-kan indicated was a cursory examination of "Good Words to Admonish the Age"

What the Taipings Failed to Take   115

and that his visions were at least subconsciously influenced by what he read.
  27. Ibid., 96.
  28. A handy, complete list of the verses quoted appears in Hamberg, 17-9. Medhurst felt that the tracts certainly treated the more important verses of Scripture. "Connection between Foreign Missionaries and the Kwangsi-Insurrection," North-China Herald, 161 (Aug. 27, 1853), 14-5.
  29. C.S.L.Y.1832.3.1b, 4 to 2.8.
  30. See principally ibid. 1.3b, 4 to 12,8. The subject comes up often throughout the pamphlets. See also ibid.2. 13b, 8-14; 19,2; 20,2; 22b,1. 3.9, 6-8; 10, 6-7; 11, 12 to 11b,1.
  31. Ibid.1. 5,6 to 1. 5b, 7.
  32. Ibid.1. 7,2.
  33. Ibid.1. 7,5 ff.
  34. Ibid.2. 2,4.
  35. The Hung family after receiving baptism threw out their household images and tablets to Confucius. Chien, op. cit., 100.
  36. C.S.L.Y.1832.1.4, 2-3.
  37. Ibid.3.14, 5-6.
  38. Hamberg, 10. Chien, op.cit., 73-4, 101.
  39. C.S.L.Y.1832.3.2, 7-8.
  40. Compare the Taiping wording for the Fifth Commandment with 孝順父母 , ibid.,9.3, 2; for the Sixth, Seventh, and Eighth Commandments with 勿行殺害之事 , 勿行奸邪淫亂之惡 , and 勿偷竊別人之物 , ibid.,2.10b, 5-7.
  41. The Atonement: Ibid.2.5, 3 to 10, 1. The term is shu-tsui. Rewards of heaven and punishments of hell: 2.5, 8-9; 26, 1 to 31, 6. 5.5, 7. 6.9b, 6-7. 8.7b, 8 to 15, 1. Immortality is called fu-sheng (to live again). The Devil and evil spirits: 1.11b, 8-12, 2 speaks of mo-kuei, hsieh-shen, and hsieh-feng. 2.18b, 8 has hsiung-shen 兇神 (malevolent gods), and o-kuei 惡鬼 (evil devils).
  42. Ibid.3.12b, 5-6.
  43. TTS, S.W.C.2.127, 3.
  44. C.S.L.Y.1832.6.9b, 8 to 10, 5. English quotation from this, Hamberg, 15.
  45. C.S.L.Y.1832.6.11, 2-6.
  46. Hamberg, 43.
  47. The resemblance of the Taiping system to Christianity is discussed thoughtfully in Latourette, A History of Christian Missions in China, 297-9. The author believes Christianity furnished only the necessary initial impulse to the Taiping movement.

7

The Role of the Christian Component in the Outcome of the Rebellion

Enough has been said in the preceding chapter to demonstrate that central features of Christian belief were absent in the religious ideology developed by the Taiping rebels. Not only were there these conspicuous omissions but the material that was borrowed was made over to suit special uses.

The Bible speaks of the "Kingdom of God"---a non-material state in the process of realization. It also mentions the "Kingdom of Heaven." The "Kingdom of God" is not mentioned in the tracts of the insurgents. The "Kingdom of Heaven" or t'ien-kuo is; indeed it is incorporated in the name of the new dynasty on earth, the T'ai-p'ing t'ien-kuo, but without the characteristic of futurity. T'ai-p'ing, the other half of the official name for the new regime, is also the name of the last and most utopian of the famous three ages mentioned in the Kung Yang interpretation of the Ch'un Ch'iu (one of the Five Classics).[1] Chien Yu-wen points out that a number of great Cantonese scholars of the Classics studied the Kung Yang and made its phraseology and idealism familiar to young students of the Kwangtung area, among them Hung Hsiu-ch'üan, K'ang Yu-wei, and Sun Yat-sen. His evidence indicates that T'ai-p'ing as a symbol of the ideal state was present in Hung Hsiu-ch'üan's earliest thought.[2] When the God-Worshippers became an anti-dynastic movement the term acquired the connotation of an ideal to be realized. Chinese tradition was thus employed to support revolution. So the official title of the rebel regime strengthened its appeal by calling in both Chinese and Western terms for the creation of a utopia on earth.

The Taipings made provision for the unique nature of their authority as follows. The Gützlaff term for the New Testament is Hsin-i chao-sheng-shu 新遺詔聖書 (new transmitted and proclaimed scripture), a title which the rebels first reproduced. Presently, however, they changed it to Ch'in-ting

<u>ch'ien-i chao-sheng-shu</u> 欽定前遺詔聖書 (authorized previously transmitted and proclaimed scripture). The intention in substituting "previously" for "new" was, I believe, to proclaim that God's communications to Hung were a more recent and hence a more authoritative body of revelation. This would imply that foreign Christians were expected to pay their respects to a new fount of revelation rather than to instruct prospective converts. It is no wonder that missionaries who visited the insurgents, even Roberts, for example, came away calling the Taiping faith blasphemy. Another case in point is the Taiping adaptation of the second commandment against the fashioning of images. This is changed into the phrase "Do not worship perverted gods (<u>hsieh-shen</u>)." The term <u>hsieh-shen</u> is at once a phrase completely foreign to translators of the Bible and an interpolation designed, it would seem, to justify attack upon the principal objects of Chinese veneration since almost legendary times. The "T'ai-p'ing chiu-shih-ko," a rebel tract, makes the statement that "in very ancient times when men's minds were still intelligent and before they had lost (sight of) the true origin (of all things), they all knew how to honor and worship the Great God, the Heavenly Father and Supreme Lord." But then at least as early as the Age of the Philosophers (which can be dated roughly 550-280 B.C.) two conditions caused Chinese to forget <u>Shang-ti</u> and worship perverse gods: a clouding of the former clarity of Chinese perceptions and deliberate deception on the part of Taoists, Buddhists, and the Devil himself. Divine sanction is thus invoked to support repudiation of the principal Chinese cultural traditions and the most thorough-going iconoclasm. Supporting arguments are studded with references to well-known figures and incidents of Chinese history.

 A notable addition to the Biblical Ten Commandments was made presumably for disciplinary purposes. On the march the Taiping host included the women and children of those who fought. Hence the commanders were confronted with a problem of maintaining a relation between the sexes that would not weaken army discipline. Their solution was strict separation. The original Seventh Commandment is simply a prohibition against adultery. The expansion of this commandment to include "strict separation of the sexes, the casting of amorous glances, the harbouring of lustful thought, . . . or the singing of libidinous songs" 3 was performed, I believe, primarily in the interest of military discipline. The prohibitions against opium in the Seventh Commandment and against the concealment of gold and silver ornaments probably had the same motivation. 4

 The addition of fabricated religious elements seems to have had as its aim the conferment of sanction upon otherwise secular political acts. The identification of **Shang-ti** with Yahweh and God the Father was a fact that permitted extensive corroboration from Chinese sources. [5] The next step was the elevation of the founder of the movement, who was declared to perform for China, albeit in more militant form, the mission of Christ for the western world. Then the way was clear to authenticate Hung's pronouncements and those of his more skilful subordinates as utterances of God and to introduce Jesus to the scene as an interested helper. The descents of God and Jesus became plausible interventions. [6] Heaven and hell, the other-worldly consequences of virtue ' and transgression, were translated into the wages of valor or cowardice in the struggle to exterminate the Manchus. God's commandments came to constitute the daily law of a military movement, his praise an expression of group solidarity. The picture was completed by the identification of their Ch'ing opponents with Satan and his legions and by the use of religious terms like "Holy" and "Heavenly" with titles of persons and names of institutions.

Borrowed Biblical elements were thus altered to suit special purposes. The next step was to translate these elements into practice. This was accomplished in a thorough-going manner.

The most conspicuous though hardly propitious manifestation of Old Testament principles was the application of the first and second of the Ten Commandments. From the first this was a clear break with Chinese custom. The first act of Hung and Feng was to substitute the name of **Shang-ti** and the Ten Commandments for their own household gods and the customary ancestral tablets. Hung Jen-kan relates that when Hsiu-ch'üan "had taken away his own idols, he placed the written name of God in their stead, and even used incense-sticks and gold paper as part of the service." [7] Jen-kan himself was one of the very first converts; in the school where he was teaching he threw out the Confucian tablets. [8] Each of the three, Hsiu-ch'üan, Jen-kan, and Feng Yün-shan, openly preached the repudiation of Buddhist deities and of traditional Confucian observances. The preaching brought converts and vigorous opposition. As the movement developed acts of idol-breaking occurred [9] and grew into organized expeditions against famous popular shrines. [10] Verses were written to celebrate each incident. Idol-breaking maintained its prominence in the program of the revolutionists when the movement assumed a military character. [11]

Thoughts of overthrowing the Ch'ing dynasty and founding a new state are believed to have crossed Hsiu-ch'üan's mind as early as 1843. [12] The following year he and Feng decided secretly that they would try to convert into true followers of God brave men who would die for the cause. Collaboration with the Triads was considered then but not favored. Hung felt that the Triads would not join in the religious part of the movement, which he believed essential, and that the failure of the Triad societies ever to unite in the past meant that their members were not sufficiently single-minded to be reliable. [13] Accordingly, the development of a political movement paralleled the growth of religious doctrine. The fact that the religion and the political revolution grew up together explains why the majority of the borrowed Christian elements were so well assimilated and secular and religious terms so consistently combined. [14]

Evidence of Hung's consciousness of mission is provided by the changes he made in his personal name, as noted previously. Hsiu-ch'üan's original personal name was Huo-hsiu 火秀. Jen-k'un 仁坤 was the name given him when he came of age. But after 1837 he insisted on being called Hsiu-ch'üan 秀全 (Accomplished and Perfect), [15] a name which he said was conferred on him by the Heavenly Father during his visions. Another reason for changing the character huo 火 (fire) to hsiu 秀 (accomplished) was to avoid using one of the characters in the transliteration for "Jehovah." Chien Yu-wen believes that the new name was a device to aid in founding the new kingdom, for after the regime was established at Nanking, Hsiu-ch'üan decreed that he be called Hung Jih 洪日 (Hung, the Sun). [16] Also, when the movement assumed organized form, Hung began using the term Chen 朕, the expression for "I" previously permitted none but the Chinese Emperor. Later, the circle of religious nomenclature was widened to include the T'ien-mu 天母 (Heavenly Mother) and the T'ien-sao 天嫂 (Heavenly Elder Brother's Wife). [17] The T'ien-wang's firstborn was naturally called the "Young Prince." [18]

Preparation of the rebellion to come proceeded through the organization of the leader group for each community and for the entire movement. [19] Then followed organization of an army in which religion was relied upon to reinforce discipline. [20] Four of the "Ten Important Rules To Be Observed In A Settled Camp" illustrate the application of the religion to military matters.
[21]
"1. Carefully obey the heavenly regulations.
2. Earnestly acquaint yourself with the commands of Heaven and the form of worship with praise and thanksgiving to be used every morning and evening, as well as the orders issued by the sovereign.
3. Cultivate good morals, do not smoke and drink wine . .
. .
5. Make the camp of the males separate from that of the females. (Men and women) must not give or take from each other's (hands)."

By the "commands of Heaven" the Taipings evidently meant the Ten Commandments, for the same characters <u>t'ien-t'iao</u> 天條 are used. The regulations quoted above were the tool whereby the "T'ien-t'iao-shu" was made part of the daily life of the army.

The T'ai-p'ing t'ien-kuo was formally inaugurated on January 11, 1851 at Chin-t'ien in Kwangsi. On this date Hung publicly took the title "King of Heaven" and the new dynasty was proclaimed. These acts were accompanied by public ceremonies of prayer and thanksgiving and the raising of a flag to mark the beginning of the Rebellion.

The descents of the Heavenly Father and Heavenly Elder Brother that occurred during the next two years were an especially effective extension of the Taiping religion for the purpose of compelling obedience and stiffening morale. [22] Their employment may have provided just the extra stimulus needed to break out of one of the critical, early encirclements. [23]

The regulations compounded with the aid of Biblical elements were enforced in a manner to win the respect of foreigners. Westerners who saw the Taipings at Nanking in 1853 commented upon their perfect order and discipline. "It was obvious to the commonest observer that they were practically a different race." [24] Dr. Taylor was present during Taiping worship at Chinkiang. He remarked upon their chanting of hymns and doxologies and the use of public prayers and grace at meals. [25] They appeared to rely on Divine guidance. It was observed that violations of Taiping regulations were punished with unusual severity. Rape and adultery in the cities taken by storm were certain to be punished by death; failure to observe the rules concerning separation of the sexes was penalized similarly. Opium-smoking merited decapitation; even tobacco-smoking called for blows with bamboo. At the same time children were carefully taken care of and taught from the religious books. [26]

There is further evidence that the use of Christian elements contributed to the military success of the movement. For one thing, before the general assembly at Chin-t'ien in the fall of 1850, the incorruptibility of Taiping leaders was well enough known to attract numbers of able men disgusted with the corruption of the Ch'ing government. [27] Two speculations should be permissible at this point. The Taiping attack on influences which would be classed today as superstitions and their abrogation of lucky days [28] must have brought the insurgents a sense of freedom that increased their single-mindedness. The enforcement of rules for the pooling of all material resources must have conveyed a sense of common effort. Taylor is of the opinion that commonly repeated promises that those who died in battle were certain of Heaven steeled the rebel soldiers to fanatical effort. This factor "made T'ai-p'ing armies a fighting force worthy of comparison with the armies of Mohammed." [29] A student of English history will recall the psalm-singing, lay preaching, use of public prayer, and occasional iconoclasm characteristic of a similarly effective group of soldiers, Oliver Cromwell's Roundheads. [30] The first part of June 1852 at a river crossing called the So-i Ford occurred the first great defeat of the Taipings by an imperialist force. This was the result of an ambush. Half the insurgents fought, half fled; in the confusion Feng Yün-shan, the Southern King, who had been badly wounded several days before in the approach to Ch'üan-chou, was transferred to shore from the boat carrying him and died. Their losses in personnel at So-i Ford were very heavy, yet the Taipings closed their ranks, re-formed, and went on to Tao-chou, the next city to the north. The ability of their army to sustain such a reverse, intensified by the loss of Feng, can be considered a true measure of the discipline which the Taiping religion had been used to instil.

The reader of Western as well as Chinese accounts carries away the impression that the Taiping host possessed a discipline and a zeal unknown to the military organizations that faced them in the first years of the Rebellion. The Ten Commandments, baptism, the keeping of the Sabbath were believed in, practiced, and ruthlessly enforced. Triad leaders could not join the movement unless they agreed to renounce Buddhist and Taoist practices and turn in their property to a common storehouse. The conclusion is inescapable that the Biblical component was an effective instrument of mass control and an important factor in Taiping military success.

The Taiping chiefs may have been successful in organizing their adherents and in disciplining an army with the use of their religion, but the faith that had been a pillar of strength to the internal structure became for them a stumbling-block in their relations with possible allies and with the Chinese people as a whole.

After several trials Taiping leaders declared that they would not compromise with the idolatry and easy-going discipline of the Triads. How much secret society aid would have meant to the success of the Taiping movement could not be known due to a basic divergence of aims. The Triads sought to overthrow the Ch'ing and restore the Ming, the Taipings to overthrow and found anew. The dogmatic use to which the Christian component lent itself prevented cooperation between the rebels and members of the secret societies.

More fateful was the handicap posed by the Taiping

religion to enlisting the support of foreign governments, merchants, or missionaries.

At first, rumors that the rebels practiced a form of Christianity attracted favorable foreign attention. Foreigners who observed Taiping communities in 1853 spoke favorably of the effect of their religion upon behavior. The North-China Herald in publishing full reports of the visit of the "Hermes" to Nanking remarked the sincere religious faith of the insurgents. At the same time the editor seemed disturbed by reports of the tone of their religious documents Reports of the visit of the "Cassini" were more reserved. The point was made that the people of the Taiping host seemed more cordial toward the French than the leaders, who were inclined to put forth arrogant pretensions. 33 Meadows, who was a member of the "Hermes" party, reports conversations which the English representatives had with the Northern King and the Assistant King. These leaders became friendly when the similarity between Christianity and the Taiping religion was discovered, but insisted that the T'ien-wang was the lord of the foreigners also. They were totally ignorant of the relative position of foreign countries. 34 The English never saw the T'ien-wang. A document from him implied that he expected their worship and adoration. 35

The year that elapsed between the expedition of the "Hermes" and the visits of the "Susquehannah," the "Rattler," and the "Styx" in no way improved the acceptability to foreigners of rebel attitudes based upon the religion. The editor of the North-China Herald after the return of "Susquehannah" noted a deterioration in the religion and complained that their professed Christianity had made the Taipings no easier to deal with than Manchu officials. 36 After the return of the "Rattler" and the "Styx" this newspaper's former favorable opinion about the Taipings changed rapidly. Their reception of the British this time was by no means encouraging. In the mind of the editor it placed "beyond all further doubt the fact that crazy and deluded fanatics are in possession of Nanking; and that among the chiefs, ignorance and imposture contend for mastery. New books have been brought down and new revelations from the Eastern and Western kings, who respectively impersonate the Holy Ghost and Jesus Christ." 37

Since the Taiping religion was not really or at least sufficiently Christian, it failed to provide a real foundation for brotherly cooperation. Further, it provided a basis for development among the rebel leaders, particularly Hung Hsiu-ch'üan, of pretensions and fanaticism that were the despair of potential friends, and at the very end, of the gifted Taiping captain Li Hsiu-ch'eng himself. Favorable trade relations were difficult with such uncompromising fanatics. Pettee remarks that revolutionary leaders are always amateurish in their conduct of foreign affairs. 38 To this predilection Taiping leaders added a stupidity born of complete ignorance and a presumptuous religious fanaticism. 39

To be more than an uprising, a revolution must persuade as well as demonstrate military strength. As an instrument of persuasion the Christian component of the ideology was a failure.

The opposition of the Chinese was provoked at first by Taiping iconoclasm, especially as expressed in overt acts of destruction. 40 The local gentry of Kwangsi and the literati first considered the ideology an expression of foreign culture and a corrupt teaching. Soon they proceeded to call it also an organized secret society. Their complaints to local officials increased in number and querulousness. Ch'ing officials in Kwangsi at first regarded the God-Worshippers as a sect of Catholic Christians. When groups formed in each community and more knowledge about them became available, these officials feared to inform the Emperor of the true state of affairs. Soon the God-Worshippers grew so numerous that they could not be ignored. Official reports then were confined to data about the religion and the nature of local opposition to it. At length a rich degree-holder, Wang Tso-hsin from Hsin-shang-kan, a village in the Thistle Mountain area, who was in charge of local troops, arrested Feng after the breaking of images at Meng-ch'ung Nov. 21, 1847. Feng's followers led by a certain Lu Liu rescued him. Wang countered by reporting the incident to the magistrate of the sub-prefecture of Kuei-p'ing, thereby causing the arrest of both Feng and Lu. The charge against them contains terms that continued to express the grounds for opposition. In addition to charges of forming a party to overthrow the government, Feng and Lu were accused of "spreading a perverted teaching," "destroying the images of gods," "possessing books on magic, corrupt books, and magical tricks," and "misleading all ignorant people." 41 Lu died in prison. Feng was banished from the province, but managed to rejoin the God-Worshippers of Kwangsi by converting the members of his escort. 42

A measure of the opposition to the Taiping ideology came from factors that caused difficulty for Christian missionaries of the time. In the opinion of the missionary William Gillespie, 43 the sources of Chinese opposition to the evangelization of China were the following: the various forms of idolatry, the practice of ancestor worship, the national pride and arrogance of the Chinese, their pride in the Chinese language, the attachment to antiquity and the extreme veneration they entertained for their sages, and Chinese embitterment toward foreigners, especially the English, arising from the first Anglo-Chinese War. Insofar as the Taiping religion could be made out to be either foreign or Christian or both it had to meet the same opposition as the Christian gospel.

The case of the Chinese people against the Taipings was eloquently put forth in the following phrases from a proclamation by the great imperialist general and Ch'ing apologist Tseng Kuo-fan. The matters which he chose to stress were points which the rebels on the basis of their record could not rebut successfully.[44]

"From the ancient days of Yao and Shun each generation of ages has upheld the far-reaching doctrines which magnify the relations of emperor and statesman, of honorable and humble, of old and young, fixed and irreversible as the position of the members in the body. But these southern rebels, borrowing the ways of the barbarian tribes, and the religion of the 'Lord of Heaven,' depose sovereigns and degrade officials, their 'officials' calling every man 'brother' and every woman 'sister.'

The farmer may not plough, but must still pay taxes; for, say they, his fields are the fields of the same 'Lord of Heaven.' The merchant may not trade, but yet must pay them; his wares, forsooth, are the property of the King of Heaven. The scholar must not study the Confucian classics any more, but instead must follow the words of Jesus in the New Testament, treating all the morality taught in China for thousands of years as so much 'swept-up dust.'

Never until these latter days have such things been--no, not from the days of creation. At such unorthodox teachings, our Confucius and Mencius must be weeping bitterly in Hades. Shall any scholar, then, or any able to read, fold his arms in his sleeves and sit in peace?

From of old, men of highest virtue have been deified to bear rule in Hades, holding official posts there corresponding to those on earth. Yet these rebels, in their fierce violence, reverence not such deities.

Li Tzu-ch'eng, arriving at Ch'u-fou (a locality sacred to Confucius), did not desecrate the sacred temple. Hsien-chung (another rebel of the same time, ca. 1644) worshipped the god of literary emolument. But the southern rebels burned the temples of the sages and destroyed the Confucian tablets, scattering their fragments on the ground. In every prefecture and subprefecture they come to, they first burn the temples with their remembrances of good statesmen and virtuous scholars, even of Kuan-ti the god of war and Yo-wang (ruler of the eastern purgatory). They defile their courts, and hew to pieces their bodies. Thus they treat Buddhist, Taoist, and local deities, and the shrines of the earth spirits. There is no temple they do not burn, no image they do not destroy. The deities are enraged; they will cool their anger (in the destruction of the rebels).

Having received the decree of the Son of Heaven, the present leader of fifty thousand troops on land or water swears that 'even in his sleep he cherishes his burning wrath!' He will prove his courage by destroying the turbulent rebels, by saving the captured boats, and by rescuing the intimidated captives, urged thereto by his indignant loyalty to the true sovereign, and from pent-up anguish at the denial of the relations proclaimed by Confucius and Mencius, the massacre of myriads of the populace, and the indignities cast upon the higher and lower deities. This proclamation is accordingly issued that all may be acquainted therewith."

With points such as Tseng Kuo-fan raises unanswered, it is little wonder that the insurgents never gained the confidence of any large part of the nation. Their creed was entirely foreign to Chinese ideology. "With the adoption of a religious creed coming from a foreign source and introduced by the barbarians themselves at Canton within a few years back, they resigned in the estimation of their countrymen all title to be considered patriots." No patriot joined such a revolution unless he had nothing in character or property to lose. Hence the power of the rebels could not rest on "sympathy felt with them, beyond the actual limits of the districts that they occupied," even though natives who witnessed it could admire the insurgents' discipline. [45]

It should be added that the medium through which the Taiping appeal was transmitted was handicapped by characteristics that often cut down its effectiveness. R.J. Forrest, at one time British consul at Ningpo, was given a set of Taiping books by Hung Jen-kan. He noted what the present-day reader always notices, that the style of the insurgent publications is far from the best Chinese. The originals he found to be badly printed on poor paper, a factor sure to inspire the contempt of Chinese literati. "The rhythm sometimes attempted is suggested by Gützlaff's translation of the Bible, and the poetry is feeble beyond expression." [46] Accomplished propagandists dare not risk ridicule by neglecting matters of style and format.

The presence of the foreign part of the ideology, its opposition to Confucian teachings, the uncompromising and un-Chinese intolerance with which it was put into practice, and possibly the inappropriate manner of its presentation caused educated Chinese like Tseng Kuo-fan to prefer the support of Manchu political control to the abandonment of Chinese culture. The cultured reaction to this type of choice raised up powerful enemies among educated men. It is no wonder that the Rebellion was eventually overthrown by Chinese scholar-officials.

Further, the leaders of successful dynastic overturn in China have usually found that they had to provide for trained civil administrators. The presence of the foreign element in the ideology meant that the rebels were denied the existing resources of educated leadership. The insurgents were never able to train their own administrators to offset the effect of this denial.

It is possible that the Christian part of the ideology handicapped the Rebellion as much as it helped it. The fact that the Taiping leaders borrowed what they did from the Bible and made the use that they did of what they borrowed seems the measure of a basic weakness of the Rebellion--incompetent leadership. Competent leaders, understanding the nature of the opportunity, would have put together a different and a more adequate ideology. Hung Hsiu-ch'üan, however, was no Chinese Lenin.

Footnotes

1. Huo Hsiu's commentary, 1st year of Yin Kung, Kung Yang Chuan. The Han Shu, the second of the twenty-four histories, in describing times in China before 700 B.C., has the following utopian characterization of t'ai-p'ing. "When there was a surplus of food (enough) for a three year period (from nine years') presentations of products of labor, it was called teng maturity. Two consecutive teng (that is, a period of eighteen years) was called p'ing 'peace,' when there would be a surplus of food (enough) for six years. Three consecutive teng (twenty-seven years) was called t'ai-p'ing 'great peace,' when there would be a surplus of food (enough) for nine years which had been accumulated during twenty-seven years. Thereafter, kindly virtue spread (among the people), and permeated them; while ceremonial rites and music became established among them. So it was said: 'If there is a (true) ruler, it must require a generation before humanity will prevail.'" Han Shu 24A, 5b-6a, translated in Nancy Lee Swann, transl., Food and Money in Ancient China

The Role of the Christian Component 127

(Princeton University Press: Princeton, 1950), 134. T'ai-p'ing has been used extensively as a reign title and a place name; it also appears often in current usage.
  2. Chien, Shou-i shih, 208-9.
  3. See p. 64. Note Rule 5 of the Taiping Army Regulations: "Make the camp of the males separate from that of the females. (Men and women) must not give or take from each other's (hands)." "T'ai-p'ing t'iao-kuei," T.S.2.1b, 5-6 under this title; S.W.C.2.131, 8.
  4. Included in Rule 4 of the Army Regulations. Ibid., T.S.2.1b, 2-4, same title. S.W.C.2.131, 7. The Taipings had the same trouble with private looting as the Israelites. Cf. Joshua 7.
  5. Taiping preference for the ancient Chinese term Shang-ti, instead of Shen-t'ien shang-ti, the term of Morrison and Liang A-fa, seems more design than accident.
  6. Chien Yu-wen, Chin-t'ien chih yu chi ch'i t'a, 30, 5-11 points out that these descents, which used Yang and Hsiao as mouthpieces, were not part of the original faith taught to the God-Worshippers nor did they particularly have Hung Hsiu-ch'üan's approval. However, these practices were so popular and increased Yang's and Hsiao's prestige so much that he had to sanction them.
  7. Hamberg, 35. Chien, Shou-i shih, 100-102.
  8. Chien, ibid., 101.
  9. Ibid., 102-3.
  10. Examples of the action of Hung and a few helpers occurred in the Liu-k'o 六窠 temple at Ch'ing-feng-hsiang 慶豐鄉, the first instance of idol-breaking in Kwangsi (Chien, ibid., 107-8); also later in the Chiu-hsien 九仙 temple, Tung-hsiang, in Wu-hsüan-hsien, Kwangsi (Ibid., 132-3). The first organized expedition was directed against a temple of the Kan-wang-yeh 甘王爺, also in Kwangsi. Ibid., 139-40; Hamberg, 36-7. Feng and a fellow leader Lu Liu were arrested after the destruction of images at Meng-ch'ung, Nov. 21, 1847. Chien, op. cit., 143; Hamberg, 38.
  11. For a summary of the later applications of the first two Commandments see Hsieh Hsing-yao, T'ai-p'ing t'ien-kuo she-hui cheng-chih ssu-hsiang (Social and political ideas of the T'ai-p'ing t'ien-kuo) (Shanghai: Commercial Press, 1935), 25, 9 to 26, 4.
  12. Chien, op. cit., 86-7. Jen-kan quotes his cousin as saying after his fourth failure to pass the government examinations, "Wait till I myself open the examinations and choose the empire's scholars!" Ibid., 86, 5.
  13. Ibid., 104-5, 211-8.
  14. For example, T'ien-chün 天軍 (Heavenly Army); T'ien-chiang 將 (Heavenly Generals); Sheng-ping 聖兵 (Sacred Troops).

Ibid., 105.
15. Chien believes that Hung's choice of the character ch' (all, perfect) was derived from Biblical phrases like 全在全能全知之上帝 (Omnipresent God, the Omnipotent and Omniscient) and symbolized to him the acquisition of God-like attributes. Ibid., 96-7.
16. Ibid., 54; 57, 2-11; 76; 127-8.
17. Ibid., 168.
18. 幼主 ibid., 149.
19. Ibid., 151-2.
20. Ibid., 161-7. Chien believes that Feng Yün-shan was responsible for whatever excellence the military organization possessed.
21. "T'ai-p'ing t'iao-kuei," T.S.2.1,2 to 1b, 1; 1b, 5-6 under this title. S.W.C.2.131, 4 to 6, 7. Medhurst's translation of the entire document is in the North-China Herald, 153 (July 2, 1853), 191.
22. For a summary of the more widely known descents see pp. 58-9. The genesis of the descent as a method is explained in Chien, op. cit., 168-9.
23. Ibid., 245. Four separate descents were necessary on this occasion, one of which ended in an execution.
24. Fishbourne, Impressions of China, 182.
25. Ibid., 184 ff.
26. Meadows, The Chinese and Their Rebellions, 243 ff.
27. Chien, op. cit., 171.
28. "Every season, therefore, may be considered as prosperous and favorable." "Kuei-hao san-nien hsin-li," T.S. 3, preface under this title, 2, 6.
29. G.E. Taylor, "The Taiping Rebellion: Its Economic Background and Social Theory," Chinese Social and Political Science Review, 16.4 (January, 1933), 590.   Rebel soldiers were "like tigers and rhinoceri escaping from (their) cages." Quoted in Chien, 229 from the report of Chou T'ien-chüeh, an imperialist general.
30. C.H. Firth, Cromwell's Army, A History of the English Soldier during the Civil Wars, the Commonwealth, and the Protectorate (London & New York, 1902), 315-6, 321-3, 330-1.
31. Chien, 300-2. Chien is convinced that the death of Feng was an irreparable loss to the spirit and original quality of a movement of which he was the chief organizer.
32. "We understand that some others of their books exhibit features of unheard-of presumption, and pretences to inspiration which no sober Christian could admit; we therefore beg our readers to suspend their judgment till they have seen the whole." North-China Herald (May 14, 1853), 163. This and the issue of May 21 treat the "Hermes" visit in full.
33. Ibid. (Dec. 24, 1853). An extra issue for Dec. 19th

The Role of the Christian Component   129

is devoted to a report of the "Cassini" expedition.
34. Meadows, The Chinese and Their Rebellions, Chap. XVII, passim.
35. Fishbourne, Impressions of China, Chap. IV, passim.
36. North-China Herald, 203 (June 10, 1854), 182. This number has a four column report in which the rebel answer to Captain Buchanan of the "Susquehannah" is termed "very extraordinary."
37. Ibid., 206 (July 8, 1854), 194.
38. G.S. Pettee, The Process of Revolution (New York, 1938), Chap. IV.
39. Chien, op. cit., 137.
40. Ibid., 139-43 describes the development of opposition to iconoclasm.
41. Ibid., 143-4 contains the charge and the nature of evidence against Lu and Feng.
42. Hamberg, Visions, 40.
43. The Rev. William Gillespie, The Land of Sinim or China and Christian Missions (Edinburgh, 1854), 91-7. The Chinese case against the spread of barbarian Christianity has seldom been as well put as in the following extract (Gillespie, 94-5) from a Chinese tract, translated by Medhurst, against the missionaries in the Straits: "It is monstrous in barbarians to attempt to improve the inhabitants of the Celestial Empire, when they are so miserably deficient themselves. Thus, introducing among the Chinese a poisonous drug (opium), for their own benefit, to the injury of others, they are deficient in benevolence. Sending their fleets and armies to rob other nations of their possessions, they can make no pretensions to rectitude. Allowing men and women to mix in society and walk arm in arm through the streets, they show that they have not the least sense of propriety. And in rejecting the doctrines of the ancient kings, they are far from displaying wisdom. Indeed truth is the only good quality to which they can lay the least claim. Deficient, therefore, in four out of the five cardinal virtues, how can they expect to renovate others? Then, while foreigners lavish money in circulating books for the renovation of the age, they make no scruple of trampling printed paper under foot, by which they show their disrespect for the inventor of letters. Further, these would-be exhorters of the world are themselves deficient in filial piety, forgetting their parents as soon as dead, putting them off with deal coffins only an inch thick, and never so much as once sacrificing to their manes, or burning the smallest trifle of gilt paper for their support in a future world. Lastly, they allow the rich and noble to enter office without passing through any literary examinations, and do not throw open

the road to advancement to the poorest and meanest in the land. From all this it appears that foreigners are inferior to Chinese, and therefore most unfit to instruct them."

44. All but the last paragraph of the text is quoted in Chinese by Hsieh, T'ai-p'ing t'ien-kuo ti she-hui cheng-chih ssu-hsiang, preface, 2,7 to 3,4 from the Ch'ing-ch'ao ch'üan-shih 清朝全史 (Complete history of the Ch'ing dynasty). The somewhat free English translation is from William Arthur Cornaby, A String of Chinese Peach Stones (London, 1895), 367-71. Tseng's anti-Taiping proclamations deserve special compilation. The one quoted is undated, but probably appeared somewhat later than the period under study, since Tseng was not assigned to a military command against the Taipings till 1854.

45. Both quotations and the point of view expressed are from Joseph Edkins, Religion in China (London, 1859, 1878), 189-95.

46. Quotations and Forrest's comments are contained in Robert James Forrest, "The Christianity of Hung Tsiu Tsuen, A Review of Taeping Books," Journal of the North-China Branch of the Royal Asiatic Society, New Series IV (Dec., 1867), 187-90.

8

Bibliographical Appendix

A. Source Materials for This Study

After the suppression of the movement the literary remains of the Rebellion were deliberately destroyed or suppressed by the Ch'ing government. As a result, numerous official documents and religious tracts published by the Taiping government almost disappeared from China. Luckily copies of rebel publications which were brought away from Nanking by foreign visiting officials or which otherwise found their way into the hands of foreigners have been preserved. Many of these official documents and religious tracts have been reprinted in China from copies preserved in British and European archives. I have relied upon the four principal published compilations of these documents. They are listed below with each title preceded by the special abbreviation used in citations in the text.

1. <u>S.L.</u> Ch'eng Yen-sheng 程演生, <u>T'ai-p'ing t'ien-kuo shih-liao ti-i chi</u> 太平天國史料第一集 (First collection of historical materials of the T'ai-p'ing t'ien-kuo), 3 <u>ts'e</u>. Peking: Peking University Press, 1926. Pages are numbered from the beginning of each document.
2. <u>S.W.C.</u> Lo Yung 羅邕 and Shen Tsu-chi 沈祖基, <u>T'ai-p'ing t'ien-kuo shih wen ch'ao</u> 詩文鈔 (Anthology of the poetry and prose of the T'ai-p'ing t'ien-kuo). 2 <u>ts'e</u>. Shanghai: Commercial Press, 1935. Numbering of the leaves is continuous.
3. <u>T.S.</u> Hsiao I-shan 蕭一山, <u>T'ai-p'ing t'ien-kuo ts'ung-shu ti-i chi</u> 叢書第一集 (First collection of books of the T'ai-p'ing t'ien-kuo). 10 <u>ts'e</u>. Shanghai: Commercial Press, 1936. Documents must first be located by title. Pages are numbered from the beginning of each document.
4. <u>Y.S.</u> Ling Shan-ch'ing 凌善清, compiler, <u>T'ai-p'ing</u>

t'ien-kuo yeh-shih 野史 (Non-official history of the T'ai-p'ing t'ien-kuo). 1 ts'e. Shanghai, 1927. This is indexed in twenty sections or chüan, with pagination from the beginning of each chuan. Reproduces with modifications part of the Tsei-ch'ing hui-tsuan (see the discussion of this in Teng, New Light).

The published official papers of the Rebellion seem to fall into two classes. Papers of the first class were issued by the highest officials of the movement and were stamped with the official Taiping seal or marked with the characters ch'in-ting 欽定 (imperially authorized). They are the source of the orthodox doctrine intended for the enlightenment of newly-won or prospective converts. To judge from the dates of publication, these were not printed in quantity until Nanking was taken and the movement had achieved a measure of permanency although several of the religious tracts were composed during the earliest days of the insurrection.[1] Even today a military movement which lacks motor transport must carry many things before it can take duplicating equipment. Papers of the second class include a large number of miscellaneous communications given out under the names of high civilian officials or military commanders.

To reproduce here a list of official Taiping documents such as are given in Teng, New Light and in the bibliography of Kuo T'ing-i, Shih-shih jih-chih seems needless; I list only the official religious documents which contain the religion as it was during the first part of the Rebellion. Each title which appears on the list has been given a number. The titles themselves are romanized, the romanization followed by the Chinese characters and an English translation. Opposite each entry is the earliest Taiping date of publication. Revisions and re-editions of a composition usually were given the same date as the earliest appearance of the composition. Where Walter H. Medhurst supplied an English translation, the North-China Herald or China Mail citation is appended. It will be observed that the Taiping Old and New Testaments, listed as numbers 1 and 2, each have three editions; an Arabic numeral in parentheses indicates the edition. A question mark is used to denote a doubtful ascription.

Various Western publications other than the North-China Herald or the China Mail either mention or contain in translation several of these Taiping documents. These references are listed alphabetically with the number of the title of eac document substituted for the full wording.

The religious documents are further classified under the three headings that follow.

Bibliographical Appendix 133

List of Official Taiping Religious Documents

A. Chinese Translations of Parts of the Bible

	Title	Date Given
1.	(1) "Chiu-i chao sheng shu" 舊遺詔聖書 (Old Testament) Genesis, Exodus only.	1853
	(2) "Ch'in-ting chiu-i chao chih" 欽定舊遺詔旨 (Authorized Old Testament) Genesis through Judges.	1853
	(3) "Ch'in-ting chiu-i chao sheng shu" 欽定舊遺詔聖書 (Authorized Old Testament) Genesis through Judges. (?)	1853
2.	(1) "Hsin-i chao sheng shu" 新遺詔聖書 (New Testament) Matthew's Gospel only.	1853
	(2) "Ch'in-ting hsin-i chao sheng shu" 欽定新遺詔聖書 (Authorized New Testament) Matthew through Luke.	1853
	(3) "Ch'in-ting ch'ien-i chao sheng shu" 欽定前遺詔聖書 (Authorized New Testament) Complete.	1853

B. Instructional Material for Children and Neophytes

	Title	Date Given	Translation, North-China Herald
3.	"T'ien-t'iao-shu" 天條書 (Book of the Laws of Heaven)	1852	146 (May 14, 1853), 163.
4.	"San-tzu-ching" 三字經 (Three Character Classic)	1853	147 (May 21, 1853), 168.

Title	Date Given	Translation, North-China Herald
5. "Yu-hsüeh-shih" 幼學詩 (Poems for the Instruction of Youth)	1851, 1852	147 (May 21, 1853)

C. Tracts for a Wider Audience

3. "T'ien-t'iao-shu"	See above.	
6. "T'ien-fu hsia-fan chao-shu" 天父下凡詔書 (Book of Declarations Made During the Heavenly Father's Descent to Earth)	Part 1, 1852 Part 2, 1853	149 (June 4, 1853), 175
7. "T'ien-ming chao-chih-shu" 天命詔旨書 (Book of Heavenly Decrees and Imperial Edicts)	1852, 1853 as part of a "T'ien-wang chao chih" 天王詔旨 (Edict of the Heavenly King)	148 (May 28, 1853) 172.
8. "Tai-p'ing chiu-shih-ko" 太平救世歌 (T'ai-p'ing Songs on Salvation)	1853	178 (Dec. 24, 1853), 83; 181 (Jan. 14, 1854), 95.
9. "T'ai-p'ing chao-shu" 太平詔書 (T'ai-p'ing Imperial Proclamations)	1852	150 (June 11, 1853), 180.
10. "T'ien-li yao lun" 天理要論 (The Essentials of Heaven's Principles)	1854	269 (Sept. 22, 1855)
11. "T'ien-fu shih" 天父詩 (Hymns on the Heavenly Father)	1857	
12. "T'ai-p'ing t'ien-jih" 太平天日 (T'ai-p'ing Days)	According to Wang Chung-min (I-ching 13.3a, 22-4), appeare as a Chao-ming 詔命 in 1848, b was not officially issued til	

Bibliographical Appendix

Western References to Titles or Translations of Taiping Religious Documents

Western Source	Number of Document Referred To
Rev. W.T.A. Barber, "The Rebel Bible," The Chinese Recorder and Missionary Journal, XXII. 7 (July, 1891), 305-8.	1 (3), 2 (3).
M.J. Beauvais, "Livres Chinois à Angoulême," T'oung Pao, Archives, 1st Series, III (May, 1892), 181-2.	1,2,3,4,5,6,7,8,9.
"Correspondence between the State Department and the late Commissioner to China," U.S. Docs. 374, 33 Congress, 1st Session (1853-54), House Exec. Docs. 16, no. 123.	1 (1), 3, 6 ?, 9 ?
Robert Kennaway Douglas, Catalogue of Chinese Printed Books, Manuscripts, and Drawings in the Library of the British Museum, London, 1877; Supplement, 1903.	1 (1,2), 2 (1), 3,4, 5,6,7,8,9.
C. De Harlez, "La Religion des Insurgés Tchang-mao," T'oung Pao, 1st series, IX, 397-401.	1 (1), 2 (1), 3,4, 5,6,7,8,9.
Robert James Forrest, "The Christianity of Hung Tsiu Tsuen, A Review of Taeping Books," Journal of the North-China Branch of the Royal Asiatic Society, New Series, IV (Dec. 1867), 187-208.	1 (3), 2 (3).
Catalogue des Livres Chinois qui se Trouvent dans la Bibliothèque de l'Université de Leide, Leyden, 1883; supplement, 1886.	1,2,3,6,7,9.
Karl Friedrich Neumann, Ostasiatische Geschichte vom Ersten Chinesischen Krieg bis zu den Vertragen in Peking (1840-1860), Leipzig, 1861.	3,5,6,7 ?, 9.
Papers Respecting the Civil War in China, Presented to the House of Lords (London, 1853), 35-41.	1 (1), 3,4,5,6, 7,9.

Wang Chung-min lists the following as the main European repositories of Taiping originals including the religious documents: Bibliothèque Nationale, Paris; Preussische Staats-Bibliothek, Berlin; British Museum; Library of Cambridge University; Library of Oxford University. ² The Library of Congress has a number of official Taiping documents in both the original printing and in photostat form. The New York Public Library reports a total of twenty-three original Taiping publications. Documents 3 through 10 of the religious compositions previously listed are among this number.

There is considerable difference between the Taiping reprints of the Bible and the publications of groups B and C, a difference which reveals the degree to which the Taipings understood or wished to make use of the Bible. The compositions of groups B and C contain a large amount of ethical and historical allusion that is purely Chinese, added perhaps to increase their persuasiveness and utility as instruments of group discipline. There is no available information on the relative number of pamphlets that were printed from each group, but it is reasonable to suppose that dissemination of the tracts and instructional material was far more widespread than was the case with the more esoteric and non-Chinese Bible. Further, the books prepared for purposes of instruction contain considerable material for public devotion. Contemporary foreign visitors who saw the Taipings worship report that they observed these pious specifications in actual practice. Their testimony makes valid the assumption that these ordinances were in force for the formative stage of the Rebellion and the period of its early military successes. Therefore, the Taiping instructional material and tracts constitute the principal repository of their religion in practice. Christian influence upon the movement must be judged in the light of what appears there.

The importance of the documents listed under B and C is sufficient to warrant their description in further detail. The writings that make up this material are listed in ascending order of the numbers assigned to them. The location in published compilations, a short synopsis, and data concerning translation into English follow each title.

Assigned No.	Taiping Religious Instructional Material and Tracts - - Titles and Comment
3	"T'ien-t'iao-shu" (Book of the Laws of Heaven), 1852: Y.S. 4. 12b, 15 to 21, 15; S.W.C. 2. 125b, 5 to 131, 1; T.S. 1. 9 leaves The principal repository of the Taiping faith containing an introductory exhortation, detailed forms for worship, the Taiping Ten

Bibliographical Appendix

Assigned No.	Taiping Religious Instructional Material and Tracts - - Titles and Comment
	Commandments, and several concluding hymns. A special commentary and hymn follow each commandment. The entire document was translated into English by Medhurst as "The Book of Religious Precepts of the T'hae-Ping Dynasty," North-China Herald, 146 (May 14, 1853), 163, reprinted in the China Mail, (June 16, 1853), 91. A synopsis and criticism of it by the Rev. W. C. Milne appeared in the same publication for July 28, 1853.
4	"San-tzu-ching" (Three Character Classic), 1853: Y.S. 4. 8, 9 to 11, 9; S.W.C. 2. 172, 7 to 174, 11. Three characters to the line. Follows the model of the well-known Chinese school-book which itself dates back to the Sung dynasty. A combination of Western and Chinese concepts and allusions intended as a textbook for new converts, this is second only to the "T'ien-t'iao-shu" in ideological importance. The document was translated into English by Medhurst as "The Trimetrical Classic," North-China Herald, 147 (May 21, 1853), 168, reprinted in the China Mail, (June 16, 1853), 91. A synopsis and criticism of it by the Rev. W.C. Milne appeared in the same publication for November 10, 1853, 182-3.
5	"Yu-hsüeh-shih" (Poems for the Instruction of Youth), 1851, 1852: Y.S. 4. 11, 10 to 12, 1 (first two stanzas only); S.W.C. 2. 169, 7 to 172, 6; T.S. 4. 14 leaves. A series of twenty-eight poems of four lines each, except for the first three, which are considerably longer. Old and New Testament influence is to be seen chiefly in the first two poems entitled respectively Ching shang-ti 敬上帝 (Revere God) and Ching yeh-su 耶穌 (Revere Jesus). The other poems state in purely Chinese fashion the duties connected with the various relationships of Chinese society and in a direct manner enjoin moral behavior. The entire document was translated into English by Medhurst as "Ode for Youth," North-China Herald 147 (May 21, 1853), reprinted in the China Mail, (June 16, 1853), 91. A synopsis and criticism of it by the Rev. W.C.

Assigned No.	Taiping Religious Instructional Material and Tracts - - Titles and Comment
	Milne appeared in the same publication for Sept. 1, 1853, 142-3.
6	"T'ien-fu hsia-fan chao-shu" (Book of Declarations Made During the Heavenly Father's Descent to Earth), Part 1, 1852; Part 2, 1853: S.L. 1. 14 pages; S.W.C. 2. 145b, 2 to 155, 7; Y.S., summary only in the Tsung-chiao 宗教 section, 3. The record of a remarkable incident in which God is represented as descending to supervise in person the exposure of a traitorous plot against the Taipings and the punishment of offenders. The narrative is written as a reminder of those attributes of God which the insurgent leaders wanted to emphasize. The entire document was translated into English by Medhurst as "Book of Declarations of the Divine Will Made During the Heavenly Father's Descent upon Earth," North-China Herald, 149 (June 4, 1853), 175. A synopsis and critique by the Rev. W.C. Milne appeared in the China Mail, (June 14, 1853) 110.
7	"T'ien-ming chao-chih-shu" (Book of Heavenly Decrees and Imperial Edicts), 1852: S.L. 1. 1, to 14b, 9; S.W.C. 1. 1, 11 to 7b 10; Y.S., selections contained in the Tsungchiao section, 4-5. A collection of the most important of the decrees and commands issued from April 1848 to April 1852 by Hung Hsiuch'üan, presumably in times of emergency when divine sanction was needed. These compositions reveal the extent to which the quasi-Christian theology of the Taipings be the tool of military necessity. For exampl the names of God the Father and of Hung's so-called Elder Brother Jesus were invoked against hoarding and to give weight to the selection of Taiping generals. The entire document was translated into English by Medhurst as "The Book of Celestial Decrees and Declarations of the Divine Will," North-China Herald, 148 (May 28, 1853), 172. A synopsis and critique by the Rev. W.C. Miln

Bibliographical Appendix   139

Assigned No.   Taiping Religious Instructional Material
                    and Tracts - - Titles and Comment

                 appeared in the China Mail, (June 7, 1853),
                 106-7.

8   "T'ai-p'ing chiu-shih-ko" (Taiping Songs
                 on Salvation), 1853: T.S. 4. 11 leaves. An
                 introduction and three poems, the first with-
                 out a title simply continuing the introduct-
                 ion, the second and third with the titles
                 Yu ko yüeh 又歌曰 (Sing for the Second Time)
                 and San ko yüeh 三歌曰 (Sing for the Third
                 Time) respectively. The introduction is
                 in the name of Yang Hsiu-ch'ing. The whole
                 composition is an example of the amalgam of
                 Christian and Chinese ideas which Taiping
                 leaders produced for practical ends. The
                 poems abound in moral instruction. The
                 English translation by Medhurst was called
                 "The Ode of the T'ai-p'ing Dynasty on
                 Saving the World" and appeared in the North-
                 China Herald, 178 (Dec. 24, 1853), 83; 181
                 (Jan. 14, 1854), 95.

9   "T'ai-p'ing chao-shu" (Taiping Imperial
                 Proclamations), 1852: S.L. 2. 10 leaves;
                 S.W.C. 1. 11 to 19, 3; T.S. 1. 13 leaves.
                 The "T'ai-p'ing chao-shu" contains four sep-
                 arate compositions of Hung Hsiu-ch'üan, com-
                 posed during the years 1845 and 1846 before
                 the author had met Roberts. (See Hamberg,
                 English text 29, Chinese text 13b.) Arranged
                 in the order in which they were printed these
                 compositions are the following:
                     (a) "Yüan-tao chiu-shih-ko" 原道救世歌 (Songs
                 of Salvation by the Basic Doctrine). S.L.
                 2. 1, 1 to 4, 3 under the above title; S.W.C.
                 1. 7b, 12 to 12, 7; T.S. 1. 1, 1 to 5b, 3
                 (this version slightly different from the
                 preceding two) under the title "T'ai-p'ing
                 chao-shu." A moralizing poem, seven char-
                 acters to the line, containing a few mono-
                 theistic ideas but relying heavily upon al-
                 lusion to Chinese tradition. The iconoclastic
                 position of the Taipings is strongly stated.
                     (b) "Pai-cheng-ko" 百正歌 (Songs of the
                 Hundred Instances of Correct Conduct). S.L.
                 2. 4, 3 to 4b, 4 under the title "Yüan-tao

Assigned No.	Taiping Religious Instructional Material and Tracts - - Titles and Comment
	chiu-shih-ko" also; <u>S.W.C.</u> 1. 12, 8 to 12b 11; <u>T.S.</u> omits this. A description of correct and incorrect conduct and the consequences of each. There are no Western allusions.

(c) "Yüan-tao hsing-shih hsün" 醒世訓 (Instruction on Rousing the World with the Basic Doctrine). <u>S.L.</u> 2. 4b, 5 to 6, 4 under the heading "Yüan-tao chiu-shih-ko;" <u>S.W.C.</u> 1. 12b, 12 to 14, 12; <u>T.S.</u> 1. 5b, 4 to 7, 9 under the title "T'ai-p'ing chao-shu." An admirable discourse on tolerance and international brotherhood.

(d) "Yüan-tao chüeh-shih hsün" 救世訓 (Instruction on Awakening the World with the Basic Doctrine). <u>S.L.</u> 2. 6, 5 to 10b, 4 under the heading "Yüan-tao chiu-shih-ko <u>S.W.C.</u> 1. 14b, 1 to 19, 3; <u>T.S.</u> 1.7, 9 to 14, 2, under the title "T'ai-p'ing chao-sh A diatribe against idolatry and superstitious practices of the Chinese; a good example of the Taiping blend of native and Western concepts.

The entire "T'ai-p'ing chao-shu" was translated into English by Medhurst as "Th Imperial Declaration of T'hae-Ping," <u>North China Herald</u>, 150 (June 11, 1853), 180. A synopsis and criticism of it by the Rev. W.C. Milne appeared in the <u>China Mail</u>, (August 4, 1853, 122-3. |
| 10 | "T'ien-li yao lun" (The Essentials of Heaven's Principles), 1854: <u>T'ai-p'ing t'ien-kuo kuan-shu shih-chung</u> (Ten officia documents of the T'ai-p'ing t'ien-kuo), 1, <u>Kuang-tung ts'ung-shu ti-san chi</u> (Third Kwangtung collectanea) (Canton, 1949). The "T'ien-li yao-lun" was taken from a revision of the first volume of an origina composition by Medhurst first published at Batavia in 1833 as <u>Shen-li tsung-lun</u> 神理總論 (General Discourse on God's Principles The revision of the first volume was print at Shanghai in 1844 under the same title the Taipings used ten years later. The Taipings introduced slight modifications. |

Bibliographical Appendix   141

| Assigned No. | Taiping Religious Instructional Material and Tracts - - Titles and Comment |

An English translation of the Taiping version by Medhurst is to be found in the North-China Herald, 269 (Sept. 22, 1855).

11   "T'ien-fu shih" (Hymns on the Heavenly Father), 1857. T.S. 7. 42 leaves. A miscellaneous collection of five hundred short poems containing (T.S. 7. 5, 5 to 5b, 1) the version of the Ten Commandments found in the "T'ien-t'iao-shu" and a number of allusions to the sayings of Jesus in the Gospels that are not characteristic of earlier Taiping religious works. E.G. T.S. 7. 2, 11 ". . . love thy neighbor as thyself." Matt. 22.39; 2b, 5 "The lamp of the body is the eye: if therefore thine eye be single, thy whole body shall be full of light. But if thine eye be evil, thy whole body shall be full of darkness." Matt. 6. 22-3; also compare 2b, 7-8 with Matt. 5. 29-30.

12   "T'ai-p'ing t'ien-jih" (Taiping Days), I-ching 逸經 (Uncanonical classics) 13 (Sept. 5, 1936), 695-700; 14 (Sept. 20, 1936), 767-70; 16 (Oct. 20, 1936), 865-9. Published with the "T'ien-li yao lun" and other documents recently discovered by Wang Chung-min in T'ai-p'ing t'ien-kuo kuan-shu shih-chung, 4, op. cit. According to Wang this appeared as a chao-ming (proclamation) in 1848, but only in 1862 as an officially published document, possibly revised by Hung Jen-kan. A detailed story of Hung's conversations with God and Jesus Christ during the period of his visions with an account of the arrest of Confucius and his punishment because his writings had led the Chinese astray. Other shorter references in Chinese to the same episode are contained in the following: Hung Hsiu-ch'üan lai-li 洪秀全來歷 (Personal History of Hung Hsiu-ch'üan), a written account which Hung Jen-kan did in 1852 for Hamberg, I-ching, 25 (March, 1937), 43-4; Wang chang tz'u-hsiung ch'in-mu Ch'in-erh kung-cheng fu-yin-shu 王長次兄親目親耳共證福音書 1860: T.S. 8. 2b; Ying-chieh kuei-

Christian Influence upon Taiping Ideology

Assigned No.   Taiping Religious Instructional Material
                 and Tracts - - Titles and Comment

chen 英傑歸真 1861: T.S. 10.

Chapter 4 lists briefly the Bibles and the tracts by
Liang A-fa which I have used in my comparisons. These materials are again listed below giving full details.

Data on Christian Religious
Materials Available for Comparison

1. Mor. 1823. Shen t'ien sheng shu 神天聖書 (Holy Bible) 21 ts'e, Malacca, 1823. The so-called Morrison Bible or what I have termed the Morrison-Milne version. Alexander Wylie, Memorials of Protestant Missionaries to the Chinese, 5 says of the New Testament belonging to this translation: "The New Testament of this version was made by Dr. Morrison on the basis of an old version of the Gospels, Acts and Epistles, which he obtained in England, and brought out with him to China. The Acts was revised from the M.S. and first printed in 1812, the Pauline Epistles being merely revised by Dr. Morrison; the New Testament was completed in 1813."
The Old Testament was the result of the joint labors of Robert Morrison and his colleague William Milne. The copy I used, according to an accompanying letter dated 1843, was sent to the United States by Peter Parker and is now the property of the American Board of Commissioners for Foreign Missions in Boston. The first ts'e bears the inscription in Chinese, "Reprinted the first month of summer of the seven year of Tao Kuang" (1827).

2. G. 1847. The Gützlaff Bible, 1847. This is evidently one of the earlier revisions of the original Medhurst-Gützlaff translation. I have called this the "Gützlaff Bible" to distinguish it from a later revision. It is in two parts, identified as follows.
   (a) Chiu-i chao sheng shu yu hsi-po-lai yin fan-i han-tzu 舊遺詔聖書由希伯來音翻譯漢字 (Old Testament, translated into Chinese from Hebrew), 4 ts'e. The cover (t'ao) bears the inscription 咪哩堅及各國聖經會印造舊遺詔聖書全函 (Old Testament, printed by the Bible societies of America and the several countries). The title page has the notation in English "Old Testament, 4 vols. Gützlaff Edition. Rec'd. in 1847, May." This volume was given to the Library of Congress by T. A. Devan, S. A. Devan, and S. C. Devan, Oct. 19, 1940. The characters are not as well cut as those of the 1855 Gützlaff Old Testament described below.

Bibliographical Appendix

(b) <u>Chiu-shih-chu yeh-su hsin-i chao shu chü shih-la yüan-pen fan-i</u> 救世主耶穌新遺詔書據實㸃原本翻譯 (New Testament of the Saviour Jesus, according to Gutzlaff's original translation). On the cover is the notation in English: "Dr. Gutslaff's 9th Edition of New Testament (n.p.) 1847."

Both Testaments of the "Gützlaff Bible" were loaned me by the Division of Orientalia of the Library of Congress.

3. <u>G. 1855.</u> The Modified Gützlaff Bible, 1855. A revision published four years after Gützlaff's death. The two Testaments are identified as follows:

(a) <u>Chiu-i chao sheng shu yu hsi-po-lai yin fan-i han-tzu</u> 舊遺詔聖書由希伯來音翻譯漢字 (Old Testament, translated into Chinese from Hebrew). This was published in 1855 by the <u>Fu-han-hui</u> 福漢會 ("Chinese Evangelization Society") and was printed at Hongkong. It bears the note in English that it was edited and revised by William Lobschied from a Gützlaff revised edition. The term <u>Yeh-ho-hua</u> 耶和華 (Jehovah) seems to have been used for God whenever possible. The nature of other alterations is indicated elsewhere. A letter attached to the cover bears the information that this copy was presented to Francis Fry (in London) by Richard Bath, Provincial Secretary (at Hongkong).

(b) <u>Chiu-shih-chu yeh-su hsin-i chao-shu</u> 救世主耶穌新遺詔書 (New Testament of the Saviour Jesus), printed in 1854 and published by the Chinese Evangelization Society in 1855. The accompanying letter in English states that it was revised and edited by William Lobschied and printed at Hongkong.

The "Modified Gützlaff Bible" was loaned me by the Library of the Yale University Divinity School.

4. <u>D. 1852.</u> <u>Hsin yüeh ch'üan shu</u> 新約全書 (Complete New Testament), London Missionary Society, Shanghai, 1852. This is commonly known as the "Delegates' Version." A note on the cover reads: "Printed at the expense of the British and Foreign Bible Society." The delegation engaged was composed of W.H. Medhurst, J. Stronach, and W.C. Milne of the London Missionary Society and Dr. E.C. Bridgman of the American Board of Commissioners for Foreign Missions, Boston.

This copy was loaned to me by the offices of the American Board in Boston.

5. <u>T.P. 1853.</u> The Taiping Bible, first officially published in fragmentary form by the Taipings in 1853. The parts which I have seen convince me that it was printed virtually character for character from a Gützlaff Bible of the kind circulated in China during the 1840's. The parts of the Taiping Bible, 1853, available to me for examination are the following.

(a) The complete Taiping Exodus, Ch'u mai-hsi-kuo chuan 出麥西國傳 (Record of leaving Egypt), 1853, with the Taiping seal. A microfilm copy of an original was supplied me by the Librarian of the American Bible Society, New York City.

(b) The first eleven verses of the first chapter of Genesis Ch'uang-shih chuan 創世傳 (Record of the Creation), the first eleven verses of the first chapter of Exodus, and the same number of verses of St. Matthew's Gospel, Ma-t'ai chuan fu-yin-shu 馬太傳福音書. The title pages of each of these three books bear the note in Chinese, "Newly-cut (printed) in kuei-hao, the third year of the T'ai-p'ing t'ien-kuo" (1853). Two of the pages of text are over-stamped with the characters chih chun 旨准 (authorized by Imperial decree). These fragments are all reproduced in T.S. 1 under Chiu hsin-i chao sheng sh (Old and New Testaments).

6. **C.S.L.Y. 1832.** Liang A-fa 梁阿發, Ch'üan shih liang yen 勸世良言 ("Good Words to Admonish the Age"), Canton, 1832. Title page notation in English: "Good Words to Admonish the Age; being Nine Miscellaneous Christian Tracts. By Leangafa, of the London Missionary Society. 1832. Printed at the expense of the Religious Tract Society. Canton, China." This copy belongs to the Library of the Harvard-Yenching Institute, Cambridge, Mass., and was given to Harvard Sept. 18, 1860 by the Rev. Andrew P. Peabody of Cambridge, Class of 1826. Hamberg, English text, 8-9, 14-19 discusses the part played by this book in the life of Hung Hsiu-ch'üan. W.H. Medhurst has a review of the contents, including a count of the various terms employed for God, in his "Connection between Foreign Missionaries and the Kwangsi Insurrection (2)," North-China Herald, 161 (August 27, 1853) 14-5.

- - - - -

In Chapter 4 mention was made of Alexander Wylie's note that there were four compositions by Roberts in existence in 1840 that could have been shown Hung. Wylie gives the following information on these compositions.

(1) Chiu-shih-chu yeh-su hsin-i chao-shu 救世主耶穌新遺詔書 ("New Testament of the Saviour Jesus"), 32 leaves, Macao, 1840. This was in fact Medhurst's version of St. Mark's Gospel only with notes by Roberts who signed himself hsiao 孝 (the filial one).

(2) Yeh-su sheng-shu 耶穌聖書 ("The Holy Book of Jesus"). A series of four small tracts.

(3) Chen-li chih chiao 真理之教 ("The Religion of Truth"), 10 leaves, Macao, 1840. A series of short dialogues, signed hsiao.

Bibliographical Appendix   145

(4) Wen-ta su hua 問答俗話 ("Catechism in (Macao) dialect"). 7 leaves, Macao, 1840. Signed hsiao.

- - - - - -

Chapter 3 refers to the existence of a number of proclamations written during the first years of the Rebellion, some of which are available both in Chinese and in English and others in English only. Several of these documents, particularly those in English only, contain legitimist ideas and evidence of Taiping association with the Triad Society. 3
The titles for these non-religious orders and proclamations and the published sources for their English and Chinese versions (where available) are given as an aid to further study of the secular part of the Taiping ideology.

1. Secular Proclamations Available in Chinese and English

Title	Published Source for Chinese Original	Source of English Translation
(1) T'ai-p'ing t'ien-kuo kuei-hao san nien hsin li 太平天國癸好三年新曆 (New Taiping Calendar for 1853)	T.S.3., separate preface, 2 leaves; text, 24 leaves. Y.S., "li-fa" section, 1,10 to 3,2. Preface only (for 1854). S.W.C.1.36b, 10 to 37,7. Preface only (for 1854). Translation of preface reproduced in full below.	North-China Herald, 154 (July 9, 1853), 194. Synopsis and critique by W.C.Milne, China Mail, (Aug. 18,1853), 134-5.
(2) Tsou chun-pan-hsing chao-shu 奉准頒行詔書 (Proclamations Published by Imperial Authority Upon Request)		
(a) Feng-t'ien chu-yao chiu-shih an-min yü 奉天誅妖救世安民諭 (Order Received from Heaven to Kill the Demons, Save the World, and Tranquilize the People)	S.L.1.1 to 3b. S.W.C.1.31,10 to 32,11.	North-China Herald, 152 (June 25,1853), 186-7. Reprinted China Mail, (Mar.31, 1853), 51; Vizetelly, The Chinese Revolution, 36-8.

Title	Published Source for Chinese Original	Source of English Translation
(b) Feng-t'ien t'ao-hu chi pu ssu-fang yü 奉天討胡檄布四方諭 (Edict Received from Heaven to Punish the Tatars and to Publish the Order Everywhere)	S.L.1.4,1 to 7b,5. S.W.C.1.32,12 to 34,12. Translation reproduced in full below.	North-China Herald, 152 (June 25, 1853), 186-7.
(c) Chiu i-ch'ieh t'ien-sheng t'ien-yang yü 救一切天生天養諭 (Order to Save All Whom Heaven Produces and Nourishes)	S.L.1.8,1 to 10b, 8 S.W.C.1.34b, 2 to 35b,11.	North-China Herald, 152 (June 25, 1853), 187.
(3) Kao chiang-nan shih-min yü 告江南士民諭 (Edict to the Scholars and People of Kiangnan), Issued by Yang Hsiu-ch'ing alone. Undated. Copied at Ning-kuo-fu, 180 miles west of Shanghai and 100 miles south of Nanking. English translation from an unknown Chinese text containing several more paragraphs than the text cited. Both may have been variants of a stock form composed for this area.	S.W.C.1.39, 3-11 with omissions.	North-China Herald, 138 (March 19, 1853), 130. Reprinted China Mail, April 7, 1853; Vizetelly, The Chinese Revolution, 55-7.
(4) T'ao-man-ch'ing chao 討滿清詔 (Proclamation on Punishing the Manchus). Undated in the original. In the translation dated Mar. 19, 1853, the date of the capture of Nanking. Bears the notation: "This proclamation is believed to be that which Mr. Ch'ai Lan-t'ing copied out in Hung's camp."	S.W.C.1.22,7 to 23,6.	"Dr. MacGowan's Notebook," North-China Herald, 159 (Aug.13,1853),7. Appended poem in ibid.,161 (Aug.27, 1853) somewhat similar to item 3 of the next list.

Bibliographical Appendix 147

2. Secular Proclamations Available in English Only

Title	Source of English Translation
(1) "Proclamation by the Insurgent Chiefs (Yang and Seaou)" Dated the first day of the fifth month, third year of the Taiping dynasty (June 6, 1853).	North-China Herald, 151 (June 18, 1853), 182.
(2) Proclamation by Lo and Huang Posted on the gate of Soochow April 2, 1853. The Lo referred to may have been Lo Ta-kang, a prominent military leader and former Triad, known to have been in command at Chinkiang during 1853-4.	North-China Herald, 141 (April 9, 1853), 142. Reprinted China Mail, (April 28, 1853), 67.
(3) Proclamation by the Insurgents in Verse Undated. Supposed to have been posted on the walls of Nanking.	North-China Herald, 140 (April 2, 1853), 138. Reprinted China Mail, (April 28, 1853), 67.
(4) Proclamation by General Shu at the Taking of Wuchang, Jan. 12, 1853. Undated in the text itself.	Cornaby, A String of Chinese Peach Stones, 202-5.
(5) Proclamation by General Sung Undated.	"Dr. MacGowan's Notebook," North-China Herald, 161 (Aug. 27, 1853), 16.
(6) Proclamation by General Wang Addressed to the Ch'ing Emperor Hsien-feng. Undated.	"Dr. MacGowan's Notebook," North-China Herald, 159 (Aug. 13, 1853), 7.
(7) Proclamation of General Kuo Dated approximately "in the first year of Emperor T'ai-p'ing of the Hou-ming or Later Ming Dynasty in the 6th day of the 3d moon (April 24, 1852)."	North-China Herald, 137 (March 12, 1853), 126-7. Reprinted China Mail, March 31, 1853, 51.
(8) Proclamation of General Hung Dated the second year of T'ien-te (Heavenly Virtue), month and day not given.	North-China Herald, 138 (March 19, 1853), 130. Reprinted China Mail, (April 7, 1853), 54,

Title	Source of English Translation
	and in Vizetelly, *The Chinese Revolution*, 54-5.
(9) Proclamation of Commissioner Liu Dated the second month, fourth year of T'ien-te. Posted on the walls of Kou-jung about 35 miles East by South of Nanking.	*North-China Herald*, 141 (April 9, 1853), 142. Reprinted in the *China Mail*, (April 28 1853), 67.
(10) Proclamation of an Anonymous Leader Undated.	*North-China Herald*, 137 (March 12, 1853), 126-7. Reprinted *China Mail*, (March 31, 1853).

A few comments on the contents of the documents listed above may be in place.

The new calendar for 1853 (No. 1 of the first list) should be noticed as an example of the insurgents' desire to found a regime within the acceptable limits of propriety. The official lunar calendar could not be approved because it was used by the Ch'ing dynasty. To borrow the Western solar calendar outright was too radical a step ever to win public approval. A compromise such as this was the only acceptable solution. The presence of one edict issued by Yang (No. 3, 1st list) and of the four (Nos. 2a, 2b, 2c, 1st list; No 1, 2d list) issued by him in conjunction with Hsiao, the Western King, is symbolic of the fact that these two kings spoke with unusual authority. The Heavenly Father was supposed to have appeared to Yang March 3, 1848 and Jesus to Hsiao Sept. 9 of the same year, performing miracles and conferring on each special authority. Reports of these and subsequent descents were delivered in such a manner as to convince Hsiu-ch'üan as well as the Taiping rank and file. As a result of these experiences, Yang assumed the title of Saviour from Calamity (Shu-ping-chu 贖病主) and Ho-nai Teacher (Ho-nai-shih 禾乃師). (Ho-nai, a term without intrinsic meaning, is believed to have been created from the components of hsiu 秀). The proclamation issued by Lo and Huang (Nos. 2 and 3, 2d list) and the specimen of verse supposed to have been pasted up on the walls of Nanking are examples of the type of order issued by subordinate leaders. Such communications were mainly devoted to reassuring local populations and giving directions. They are not as representative of the Taiping argument as the edicts of Yang and Hsiao.

Bibliographical Appendix 149

Four of the documents (No. 4, 1st list; Nos. 4,5,6, 2d list) make a point of the illegal seizure of the Chinese Empire by the Manchus who took advantage of an invitation to render assistance to the Ming general, Wu San-kuei. These all refer to two hundred years of Manchu misgovernment. No. 4, 1st list and No. 6, 2d list are written in praise of the seventh descendant of the Ming Emperor Kuang-tsung, the purported head of the rebellion against the dynasty.

The first of the documents in the series 7 through 10, 2d list refers to the leader of the insurrection as "our Emperor T'ien-te" who in the same edict is called the "Emperor T'ai-p'ing of the Hou-ming or Later Ming Dynasty." The second proclamation speaks of "aiding in the advancement of the T'ai-p'ing . . . Dynasty," but is dated in the second year of T'ien-te. The proclamation of Commissioner Liu, with a T'ien-te dating likewise, refers to a Captain-General Yang as a colleague. Liu's associate has the name and approximate title to fit Yang Hsiu-ch'ing, the Eastern King. The fourth composition is the work of an unnamed, unsuccessful candidate in the civil service examinations who claims lineal descent from subjects of the Ming Dynasty. The revolutionists he leads are said to "reverently worship the Deity (Shang-ti) in order to protect the people."

B. Translated Illustrations of the Taiping Ideology as a Whole

To illustrate properly the way in which non-religious were combined with religious elements in the typical Taiping secular proclamation two of the documents listed above have been selected for quotation in extenso.

1. (No.1, 1st list)

"New Calendar for Kuei-hao, the Third Year of the T'ai-p'ing t'ien-kuo

Ordered to be published throughout the empire.

Yang, the eastern king, chief minister of state, and generalissimo, the Ho-nai teacher and saviour from calamity,
Hsiao, the western king, second minister of state, also generalissimo,
Feng, the southern king, and general of the advance guard,
Wei, the northern king, and general of the rear guard, and
Shih, the assistant king, and general of the left wing.

---all high officers of the heavenly dynasty of T'ai-p'ing, kneeling before our sovereign, and elder brother, the King of Heaven, whom we wish to live for myriads of years added to myriads of years, and myriads of myriads of years, report that we have prepared a calendar and fixed the seasons.

Now that our heavenly Father, the supreme Lord and great God, has of his great goodness sent down our lord into the world to become the monarch of the universal dynasty of T'ai-p'ing, we consider that it is truly a period of great peace (when all things ought to be) equally adjusted, and filled up, without a single deficiency. We therefore, your majesty's servants, have made a calendar considering 366 days as a year, the odd months as containing 31 days and even months as containing 30 days; (the terms) Li-ch'un (commencement of spring), Ch'ing-ming (clear and bright (season)), Mang-chung ((period) of bearded grain), Li-ch'iu (commencement of autumn), Han-lu ((season) of cold dew), and Ta-hsüeh ((season) of great snow) (are reckoned) at 16 days, the other (eighteen terms) at 15 days each. Our heavenly dynasty and heavenly kingdom, (possessing) the hills and rivers for myriads and myriads of years, without end, is to be ascribed to the determination of our heavenly Father, the supreme Lord and great God, who has sent our lord down into the world.

All the corrupt doctrines and perverted customs of previous almanacs are the result of the devil's cunning devices to deceive and delude mankind; we, your majesty's servants, have set them all aside; for the years, months, days, and hours are all determined by our heavenly Father; thus, every year is lucky and favorable, every month is lucky and favorable, every day is also generally lucky and favorable. Why have good ones and bad ones? What is the need of selection? Whoever truly venerates our heavenly Father, the supreme Lord and great God, is under the protection of Heaven, and can engage in his duties whenever he thinks proper. Every season, therefore, may be considered as prosperous and favorable. Now we, your majesty's servants, having completed (this) almanac, reverently present it to our sovereign (wishing that he may live) myriads of years upon myriads of years, added to myriads of myriads of years, and that he will order the almanac to be published.

The imperial reply having been given as 'let the request be granted,' we now in obedience thereto issue this new almanac for <u>Kuei-hao</u>, the third year (1853), directing it to be published throughout the empire."

    (The foregoing is the preface. The calendar itself
      follows, but is omitted here.)

In the form of the document quoted above the authors are careful to follow traditional Chinese procedure. The "kings" petition that they may compose and publish a new calendar.

Bibliographical Appendix 151

The King of Heaven gives his assent, even to the extent of using the characters [5] employed by the Ch'ing emperor in approving a memorial. Then the "kings" publish it. Wishes for the T'ien-wang's long life are couched in traditional phraseology. [6]

2. (No. 2b, 1st list)

"Edict Received from Heaven to Punish the Tatars and to Publish the Order Everywhere

Yang, entitled the eastern king, chief minister of state and generalissimo, with Hsiao, entitled the western king, second minister of state, and general-in-chief, (both of) the true, heaven-appointed, heavenly kingdom of great peace, (together announce) that they have received the commands of Heaven to punish the Tatars.

We (hereby) promulgate our orders in every place, and say, Oh, you multitudes, listen to our words. We conceive that the empire belongs to the Chinese, and not to the Tatar barbarians; the food and clothing therein belong to the Chinese and not to the Tatars; the men, women, and children inhabiting this region are subjects and people of China, not of the Tatars. But alas! The Ming (dynasty) lost the rule, and the Manchus took advantage of a quarrel to throw China into confusion, and deprive the Chinese of their empire; they robbed them of their food and clothing and debauched and oppressed their sons and daughters. Yet the Chinese, although having an extensive territory and a large population, allowed the Tatars to do as they pleased without making (the least) objection. Can the Chinese still consider themselves men? Ever since the Manchus poisoned China, the flame of oppression has risen up to heaven, the poison of corruption has defiled the emperor's throne, the offensive odor has spread over the four seas, and the influence of demons has distressed the empire, while the Chinese with bowed heads and dejected spirits willingly become subjects and servants. How strange it is that there are no men in China! Now China is the head, Tartary the feet; China is the land of gods, Tatary the land of demons. Why may China be considered the land of gods? Because the true God, the great God and heavenly Father, made heaven and earth and the land and sea. Therefore from of old China has been termed the land of gods. Why are the Tatars to be considered demons? The devilish serpent, the king of Hades, is a corrupt demon. The Tatars worship him. Therefore the Tatars may be considered demons. Alas! the feet have assumed the place of the head, and demon-men have usurped the land of gods while they have compelled our Chinese (people) all to become demons.

If all the bamboos of the southern hills were to be used for writing, they would not be enough to detail the obscenities of these Tatars; and if all the waves of the eastern sea were to be employed, they would not be sufficient to wash away their sins, which fill the heavens. We shall merely enumerate a few general circumstances that are well known among men. The Chinese have a form of their own, (but) now the Manchus have commanded all to shave the hair round their heads and wear a long tail behind, thus causing the Chinese to become animals. The Chinese have a dress peculiar to themselves but these Manchus have caused them to wear knobs on their cap with Tatar clothes and monkey caps, while they discard the robes and head-dress of former dynasties, thus causing the Chinese to forget their origin. The Chinese have their own relations and descendants, but that false devil K'ang-hsi (Manchu emperor 1662-1722) secretly commanded his Tatar (followers) each to take control of ten families and defile wives and daughters of Chinese; he wanted thereby to make the Chinese all into Tatars. The Chinese have their own connections by marriage, but the Manchu fiends have all taken to themselves the beautiful women of China to be their slaves and concubines thousands of our young women have been defiled by these rammish dogs, and myriads of our ruddy daughters have been ravished by these lustful foxes, the very mention of which distresses the feelings, and pollutes the tongue, for the women of China have all been thus debauched. The Chinese have their own laws and regulations, (but) the Manchus have manufactured devilish enactments so that our Chinese people cannot escape the meshes of their net nor can they move hand or foot. This is the way in which all the Chinese young men are brought under their control. The Chinese have their own language, (but) now the Manchus have made it into the slang of the capital and changed Chinese pronunciation, designing thus to seduce China by their Tatar speech. Whenever drought and inundations occur, the government manifests no compassion, but quietly sees our people scattered abroad or dying of hunger, their bleaching bones like mustard, seeking in this way the depopulation of our country. The Manchus, moreover, have allowed corrupt magistrates and covetous officers to spread themselves all over China, flaying the people and devouring their substance (until) both men and women weep by the roadside. They seek in this way to see our fellow subjects reduced to want and poverty. Offices are to be obtained by bribes; crimes are to be pardoned with money. The rich engross all authority while heroes despair. They seek in this way to cause the noble spirits in our China to despair and die. Those who are animated by patriotic feeling and who seek to revive China are falsely accused of fostering rebellion and their whole families exterminated. In this way they aim to cut off all heroic planning in China. There is no way in which the Manchus have not deceived and insulted China, for they are ingenious in the extreme. In former times Yao I-chung 姚弋仲, though (himself) a Tatar, warned his son Hsiang to submit to China. Fu Yung 苻融 was also a Tatar, but he often admonished his elder brother Chien not to invade China. But now these Manchus, forgetting the meanness and lowness of their origin, and taking advantage of Wu San-kuei's introduction, have usurped dominion in China and have carried their villainies to the utmost. . . . (The six lines omitted here describe in highly figurative terms the low origin of the Manchus and the outrageous nature of their rule.)

You have read books, and are acquainted with history, and do you not feel in the slightest degree ashamed? In former times Wen T'ien-hsiang 文天祥 and Hsieh Fang-te 謝枋得 swore that they would die rather than serve the Mongols. Shih K'o-fa 史可法 and Ch'ü Shih-ssu 瞿式耜 swore that they would rather die than serve the Ch'ing. These (facts) must all be familiar to you. According to our calculation the Manchus cannot be above a hundred thousand in number and we Chinese amount to more than fifty millions(sic); but for fifty millions to be ruled over by a hundred thousand is very disgraceful. Now happily, with the way of God about to return and China having some prospect of a revival, men's minds are bent on good government. It is evident that the Tatars will certainly be destroyed. . . . The iniquities of the Tatars are full; high Heaven in thundering anger has commanded our heavenly king sternly to display his heavenly majesty, and erect the standard of righteousness, sweeping away the demoniacal brood and cutting away the Ch'ing from China. He reverently carries out Heaven's punishment and says to all, whether far or near, 'Who is there that is not ready to bare the arm in my cause? Whether officers, or people, who is there that is not willing to meet the emergency and raise a flag (in my defence)?'

Let the armed bands display their glittering lances, raise the animating shout, and present a bold front; let husbands and wives and men and women develop their righteous indignation and press forward in the van. Let us swear to exterminate the eight banners (Manchu army) in order to tranquillize the nine provinces (China). We especially call upon the noble-minded of every region to venerate God in order to support the mind of Heaven; (let us win over again our former battles when our ancestors) seized Shou Hsü 守緒 in Ts'ai-chou 蔡洲 and took T'o Huan 妥懽 in Yingch'ang 應昌 (both Mongol chiefs at the end of the Yüan dynasty); let us recover the territory that has been long lost and reverently comply with the rules and commandments of

God. Whoever can succeed in catching that Tatar dog (the) Hsien-feng (Emperor) and will bring him before us, or whoever is able to cut off his head and present it to us; or whoever can seize or decapitate any one of the Manchus shall be rewarded with high offices. We will certainly not (break our word. Now that we have obtained the eminent favor of the great God who commands our lord the heavenly king to set in order our Chinese empire, can the Tatars keep it any longer in confusion? Who among you, inhabitants of China, is not a son or daughter of God? If now you set about slaughtering the demons in obedience (to the command) of Heaven, if, seizing the standard you are among the first to mount the wall, and are careful to avoid the error of Fang Feng 防風 who was the last to come (to the help of the prince Yü, 2204 B.C.), you shall in the present world be considered a matchless hero, and in heaven above obtain eternal glory. If, perhaps, you (still) retain your delusions, and will not awaken, protecting the false and resisting the true, (then) while you are alive you will be Tatar men and at death will be Tatar devils. Obedience and disobedience have their properties; Chinese and barbarians have their definite designations; let everyone obey Heaven, free himself from demoniacal (influences), and become a man. You have suffered calamity from the Manchus long (enough). If now you do not change your plans and with united strength and courage sweep away the Tatar dirt, how can you answer for it to God in the highest heavens? We have now set in motion our righteous army, above to revenge (the insult offered to) God in deceiving Heaven, and below to deliver China from its inverted position. We are devoting ourselves sternly to sweeping away every vestige of Tatar influence and unitedly enjoying the happiness of the T'ai-p'ing dynasty. Those who obey Heaven shall meet with large rewards; those who disobey shall be openly put to death. This is our announcement to the whole empire; let all hear!"

Bibliographical Appendix   155

   C. General Bibliography

   In the listings that follow items that have already been
given on pages 131-2 and 142-4 in this chapter are omitted.

       I. Primary Sources

Chang Te-chien 張德堅. Tsei ch'ing hui tsuan 賊情彙纂
(Collections on the conditions of the robbers). 6 ts'e.
Nanking, 1932. An important and original source, con-
taining the reports of subordinates of Tseng Kuo-fan.
Hard to use, no pagination, but with many diagrams and
hand drawn illustrations.

Dispatches from United States Ministers to China (microfilm), Vol. 8 (August 5, 1852 - February 22, 1854).

Great Britain. Parliamentary Publications (hereafter abbreviated P.P.), 1853. House of Lords, Sessional Papers.
"Papers Respecting the Civil War in China." London,
1853.

P.P. 1861. House of Commons 66, Accounts and Papers 33,
(2754) "Correspondence respecting Affairs in China,
1859-60." London, 1861. 265 pages.

P.P. 1861. House of Commons 66, Accounts and Papers 33,
(2840) "Correspondence respecting the Opening of the
Yang-tze-kiang River to Foreign Trade." London, 1861.
33 pages.

P.P. 1862. House of Commons 63, Accounts and Papers 35,
(2976) "Papers Relating to the Rebellion in China and
Trade in the Yang-tze-kiang River." London, 1862.
158 pages.

P.P. 1862. House of Commons 63, Accounts and Papers 35,
(2992) "Further Papers relating to the Rebellion in China
(in continuation of Papers presented to Parliament, May 2,
1862)." London, 1862. 17 pages.

P.P. 1862. House of Commons 63, Accounts and Papers 35,
(3057) "Correspondence on the Employment of British
Officers by the Government of China." London, 1862.
5 pages.

P.P. 1862. House of Commons 63, Accounts and Papers 35,
(3058) "Further Papers Relating to the Rebellion in
China." London, 1862. 55 pages.

Great Britain. P.P. 1864. House of Commons 63, Accounts and Papers , (3408) "Correspondence relative to Lieutenant-Colonel Gordon's Position in the Chinese Service after the Fall of Soochow." London, 1864. 36 pages.

State Papers 52. p. 482; 53. p. 312.

Hertslet, Geoffrey E.P. Treaties, etc., between Great Britain and China and between China and Foreign Powers. London, 1908.

The Holy Bible Containing the Old and New Testaments Translated Out of the Original Tongues, etc. American revision of the 1611 version. Ed. 1901, American Revision Committee. Standard edition. New York: Thos. Nelson & Sons, 1901.

Hsieh Hsing-yao 謝興堯 ed., T'ai-p'ing t'ien-kuo ts'ung-shu shih-san chung 太平天國叢書十三種 (Collectanea of the T'ai-p'ing t'ien-kuo, thirteen items). Peiping: Yao-ch ts'ung-k'o, 1938.

Kyū-shin-yaku seishō 舊新約聖書 (Complete Holy Bible). Tokyo Japanese Bible Society, 1940.

T'ai-p'ing t'ien-kuo kuan-shu shih-chung 太平天國官書十種 (Ten official documents of the T'ai-p'ing t'ien-kuo). Kuang-tung ts'ung-shu ti-san chi 廣東叢書第三集 (Third Kwangtung collectanea). Canton, 1949.

U.S.Doc. 374, House Exec. Docs. 16, no. 123, 33 Cong., 1st sess. (1853-54). "Correspondence between the State Department and the late Commissioner to China (Humphrey Marshall)."

U.S.Doc. 819, Sen. Exec. Docs. 10, 34 Cong., 1st & 2d sess. (1855-56). "Report relative to regulations with China, in conformity with the 6th section of the act of Aug. 11, 1848." Notable for Commissioner McLane's proclamation of neutrality for Americans residing in China, date Canton, Dec. 5, 1854.

U.S.Doc. 887, Sen. Exec. Docs. 22, part 1, 35 Cong., 2d sess. Contains I, 47-92 Commissioner McLane's report o the visit of the "Susquehannah" to Nanking.

U.S.Doc. 901, Sen. Exec. Docs. 39.3. 36 Cong., 1st sess. Contains Secretary of State Marcy's instructions, Nov.

1853, to Commissioner McLane, authorizing the latter to recognize the rebels at his discretion as the de facto government of China.

Wang Chung-min 王重民 ed., "T'ai-p'ing t'ien-jih" 太平天日 (T'ai-p'ing days), I Ching 逸經 (Uncanonical classics), 13 (Sept. 5, 1936), 695-700; 14 (Sept. 20, 1936), 767-70; 16 (Oct. 20, 1936), 865-9.

II. Secondary Works

1. Catalogues

Catalogue des livres Chinois qui se trouvent dans la bibliothèque de l'Université de Leide. Leyden, 1883. Supplement, 1886.

Cordier, Henri. Bibliotheca Sinica, I, 1 (Paris, 1904), 645-64. Lists most of the Western language titles concerning the Rebellion that had appeared up to 1904.

Douglas, Robert Kennaway. Catalogue of Chinese Printed Books, Manuscripts, and Drawings in the Library of the British Museum. London, 1877.

Teng Yen-lin 鄧衍林. "T'ai-p'ing t'ien-kuo shih-liao shih-chi chi-mu" 太平天國史料史籍集目, Pei-p'ing t'u-shu kuan hsüeh chi-k'an 北平圖書館學季刊 (Bulletin of the National Library, Peiping), 9.1 (March, 1935), 109-26.

Wang Chung-min 王重民 ed. "T'ai-p'ing t'ien-kuo shu pu pien hsü-lu" 太平天國官書補編敘錄 (Introduction to additional official documents of the T'ai-p'ing t'ien-kuo), Bulletin of the National Library of Peiping, 10.6 (Nov. - Dec., 1936), 25-9.

Wylie, Alexander. Memorials of Protestant Missionaries to the Chinese: Giving a List of Their Publications, and Obituary Notices of the Deceased, with Copious Indexes. Shanghai: American Presbyterian Mission Press, 1867.

2. Dictionaries and Gazetteers

Hsieh Ch'i-k'un 謝啓昆 et al. Kuang-hsi t'ung-chih 廣西通志 (Gazetteer of Kwangsi Province). 1st ed. 1800; rev. ed. 1891. 80 v. without pictures or maps.

Li Shih-hua 黎士華 and Chang Hsien-hsiang 張顯相. P'ing-nan hsien chih 平南縣志 (Gazetteer of P'ing-nan Sub-prefecture). 1835. 6 v., illustrated. P'ing-nan was a

Taiping center southeast of Chin-t'ien.

Soothill, William Edward and Hodous, Lewis. A Dictionary of Chinese Buddhist Terms. London: Kegan Paul, 1937.

Wei Tu 魏篤. Hsün-chou-fu chih 潯州府志 (Gazetteer of Hsün chou Prefecture). 1874. Contains descriptions of the localities and regions of Kwangsi where the first Taiping preaching was done. Note maps (1.12b-13; 14b-15) and description (5.6b, 8 to 7,4) of Tzu-ching-shan (Thistle Mountain), the area of the first military assembly and the first engagements with Ch'ing troops.

Werner, E.T.C. A Dictionary of Chinese Mythology. Shanghai: Kelly & Walsh, 1932. Based on long study and considerable residence in China. The author uses Chinese sources.

3. Newspapers and Magazines

The China Mail (Hongkong), 1851-3.

I Ching 逸經 (Uncanonical classics), 1936-37.

The North-China Herald (Shanghai), 1851-5, 1857.

4. Books

Author unknown. A History of China to the Present Time, Including an Account of the Rise and Progress of the Present Religious Insurrection in the Empire. London, 1854. Contains copies of edicts and proclamations not obtainable elsewhere.

Bales, W.L. Tso Tsungt'ang, Soldier and Statesman of Old China. Shanghai: Kelly & Walsh, 1937.

Biernatzki, R.L. Die Gegenwartige Politisch-religiöse Bewegung. Berlin, 1854.

Bredon, Juliet and Mitrophanov, Igor. The Moon Year--A Record of Chinese Customs and Festivals. Shanghai: Kelly & Walsh, 1927.

Brine, Lindesay. The Taeping Rebellion in China. London, 1862.

Brinton, Crane. The Anatomy of Revolution. New York, 193 An analysis of the French, American, English, and Russia revolutions in the attempt to discover common patterns.

Broomhall, Marshall. Islam in China. London, 1910.
Chinese Moslem evangelists made use of China's supposedly monotheistic past in a manner similar to that of Taiping apologists.

Burns, Edward McNall. Western Civilizations, Their History and Their Culture. 3d ed. New York: W.W. Norton, 1949.

Burns, Robert. The Complete Writings of Robert Burns. Boston: Houghton Mifflin, 1926.

Callery, J.M., and Yuan, M. History of the Insurrection in China, etc. Translated from French by John Oxenford. London, 1854. A standard work for the early part of the Rebellion.

Canton, W. History of the British and Foreign Bible Society. 2 vols. London, 1904.

Chang Hsiao-wu 張霄鳴. T'ai-p'ing t'ien-kuo ko-ming shih 太平天國革命史 (History of the revolution of the T'ai-p'ing t'ien-kuo). Shanghai, 1932. A general text. No sources indicated.

Ch'en Kung-lu 陳恭祿. Chung-kuo chin-tai shih 中國近代史 (Modern history of China). Shanghai: Commercial Press, 1935. A general account of the Rebellion given pp. 131-219.

Cheng Hao-sheng 鄭鶴聲 ed. Chin-shih chung-hsi shih jih tui-chao piao 近世中西史日對照表 (Comparative table of dates for recent Chinese and Western history). Shanghai: Commercial Press, 1936. Covers the period from 1516 to the present.

Chien Yu-wen 簡又文. Chin-t'ien chih yu chi ch'i t'a 金田之遊及其他 (A journey to Chin-t'ien and other articles) Chungking: Commercial Press, 1944. Based upon an eleven months' trip (1942-43) through the areas where the Rebellion began. Useful for atmosphere, local records, and local traditions.

Chien Yu-wen. T'ai-p'ing chün kuang-hsi shou-i shih 太平軍廣西首義史 (History of the uprising of the Taiping army in Kwangsi). Chungking: Commercial Press, 1944. Based on life-long interest and more than a decade of research and publication. This is to date one of the most important books by a Chinese on the Rebellion.

Chien Yu-wen. T'ai-p'ing t'ien-kuo tsa chi 太平天國雜記 (Miscellaneous records of the T'ai-p'ing t'ien-kuo). Shanghai: Commercial Press, 1935.

Cornaby, William Arthur. The Call of Cathay. London, 1910.

Cornaby, William Arthur. A String of Chinese Peach Stones London, 1895. Pictures village life of central China during the period 1849-67. Source of useful translation of both Taiping and Imperialist originals.

Cornelssen, Lucy. Tai Ping Tien Guo - Rebellen unterm Kreuz. Berlin, 1938. A romanticization of the Taiping story based on available sources in Western languages. Following them the preponderance of attention is devoted to the years 1859-64.

Creel, Herrlee Glessner. The Birth of China. London: Jonathan Cape, 1936.

Creel, Herrlee Glessner. Confucius, the Man and the Myth. New York: John Day, 1949.

Davis, John Francis. China, A General Description, etc. 2 vols. London, 1857. The Rebellion is treated by this author in an arbitrary manner typical of the British attitude after all hope of rapprochement with the rebels was gone.

Dean, William. The China Mission. New York, 1859.

De Groot, J.J.M. Sectarianism and Religious Persecution in China. 2 vols. Amsterdam, 1903. The author is persuaded that religious persecution was a major cause of the Rebellion, a conclusion scarcely borne out by the facts as known now.

Dennett, Tyler. Americans in Eastern Asia. New York, 19 Valuable for official American attitudes toward the rebe and relations with them.

Edkins, Joseph. The Religious Condition of the Chinese. 1859.

Edkins, Joseph. Religion in China. London, 1878. This and the preceding title are the thoughtful observations of an early missionary.

Bibliographical Appendix   161

Fan Wen-lan 范文瀾. T'ai-p'ing t'ien-kuo ko-ming yün-tung
   太平天國革命運動 (The Taiping revolutionary movement).
   Shanghai: Hsin Hua Shu Tien, 1949.

Fan Wen-lan, editorial director, Hua-pei ta-hsüeh li-shih
   yen-chiu shih 華北大學歷史研究室 (Historical research
   group of North China University). T'ai-p'ing t'ien-kuo
   ko-ming yün-tung lun wen-chi 太平天國革命運動論文集
   (Collection of writings on the T'ai-p'ing revolutionary
   movement). Centennial volume. Peking: San Lien Shu
   Tien, 1951.

Feng Tzu-yu 馮自由. Chung-hua min-kuo k'ai-kuo ch'ien ko-
   ming shih 中華民國開國前革命史 (History of the revolution
   preceding the foundation of the Chinese Republic).
   Chung-kuo Wen-hua Fu-wu She, 1944, 1946.

Firth, C.H. Cromwell's Army, A History of the English
   Soldier during the Civil Wars, the Commonwealth and the
   Protectorate. Being the Ford Lectures delivered in the
   University of Oxford in 1900-1. London, New York, 1902.
   Documentation for an analogous use of religion for mil-
   itary purposes.

Fishbourne, E.G. Impressions of China and the Present
   Revolution, Its Progress and Prospects. London, 1854.
   A full account by the commander of the "Hermes" on her
   visit to Nanking.

Gillespie, William. The Land of Sinim or China and Christian Missions. Edinburgh, 1854. The author for seven
   years was agent for the London Missionary Society at
   Hongkong and Canton.

Group for the Study of Recent Chinese History 中國現代史研究
   委員會. Chung-kuo hsien-tai ko-ming yün-tung shih 中國現
   代革命運動史 (History of recent Chinese revolutionary movements). Hsin Hua Shu Tien, 1942. Vol. I.

Gützlaff, Charles Friedrich August. Journal of Three Voyages along the Coast of China in 1831, 1832, and 1833, etc.
   2d ed. London, 1834.

Hail, William James. Tseng Kuo-Fan and the Taiping Rebellion. New Haven: Yale University Press, 1927. One of the
   more important books about the Rebellion, based upon
   Chinese as well as Western sources. The author in defend-
   ing Tseng Kuo-fan against his detractors devotes his
   principal attention to the suppression of the uprising.
   His remarks on the earlier years of the movement are
   valuable though introductory.

Hamberg, Theodore. The Visions of Hung-Siu-Tshuen and Origin of the Kwang-si Insurrection. Hongkong, 1854. Reprinted Peiping: Yenching University Library, 1935 with Chinese translation by Chien Yu-wen under the title T'ai-p'ing t'ien-kuo ch'i-i chi 太平天國起義記 (Origin of the Rebellion of the T'ai-p'ing t'ien-kuo). Written from material furnished Hamberg by Hung Jen-kan, a second cousin of Hung Hsiu-ch'üan, who, however, did not participate in military activity during the years 1851-3. This work is the chief source for knowledge of the Rebellion as far as the early experiences of Hung and the organization of the first communities of God-Worshippers is concerned. It is now believed to have been based in part on an early work of Hung Hsiu-ch'üan, T'ai-p'ing t'ien-jih 太平天日 (T'ai-p'ing days). The written account which Jen-kan did for Hamberg is known as Hung Hsiu-ch'üan lai-li 洪秀全來歷 (Personal history of Hung Hsiu-ch'üan) and is reproduced in I Ching 25 (March, 1937).

Hayes, L. Newton. The Chinese Dragon. Shanghai: Commercial Press, 1923.

Hsieh, Hsing-yao 謝興堯. T'ai-p'ing t'ien-kuo shih shih lun ts'ung 太平天國史事論叢 (Collection of essays on the history and affairs of the T'ai-p'ing t'ien-kuo). Shanghai: Commercial Press, 1935. Twelve essays, many of considerable importance, each accompanied by a bibliography.

Hsieh, Hsing-yao. T'ai-p'ing t'ien-kuo ti she-hui chengchih ssu-hsiang 太平天國的社會政治思想 (Social and political theories of the T'ai-p'ing t'ien-kuo). Shanghai: Commercial Press, 1935. Introductory essays on the origin of Taiping theory. The author's position is that rebel social and political thought came from three sources, viz. Protestantism, the Rites of Chou (a work of the Han dynasty), and Chinese secret societies.

Hsieh, Pao-chao. The Government of China (1644-1911). Baltimore: Johns Hopkins Press, 1925.

Hua Kang 華岡. T'ai-p'ing t'ien-kuo ko-ming chan-cheng shih 太平天國革命戰爭史 (History of the Taiping revolutionary war). Shanghai: Hai Yin, 1949.

Hummel, Arthur W., ed. Eminent Chinese of the Ch'ing Period. Washington: U.S. Govt. Printing Office, 1943-4. 2 vols. Invaluable for biographical and bibliographical data.

Hykes, John R. Translations of the Scriptures into the
Languages of China and Her Dependencies. American Bible
Society Centennial Pamphlet # 22. New York, 1916.

Kretzmann, P.E. The God of the Bible and Other Gods.
St. Louis, 1943.

Kuo T'ing-i 郭廷以. T'ai-p'ing t'ien-kuo li-fa k'ao-ting
太平天國曆法考訂 (A study of the calendar of the T'ai-
p'ing t'ien-kuo). Shanghai: Commercial Press, 1937.

Kuo T'ing-i. T'ai-p'ing t'ien-kuo shih-shih jih chih 太平
天國史事日誌 (Day to day records of the historical events
of the Heavenly Kingdom of Great Peace). 2 vols. Shanghai: Commercial Press, 1946-47. An indispensable reference work with extensive bibliographies.

Latourette, Kenneth Scott. The Chinese Their History and
Culture. New York: MacMillan, 1947. 3d ed. rev.

Latourette, Kenneth Scott. The Great Century in Northern
Africa and Asia, A.D. 1800 - A.D. 1914. Vol. VI of
A History of the Expansion of Christianity by the same
author. New York and London, 1944.

Latourette, Kenneth Scott. A History of Christian Missions
in China. New York: MacMillan, 1929.

Lindley, A.F. Ti-Ping Tien-Kwoh--The History of the Ti-
Ping Revolution. London, 1866. 2 vols. Lindley was
associated with the rebels for four years from 1860 on
and was especially well acquainted with Li Hsiu-ch'eng,
the leading Taiping military chief after the death of
Yang Hsiu-ch'ing. Where its statements can be checked,
this book is of value. The author is strongly anti-
British and anti-Manchu.

Lo Erh-kang 羅爾綱. T'ai-p'ing t'ien-kuo shih kang 太平天國
史綱 (Resume' of the history of the T'ai-p'ing t'ien-kuo).
Shanghai: Commercial Press, 1937.

Lowenthal, Rudolf; Ch'en Hung-shun; Ku T'ing-ch'ang; and
Liang Yun-i. The Religious Periodical Press in China.
Series Sinologica 57. Peking: The Synodal Commission in
China, 1940. Helpful as an index of early missionary
publishing activity.

MacFarlane, Charles. The Chinese Revolution, etc. London,
1853. A pocket-size, contemporary account giving details
of Taiping religious beliefs.

MacGillivray, D. A Century of Protestant Missions in China
(1807-1907), Being the Centenary Conference Historical
Volume. Shanghai, 1907. The author was a distinguished
missionary sinologue of two generations ago.

MacGillivray, D., ed. The China Mission Year Book 1915.
Shanghai, 1915.

Mackie, J. Milton. Life of Tai-ping-wang. New York, 1857
Has translations of several insurgent documents and extracts from contemporary letters.

MacNair, Harley Farnsworth. Modern Chinese History:
Selected Readings. Shanghai, 1923.

Martin, Alfred W. Seven Great Bibles. New York, 1930.
Explains in detail the covenant relationship between
Yahweh and the Hebrews of the Old Testament.

Martin, W.A.P. A Cycle of Cathay. New York, 1897.

Meadows, Thomas Taylor. The Chinese and Their Rebellions.
London, 1856. A valuable reflective study by a British
Chinese interpreter with the "Hermes" on her visit to
Nanking in 1853. Meadows and Medhurst are the two best,
contemporary Western interpreters of the early part of
the Rebellion.

Medhurst, Walter Henry. China: Its State and Prospects wi
Especial Reference to the Spread of the Gospel, etc.
London, 1838.

Medhurst, Walter Henry. Pamphlets Issued by the Chinese
Insurgents; to Which is Added a History of the Kwangse
Rebellion . . . and . . . Connection between Foreign
Missionaries and the Chinese Insurrection. Shanghai,
1853. A reprint of material that appeared serially in
in the North-China Herald. The major part of translations of Taiping originals that were read by Westerners
during the early years of the Rebellion are the work of
Medhurst.

Mercier, R.P. Campagne du "Cassini" dans les Mers de
Chine 1851-1854 d'après les Rapports, Lettres, et Notes
de Commandant du Plas, Enrichie de Plusieurs Cartes pou
l'Intelligence du Texte. Paris, 1889.

Milne, William. A Retrospect of the First Ten Years of t
Protestant Mission to China. Malacca, 1820. A detaile

account of Christian beginnings in the China mission and of early difficulties by the associate of Robert Morrison. Liang A-fa was baptized by William Milne.

Milne, William C. Life in China. London, 1858. The author, the son of William Milne, shows little sympathy with the Taiping movement.

Morgan, Harry T. Chinese Symbols and Superstitions. South Pasadena, Calif.: Perkins, 1942.

Moule, Arthur Evans. Half a Century in China. London, 1911. Illustrates (p. 30) and describes a stone set up at the entrance to the Taiping Palace in Nanking which bore an engraving of the Christian Beatitudes. The stone was destroyed when the imperial troops took the city. The author's comments are concerned with the latter part of the Rebellion.

Muirhead, William. China and the Gospel. London, 1870.

Neumann, Karl Friedrich. Ostasiatische Geschichte vom ersten Chinesischen Krieg bis zu den Vertragen in Peking (1840-1860. Leipzig, 1861.

Norris, Frank L. China. London, 1908. Interesting comments on the Taiping rebels by an English missionary for the Society for the Propagation of the Gospel.

North, Eric M., ed. The Book of a Thousand Tongues. New York, 1938. A compendium of information concerning translations of the Bible.

Oehler, Wilhelm. Die Taiping Bewegung Geschichte eines Chinesisch-Christlichen Gottesreichs. Gutersloh: C. Bertelsmann, 1923.

P'eng Tse-i 彭澤益. T'ai-p'ing t'ien-kuo ko-ming ssu-ch'ao 太平天國革命思潮 (The dynamic thought of the Taiping Rebellion). Shanghai: Commercial Press, 1946.

Pettee, G.S. The Process of Revolution. New York, 1938. A thoughtful attempt to formulate an adequate theory of revolution considered either as the political failure of a government or the general failure of a whole social system. Based upon the Russian and French Revolutions.

Platonov, S.F. History of Russia. New York, 1929. A standard work.

Richard, Timothy. *Forty-five Years in China.* New York, 1916

Richards, I.A. *Mencius on the Mind.* New York: Harcourt, Brace, 1932.

Rowbotham, Arnold H. *Missionary and Mandarin-The Jesuits at the Court of China.* Berkeley: University of California Press, 1942.

Scarth, John. *Twelve Years in China The People, the Rebels the Mandarins.* Edinburgh, 1860. Pro-Taiping. Gives valuable supplementation, especially about British attitudes and the activities of secret societies.

Schlyter, Herman. *Karl Gützlaff als Missionar in China.* Lund, Sweden: C.W.K. Gleerup, 1946. No. 1, Publications by the Swedish Society for Missions Research. The best work to date on Gützlaff, based on letters, archives of mission societies, and a wide range of printed matter. The text of the volume is in German, to which a summary in English is appended.

So Kwan-wai and Boardman, Eugene P. *Hung Jen-kan, Taiping Prime Minister, 1859-64.* Unpublished manuscript, University of Wisconsin, 1950.

Spielmann, Christian. *Die Taiping-Revolution in China (1850-1864).* A general account. No sources cited.

Stanton, William. *The Triad Society.* Shanghai: Kelly and Walsh, 1900. By a former detective in Shanghai and Hongkong. Good for a historical sketch of the Triads. Contains data on the Triad initiation ceremonies.

Swann, Nancy Lee. Transl. and annotator. *Food and Money in Ancient China* (Han Shu 24 with related texts, Han Shu 91 and Shih-chi 129). Princeton: Princeton University Press, 1950.

Tai Chi-t'ao 戴季陶. *Kuo-min ko-ming yü chung-kuo kuo-min-tang* 國民革命與中國國民黨 (The people's revolution and the Chinese Kuomintang). Chung-kuo wen-hua fu-wu she, 1943, 1946.

Teng Ssu-yü. *New Light on the History of the Taiping Rebellion.* Cambridge: Harvard University Press, 1950. 132 pages. A resume with critical comment of the state of research on the Rebellion by the author of most of the biographies of government and rebel leaders of the Taiping period in *Eminent Chinese of the Ch'ing Period.* An indispensable aid.

Tsou Lu 鄒魯. Chung-kuo kuo-min-tang shih lüeh 中國國民黨史略 (Historical sketch of the Chinese Kuomintang). Chungking: Commercial Press, 1945.

Tu Wen-lan 杜文瀾. P'ing-ting yüeh k'ou chi lüeh 平定粵寇紀略 (A general account of the pacification of the Canton rebels). Date of publication unknown. 4 vols. A standard official history.

Vinacke, Harold M. A History of the Far East in Modern Times. New York: Crofts, 1946. 4th ed.

Vizetelly, Henry. The Chinese Revolution: The Causes which Led to It--Its Rapid Progress and Anticipated Result; with abstracts of all the known publications emanating from the insurgents. London, 1853. Chiefly useful as a source of translations.

Walker, Williston. A History of the Christian Church. New York: Scribner's, 1947.

Wang Chung-ch'i 王鍾麒. T'ai-p'ing t'ien-kuo ko-ming shih 太平天國革命史 (History of the revolution of the T'ai-p'ing t'ien-kuo). Shanghai: Commercial Press, 1931. A general account with bibliography.

Ward, J.S.M. and Sterling, W.G. The Hung Society, or the Society of Heaven and Earth. London, 1925.

Whale, J.S. Christian Doctrine. New York: MacMillan, 1941.

Williams, Frederick Wells. The Life and Letters of Samuel Wells Williams. New York, 1889.

Williams, S. Wells. The Middle Kingdom. Rev. ed. New York: Scribners', 1913. 2 vols.

Wittfogel, Karl A. and Feng Chia-sheng. History of Chinese Society, Liao (907-1125). Transactions of the American Philosophical Society. Vol. 36 (1947).

Wolferstan, Bertram, S.J. The Catholic Church in China from 1860 to 1907. London, Edinburgh, St. Louis, 1909. An able exposition of the Catholic philosophy regarding missions in China.

Wu Sheng-hai 吳繩海. T'ai-p'ing t'ien-kuo shih 太平天國史 (History of the T'ai-p'ing t'ien-kuo). Place and date of publication not indicated. Written as a textbook with topics for discussion at the end of each chapter.

Yang Sung 楊松 and Teng Li-ch'ün 鄧力羣. Chung-kuo chin-tai shih ts'an-k'ao ts'ai-liao 中國近代史參考材料 (Materials for the study of modern Chinese history). Chieh-fang She, 1942. Vol. I.

Yung Wing. My Life in China and America. New York, 1909. One of the first Chinese to be sent to the United States for higher education, Yung Wing made two trips into Taiping territory in 1859 and later engaged in tea-running through the rebel lines. In 1863 Yung entered government service under Tseng Kuo-fan. Yung was thoroughly convinced that neither the reformation nor the regeneration of China were to be expected from the Taipings as he saw them.

Yates, Matthew Tyson. The T'ai-p'ing Rebellion. A lecture for the benefit of the Shanghai Temperance Society. Shanghai, 1876. In 1853 the author talked with two young Chinese believed to be the sons of Feng Yün-shan, the Southern King. Yates gathered from them that the first germs of the Taiping movement were religious and that the patriotic and political motives entered only after it became apparent that it was necessary to resist the Manchu government. This interpretation is echoed in a number of contemporary Western works.

5. Articles in Periodicals and Composite Publications

"The Sixty-third Annual Meeting," American Historical Review LIV.3 (April, 1949), 727. Comments by Teng Ssu-yü on a paper presented by the author.

Barber, W.T.A. "The Rebel Bible," The Chinese Recorder and Missionary Journal, XXII.7 (July, 1891), 305-8.

Beauvais, M.J. "Livres Chinois à Angoulême," T'oung Pao, Series 1.3 (Mai, 1892), 181-2.

Cunningham, Edward. "Our Commercial and Political Relations with China," Hunt's Merchants' Magazine and Commercial Review, 33.3 (Sept., 1855), 275-82. By a member of the firm of Russell & Company. Unsympathetic with the Taiping side.

De Courcy, René. "L'Insurrection Chinoise--Son Origine et Ses Progrès," Revue des Deux Mondes, 34.1 (July 1, 1861), 5-35; and 34.2 (July 15, 1861), 312-60. Based on Peking Gazettes, a competent account for its date. Especially full on the siege of Nanking.

De Harlez, C. "La Religion des Insurgés Tchang-mao," T'oung Pao, Series 1.9, 397-401.

De Harlez, C. "T'ien Fu Hsia Fan Chao Shu 天父下凡詔書," T'oung Pao, Series 1.10 (1899). Partial translation, partial digest of the exposure of Chou Hsi-neng by the Heavenly Father. The Chinese text follows.

Fairbank, J.K., and Teng, S.Y. "On the Types and Uses of Ch'ing Documents," Harvard Journal of Asiatic Studies, 5.1 (January, 1940), 1-71.

Forrest, Robert James. "The Christianity of Hung Tsiu Tsuen, A Review of Taeping Books," Journal of the North-China Branch, Royal Asiatic Society, New Series, 4 (Dec., 1867), 187-208.

Foster, John, D.D. "The Christian Origins of the Taiping Rebellion," The International Review of Missions, XL. 158 (April, 1951), 156-67.

Hinton, Harold C. "Grain Transport Via the Grand Canal," Papers on China from the Regional Studies Seminars, Harvard University, IV (1950), 36.

Littell, John B. "Missionaries and Politics in China-- The Taiping Rebellion," Political Science Quarterly, XLIII.4 (Dec., 1928), 566-99.

Medhurst, W.H. "Connection between Foreign Missionaries and the Kwangsi-Insurrection (2·)," North-China Herald, 161 (Aug. 27, 1853), 14-5.

Medhurst, W.H. "Critical Review of the Books of the Insurgents," North-China Herald, 162 (Sept. 3, 1853), 19.

Roberts, Issachar J. "Tae Ping Wang," Putnam's Magazine, VIII.xlvi (Oct., 1856), 380-3.

Roberts, Issachar J. Untitled article in The Chinese and Missionary Gleaner, Oct., 1852.

Sargent, W. "The Chinese Rebellion," The North American Review, 79 (July, 1854), 158-200.

Stelle, Charles C. "Ideologies of the T'ai P'ing Insurrection," Chinese Social and Political Science Review, 20.1 (April, 1936), 140-9.

Taylor, G.E. "The Taiping Rebellion--Its Economic Background and Social Theory," Chinese Social and Political Science Review, 16.4 (January, 1933), 545-614. An important pioneer contribution.

Wang Chung-min 王重民. "T'ai-p'ing t'ien-kuo kuan-shu pu-pien hsü-lu" 太平天國官書補編叙錄 (Introduction to additional official documents of the T'ai-p'ing t'ien-kuo), Pei-p'ing t'u-shu-kuan kuan-k'an 北平圖書館館刊 (Bulletin of the National Library of Peiping), 10.6 (Nov. - Dec., 1936), 25-9.

Wang Yu-ch'üan. "The Rise of Land Tax and the Fall of Dynasties in Chinese History," Pacific Affairs, IX.2 (June, 1936), 201-20. Demonstrates the agrarian basis of the T'ai-p'ing Rebellion and of other revolts in Chinese history.

"The War in China," The British Journal, I.4 (1853), 289-96. Contemporary summary and report, principally of the "Hermes" visit.

Wylie, Alexander. "The Bible in China," Chinese Researches (Shanghai, 1897), 81-109. A printing of one of the more valuable of Wylie's shorter essays.

Footnotes

1. Several documents are believed to have been composed by Hung Hsiu-ch'üan himself at home during the years 1845 and 1846. See item 9, pp. 139-40, in the List of T'ai-p'ing Instructional Material and Tracts given in this chapter. For the existing differing versions of these compositions compare these titles as reprinted in T.S., S.L., and S.W.C. and consult Kuo T'ing-i, II, 185-7.
2. Wang Chung-min,"T'ai-p'ing t'ien-kuo kuan-shu pu-pien hsü-lu (Introduction to additional official documents of the T'ai-p'ing t'ien-kuo)," Pei-p'ing t'u-shu-kuan kuan-k'an (Bulletin of the National Library of Peiping), 10.6 (Nov. Dec. 1936), 25-9.
3. After Nanking fell in 1853 a deliberate attempt was made to falsify traces of the early association with the Triads. Earlier appeals to restore the rule of the Ming emperors and return to true Chinese customs in contrast with what the Manchus had imposed upon China were no longer heard. An increasing emphasis was placed upon a theocracy divinely-ordained and possessed of a new fount of revelation. The original and an altered text of the proclamation Feng-t'ien

Bibliographical Appendix   171

chu-yao chiu-shih an-min yü 奉天誅妖救世安民諭 (Command Received from Heaven to Kill the Imps, Save the World, and Pacify the People) show the nature of the falsification. In the original, members of the Triad Society are called upon to live up to an original bargain in which they had promised to help the Taipings in overthrowing the Manchu dynasty. After its alteration this part of the document simply calls on Chinese to be true to their natural conscience and exterminate the Manchus. One copy of the original reached Medhurst in time to be translated and published in the March 12, 1853 number of the North-China Herald. Another was brought from Nanking by the "Hermes" in May. The altered text was secured from Chinkiang the following month. North-China Herald, June 25, 1853. For the original text see S.W.C. 1. 31, 10 to 32, 11; the deleted passage (32, 3-4) begins with k'uang 況 and ends with ti-che-yeh 敵者也. The altered text is given in S.L. 1. 1-3b. The substituted passage may be found between the characters ai-hsi-yeh 愛惜也 and chin-ko-sheng 今各省 on page 2b, 5-7.

4. Chien, T'ai-p'ing chün kuang-hsi shou-i shih, 168-70. Hamberg, 45-6. The descent to Yang became known as the Yeh-hsiang-chieh 爺降節 (Occasion of the Father's Descent), that to Hsiao as the Ko-hsiang-chieh 哥降節 (Occasion of the Elder Brother's Descent). The incidents are officially recorded in the TMCCS, S.W.C.1. 1, 11 to 7b, 10.

5. Yü-p'i 御批. Fairbank and Teng, "On the Types and Uses of Ch'ing Documents," op. cit., 71. In the preface to the calendar for the following year this was changed to T'ien-wang p'i 天王批 (Endorsed by the King of Heaven). S.W.C.1, 37,7.

6. Wan-sui (Ten thousand years), the same characters as in the more familiar Japanese Banzai.

D. Characters for Names of Persons Appearing in the Text

Chang Pi-lu 張必祿
Chang Te-chien 張德堅
Ch'en Yü-ch'eng 陳玉成
Chiao Liang 焦亮
Feng Yün-shan 馮雲山
Hsiao Ch'ao-kuei 蕭朝貴
Hsiang Jung 向榮
Hu I-kuang 胡以晃
Hung Ching-yang 洪鏡揚
Hung Hsiu-ch'üan 洪秀全
Hung Jen-kan 洪仁玕
Hung Ta-ch'üan 洪大全
Li Hsiu-ch'eng 李秀成

Li Hung-chang 李鴻章
Li K'ai-fang 李開芳
Li Tzu-ch'eng 李自成
Liang A-fa 梁阿發
Lin Feng-hsiang 林鳳祥
Lin Tse-hsü 林則徐
Lo Ta-kang 羅大綱
Lu Liu 盧六
Min Cheng-feng 閔正鳳
Seng-ko-lin-ch'in 僧格林沁
Sheng Pao 勝保
Shih Ta-k'ai 石達開
Su San-niang 蘇三娘

D. Characters for Names of Persons Appearing in the Text (cont'd.)

Tseng Kuo-ch'üan 曾國荃
Tseng Kuo-fan 曾國藩
Tso Tsung-t'ang 左宗棠
Wang Tso-hsin 王作新

Wei Ch'ang-hui 韋昌輝
Wu K'o-i 吳可憶
Wu San-kuei 吳三桂
Yang Hsiu-ch'ing 楊秀清

E. Characters for Place Names Appearing in the Text

Chiang-k'ou-hsü 江口墟
Chin-t'ien 金田
Chiu-kuan 九關
Ch'üan-chou 全州
Hsin-shang-kan 新上甘
Hsün-chou 潯洲
Hua-chou 花州
Hua-hsien 花縣
Kua-chou 瓜州
Kuei-p'ing 桂平

Kuan-lu-pu 官祿埗
Meng-ch'ung 蒙冲
P'ing-nan hsien 平南縣
Po-pai 博白
So-i ford 蓑衣渡
Tao-chou 道洲
Tzu-ching-shan 紫荆山
Tz'u-ku 賜谷
Wu-hsüan 武宣
Yung-an 永安

Index

Abbreviations: titles of published compilations, 37; of Taiping religious documents, 38n
America: supports intervention, 26
American Baptist Mission: doxology of, similar to Taiping doxology, 72
American Bible Society: aids missionary efforts, 42; spends money for translation and revision, 49n
American Board of Commissioners for Foreign Missions: sends first missionaries to China, 42; collection of tracts, 51n, 52
Amoy: treaties permit foreign residence in, 45
Ananias: 82
Anglo-Chinese War (1839-42): test for Ch'ing regime, 9; destroys Manchu military reputation, 10; highlights Ch'ing failures, 11; Christian literature distributed before, 44; facilitates treaties permitting residence, 45
Anglo-Chinese War (1858-60): fails to produce Western-Taiping cooperation, 20
Anking, Anhwei: Taiping capture of, 21; overthrow of, by Tseng Kuo-ch'üan, 24; Taiping failure to recapture, 24

Arabic: choice of styles of, 41
Assistant King: See Shih Ta-k'ai
Atonement: part of Taiping dogma, 79
An-wei-che: term for Comforter, 72

Baptism: learned from tracts, 13; by Hung Hsiu-ch'üan, 76; Taiping ceremony of, 77; confers freedom from sin, 77; self-baptism sanctioned, 77; Liang's thought regarding, followed, 113
Batavia: mission stations at, 42
Beatitudes: carved on Taiping slab, 97-98n
Bible: indiscriminate use of, linked to Taiping failure, 8n; Protestant translations into Chinese, available for present study, 47; abbreviations for titles of Chinese translations used in present study, 48; authoritative position of, in the minds of missionaries, 52; scantiness of Taiping borrowing from, 53; early Chinese versions, absence of commentaries for, 54; New Testament material borrowed by Taipings, summarized, 54; Old Testament material borrowed by Tai-

173

pings, summarized, 54
American Revised Version, 1901: source of English quotations, 55; used in comparisons, 62 ff.
Delegates' Version: completion of, 7n; produced by Protestant committee, 47; first printed, 47; use of shen for God in, 59; copy used in present study described, 143
Lassar-Marshman Version: 47
Medhurst-Gützlaff Version: probable use of, by Roberts, 44; distributed by the Chinese Union, 47; first printed, 47; reprinted by Taipings, 47; designations for God borrowed, 55, 60; copied by Taipings, 56; 1847 copy used described, 142-43
Medhurst-Gützlaff Modified Version: 1855 copy used described, 143
Morrison-Milne Version: inferior to Medhurst-Gützlaff Bible, 44; published at Malacca, 47; used by Liang A-fa, 47; copy used described, 142
Bodhisattva: object of Taiping destruction, 66
Bonham, Sir George: exchanges tracts for rebel publications, 46
Book of Declarations Made During the Heavenly Father's Descent to Earth: See "T'ien-fu hsia-fan chao-shu"
Book of Heavenly Decrees and Imperial Edicts: See "T'ien-ming chao-chih-shu"
Book of History: quoted in "Yüan-tao chüeh-shih hsün", 35
Book of the Laws of Heaven: See "T'ien-t'iao-shu"
Book of Songs: quoted in "Yüan-tao chüeh-shih hsün", 35
Brave King: See Ch'en Yü-ch'eng
Bridgman, Elijah Coleman: useless effort of, 5; aboard "Susquehannah", visits Nanking, 21, 42; told of "Northern Expedition", 21; represents American Board, 42; member of Bible revision committee, 47, 143
British: decision to support Manchus, reasons for, 25-26; loan of officers to anti-Taiping forces, 26; use regulars about Shanghai, 26; rules for loan of officers, 32n
British and Foreign Bible Society: aids missionary activities, 42; aids Chinese Union, 43
Buddha, the: mentioned, 67
Buddhism: Taiping treatment of, 35; influences of, on Taiping religious ideology, mentioned, 37; many divinities recognized by, 65; proscribed, 68; terms of, scarcity of, 84; attacked by Liang A-fa, 112
Buddhists: property of, Taiping promise to confiscate, 36; responsible for neglect of Shang-ti, 67

Canton: resident missionary work permitted in factories at, 45; treaties allow foreign residence in, 45
"Cassini": visit of, to Nanking, comments on, 122
Catholic: failure to influence Taipings, 4; lack of responsibility for Taiping religion, 41
Chan-yao (behead the demons): source of Hung's use of, 112
Ch'an-ch'u: term, 61
Changchow, Kiangsu: Taiping seizure of, 23
Chang Pi-lu: ordered to suppress God-Worshippers, 17
Chang Yüeh liang yu hsiang-lun: possibly disseminated by China Union, 46
Ch'ang-mao-tsei: God-Worshippers called, 17
Changsha, Hunan: Hsiao Ch'ao-kuei dies near, 19; Taiping failure to capture, 21
Chao-shu: explained, 33

Index

Chen: imperial term, Hung's use of, 11
Chen-shen: term for God in Baptist doxology, 72
Ch'en Yü-ch'eng: assumes direction of military affairs, 23; campaigns in Yangtze Valley area, 23-24; death of, 24
Chia-ch'ing Emperor (1796-1820): difficulties of, 11
Chiang-k'ou-hsü: seizure of, 18
Chiang-nan: great camp of, established, 20; reestablished, 23
Chiao Liang: identified with Hung Ta-ch'üan, 19
Chieh-yang, Kwangtung: Lo Ta-kang from, 18
Ch'ien-lung Emperor (1736-96): inferiority of successors to, 9
Chin-hsi: Taiping term for baptism, 77
Chin-t'ien, Kwangsi: Wei Ch'ang-hui from, 16; rebel headquarters, 16-7; Taipings leave, 18; Hung Jen-kan fails to reach, 22; formal Taiping beginnings at, 120
Ch'in dynasty: changed attitude of, toward Shang-ti, 68; mentioned, 35
Chinese Union: organized by Gützlaff, 43; possible dissemination of Bibles and tracts to Taipings, 47; mentioned, 44
Ch'ing dynasty: Hung's first thought of overthrow of, 118
Chinkiang, Kiangsu: Taiping loss of, 23
Chiu-kuan: school at, 13
Chiu-shih-chu Yeh-su: Taiping term for "Jesus the Lord and Saviour," 73
Chou dynasty: mentioned, 35
Chou Hsi-neng: Taiping traitor exposed, 58-59
Chou-li: used for Taiping military organization, 16
Christ: acceptable because acting in Chinese manner, 35; concern for mankind of, Taiping allusion to, 35; Taiping information about life of, 73; Taiping phraseology for, 73; Taiping neglect of his ministry, 109
Christianity: official toleration proclaimed for, 45; Taiping contact with doctrine of, 41-47; Taiping use of dogma of, described, 79-80
Christian faith: essentials of, 107-9
Christian literary activity: increase in, after 1842, 45
Christian tracts: production of, to 1852, 45-46
Ch'üan-chou, Kwangsi: So-i ford near, 19; Feng wounded near, 121
Ch'üan shih liang yen: neglect of, by Chinese historians, 6; reaches Hung Hsiu-ch'üan, 42; availability of, for present study, 47; as established contact with Taipings, 47; abbreviation for, 48; absence of commentaries for, 54; term for God neglected, 60; presence of Golden Rule in, 107; use made of, by Hung, 109-110; contents described, 110; presence of acceptable Bible section in, 111-13; digressive style of, 112; source of Hung's theory of Shang-ti, 112; Christian doctrine in, not borrowed, 113; copy used described, 144; mentioned, 44, 76
Ch'üan-wei-shih: Chinese for Comforter, 72
Comforter: Chinese translations of, 72
Confucius: doctrine of, Taiping treatment of, 35; influence of, on Taiping religious ideology, 37; many deities recognized by state cult of, 65; dishonored by

Manchus, 34; example to Taipings, 35; quoted, 35; doctrines of, attacked by Liang A-fa, 112
Covenant: with Shang-ti, absence of, 66
Creation: Biblical account of, borrowed, 60
Cromwell, Oliver: soldiers of, compared with Taipings, 121
Cross: as symbol, Taiping neglect of, 78
C.S.L.Y. 1832: explained, 48; see Ch'üan-shih liang yen
D. 1852: explained, 48; see Bible: Delegates' Version
"Descents" of God and Jesus: begin, 16; summarized, 58-59; explained, 68; made plausible, 118; aid to morale, 120; addition to original Taiping faith, 127n; strengthen authority of leaders, 148
Devil, the: responsible for neglect of Shang-ti, 67; liberal references to, 80; widespread activities of, 80-81; Taiping terms for, 81; many helpers for, 81; allusions to, in New Testament, 82; mentioned in Old Testament, 82; portrayal as serpent, Taiping fondness for, 82; early Chinese Bible terms for, 83; identified with Taiping opponents, 118
Dialogue between Two Friends: See Chang Yüeh liang yu hsiang-lun
Discourse on Theology: printed, 46; revised "T'ien-li yao-lun", 46; see "T'ien-li yao-lun"
Divinity, of Christ: denied by Taipings, 79
"Dr. MacGowan's Notebook": See MacGowan, Dr. William
Doxology: Taiping version of, mentioned, 72; reasons for correspondence between Taiping and Baptist versions of, 73; Sabbath use of, 78; Taiping and missionary versions of, 96n
Dragon: as symbol, Taiping use of, 78, 82; Chinese conception of, 102-3n

Earth: See Hou-t'u
Eastern King: See Yang Hsiuch'ing
Egypt: Israelite experience in, Taiping reference to, 60-1
Elevation of characters: Taiping use of, 54-55; to indicate Christ's subordination to God, 79
Eschatology: Taiping need for, 84; availability of, from New Testament sources, 85
Essentials of Heaven's Principles: See "T'ien-li yao-lun"
Eucharist: See Lord's Supper
"Ever Victorious Army": in Shanghai vicinity, 24; under Gordon, 25; mustered out, 26
Evil spirits: frequency of reference to, 80; Taiping terms for, 81; allusions to, in New Testament, 82; Taiping treatment of New Testament allusions to, 82; early Chinese Bible terms for, 83; identified with Taiping opponents, 118

"Father of His Country": use of, 70
Fatherhood of God: stressed in Gospels, 69-70; prominent Taiping use of, 70; neglect of gentler aspects of, 70
Feng Yün-shan: religious conversion of, 13; moves to Kwangsi to preach, 14; preaches in Tzu-ching-shan area, 14; imprisonment of, unifies God-Worshippers, 14-15; returns to Hua-hsien, 1848, 15;

Index

begins political planning, 15; last trip to Kwangsi of, 15; released from prison, 16; participates in anti-Manchu planning, 16; given military titles, 18; death of, 19, 121; sees Ch'üan shih liang yen, 43; baptized by Hung Hsiu-ch'üan, 76; preaches against Chinese cultural traditions, 118; first connects converts with Ch'ing overthrow, 118-19; arrested, 123
Five relations: Taiping praise for, 35
Flood, the: Taiping reference to, 60
Foochow: treaties permit foreign residence in, 45
Foreign missionaries: attracted by Taiping religion, 122; repelled by Taiping religious pretensions, 122
Foreigners: China residence of, forbidden, 41; treaties allow hiring of native teachers for, 45
Forgiveness: lack of individual obligation for, 80; terms for, 98n
Forgiveness of sin: Christian attitude toward, 75; Taiping concern for, 75-76; Taiping neglect of profounder aspects of, 76
Forrest, Robert James: comments on ineffective presentation of Taiping ideology, 125
French: armed support of intervention, 26
French Revolution: debates before, compared with Taiping preparations, 36
Fu-chu incident: 17
Fundamentalism: closer to Taiping religion than "social gospel", 113

G. 1847: explained, 48; see Bible: Medhurst-Gützlaff Version

G. 1855: explained, 48; see Bible: Medhurst-Gützlaff Modified Version
Gillespie, William: lists reasons for Chinese opposition to Christian missions, 123-24; quotes Chinese tract, 129-30
God: as Heavenly Father in Hung's visions, 12-13; begins "descents", 16; personal nature of, stressed by Taipings, 71
God-Worshippers: See Pai Shang-ti Hui
Golden Calf: mentioned, 66
Golden Rule: omission of, in Taiping dogma, 107
"Good Words to Admonish the Age": See Ch'üan shih liang yen
Gordon, Charles George: commands "Ever-Victorious Army", 25; permission to serve imperialists withdrawn, 26
Gospels: stress God to man relationship, 71
Great Supreme Ruler: See Huang Shang-ti
Gützlaff, Karl Friedrich August: activities of, 43; distributes tracts during voyages, 44; uses Roberts as assistant, 44; prolific author of tracts, 45; member of Bible revision committee, 47; philosophy of evangelization, 49n

Hakkas: Hung Hsiu-ch'üan's connection with, 12; converts of Feng's preaching, 14; God-Worshippers attractive to, 15; origin of, 30n
Hamberg, Theodore: connection of, with Hung Jen-kan, 13; Hung Jen-kan informant for, 29n
Han Yü: reproves Hsien-tsung, 68
Hangchow: Taiping seizure of, 24; Franco-imperialist

capture of, 25
Hankow: repeated Taiping capture of, 21
Hanyang, Hupeh: repeated Taiping capture of, 21
Heaven: in Old Testament, absence of references to, 85; in New Testament, abundance of references to, 85-86; Taiping description of, 86-87; Taiping use of, as attribute, 120
Heavenly: ubiquitous Taiping use of as a term, 86; as prefix, 119
Heavenly King: See Hung Hsiu-ch'üan
Heavenly Kingdom of Great Peace: See T'ai-p'ing t'ien-kuo
Hebrews: attitude of, toward other gods, 66; same, not followed by Taipings, 67
Hell: as Old Testament concept, limited development of, 85; as New Testament concept, full development of, 85-86; Taiping description of, 87
"Hermes": visit of, to Nanking, reported, 122; mentioned, 46
"Himmaleh": used to carry tracts, 45
Holy Spirit: New Testament concept of, 71; Taiping misconception of, 71-73
Ho-nai Teacher: title conferred on Yang Hsiu-ch'ing, 57, 148
Hongkong: center for Chinese Union, 43
Hou-t'u: sacrifices to, 68
Hsiang Jung: ordered to suppress God-Worshippers, 17
Hsiangtan, Hunan: Taiping possession of, 21
Hsiao Ch'ao-kuei: participates in anti-Manchu planning, 16; given military titles, 18; death before Changsha, 19; yü issued under the name of, 33; authority of, strengthened by "descents", 148

Hsieh-mo: Taiping use of, similar to that of Gützlaff and Liang A-fa, 69
Hsieh-shen: God's intolerance of, 67; Taiping use of, similar to that of Gützlaff and Liang A-fa, 69; in tabulation of terms, 81; special rebel use for, 117
Hsien-feng Emperor (1851-61): inherits difficulties, 11
Hsien-tsung, T'ang emperor: welcomes Buddha's bones, 68; reproved, 68
Hsin-shang-kan: Wang Tso-hsin from, 123
Hsiu-ch'üan: acquired by Hung as given name, 13
Hsüan, Han emperor: sacrifices to Earth, 68
Hsün-chou, Kwangsi: Taiping beginnings near, 11
Hu I-kuang: mentioned, 16
Hua-chou, Kwangsi: rebel leaders hide in, 17
Hua-hsien, Kwangtung: Hung Hsiu-ch'üan born at, 11
Huan, Sung emperor: calls highest Taoist deity Shang-ti, 68
Huang I-chen: disobedient Taiping leader, 58
Huang-shang-ti: Taiping use of, 49n, 55; illustrated, 55-56; use in T.P. 1853 and G. 1847, 56; mentioned, 59, 61
Hui-fei: God-Worshippers denounced as, 14
Humility: Taiping failure to exalt Christian virtue of, 109
Hung Ching-yang: father of Hung Hsiu-ch'üan, 12; God-Worshipper ceremonies at death of, 15
Hung Hsiu-ch'üan: receives later revelation than Western Christians, 4-5; early life of, 11-12; fails government examinations, 12; receives Christian tracts, 12; visions of, 12-13; identifies visions with Biblical dogma, 13;

Index

loses teaching position, 13; moves to Kwangsi, 14; returns to Hua-hsien, 1844, 14; second trip to Kwangsi of, 14, 44; begins political planning, 14-15; returns to Hua-hsien, 1848, 15; third trip to Kwangsi of, 15; last trip to Kwangsi of, 15; begins military and political development of God-Worshippers, 15-16; official foreign missions fail to see, 20; reproached by Yang Hsiu-ch'ing, 21; causes murder of Eastern and Northern Kings, establishes nepotism, 22; withdraws from active direction of affairs, 22; refusal of, to leave Nanking or lay in supplies, 24; son escapes from Nanking, executed, 25; sets poor example, 28; <u>chao-shu</u> and <u>yü</u>, lack of association with, 33; advises followers to be content, 35; first receives <u>Ch'üan shih liang yen</u>, 42; likelihood of having received Bible from Roberts, 43-44; divine agent for China, 57; "descent" of, with Jesus, 68; authority of, strengthened, 70; lectures Taipings on nature of God, 70; Holy Spirit, ideas of, concerning, 72-73; neglects teachings of Christ, 74; occasions for personal knowledge of Christian religious observances, 76; first baptism of converts, 77; date of first preaching heard by, 98-99n; first evangelists seen by, 98-99n; invites Roberts to Nanking, 100n; use made of <u>Ch'üan shih liang yen</u>, 109-110; influenced by Liang A-fa's iconoclasm, 112; arbitrary character of, 114n; uses <u>T'ai-p'ing</u> in utopian sense, 116; preaches against Chinese cultural traditions, 118; first ponders Ch'ing overthrow, 118-19; changes personal name, 119; inflates religious pretensions, 122; describes visions, 141-42

Hung Jen-kan: religious conversion of, 13; to Canton, 14; given high rank on arrival in Nanking, 22; flees Nanking, executed, 25; in Hongkong, 27; tells story of Rebellion to Hamberg, 29n; receives instruction from Roberts, 44; baptized, 76; has Beatitudes carved, 97-98n; preaches against Chinese cultural traditions, 118; relates earliest iconoclasm, 118

Hung Jih: See Hung Hsiu-ch'üan

Hung Ta-ch'üan: confession of, 19; identity of, 19

Huo-hsiu: childhood name, 13

Hymns on the Heavenly Father: See "T'ien-fu shih"

I-chu: See Hsien-feng Emperor

Incarnation: Taiping denial of, 79

Instruction on Awakening the World with the Basic Doctrine: See "Yüan-tao chüeh-shih-hsün"

Instruction on Rousing the World with the Basic Doctrine: See "Yüan-tao hsing-shih hsün"

I-se-lieh: term for Israel, 61

Israelites, in Egypt: Taiping reference to, 60

Jade Emperor: See Yü-huang-ta-ti

Jen-k'un: given name, 13

Jesus: "descents" of, with God, summarized, 58-59; "descent" of, with Hung, 68

Jesus, the Heavenly Elder Brother: in Hung's visions, 12-13; begins "descents"

Job: mentioned, 82

K'ai-feng: Taipings cross

Yellow River at, 21
K'ang-hsi Emperor (1662-1723): villified, 152
Kew A-gang: carries Christian materials into China, 42
Kiangnan: See Chiang-nan
King of Hades: See Yen-lo-yao
King of Heavenly Virtue: See Hung Ta-ch'üan
"Kingdom of God": not mentioned by Taipings, 116
"Kingdom of Heaven": origin of Taiping use of, 86; Taiping failure to comprehend otherworldly nature of, 108; use of, in title of regime, 116
Kitchen God: See Tsao Chün
Kiukiang, Kiangsi: Taiping capture of, 21; imperialist recovery of, 23
Ku: term, 61
Kuai-shih: term, 68
Kuan-lu-pu: Hung Hsiu-ch'üan attended school at, 12
Kuang-tsung, Ming emperor: mentioned, 149
Kuei: importance of, for Chinese polytheism, 65
Kuei-p'ing-hsien, Kwangsi: Shih Ta-k'ai from, 16
Kung Yang: use by Kwangtung scholars of, 116
Kuo-chou, Kiangsu: Taiping loss of, 23

Li: calls attention to Ch'üan shih liang yen, 13
Li Hsiu-ch'eng: Taiping commander-in-chief, 23; campaigns in Yangtze Valley, 23-25; flees Nanking, executed, 25; disappointment with Hung, 122
Li Hung-chang: imperialist leadership of, 23; menaces Soochow, 24; besieges Soochow, 24
Li K'ai-fang: commander for "Northern Expedition", 21
Liang A-fa: author of Christian tracts given to Hung, 12, 42; carries Christian materials into China, 42; possible contact with Hung, 99n; includes basic Christian ideas in Ch'üan shih liang yen, 110-11; preference of, for Epistles over Gospels influences Taipings, 111; copy of Ch'üan shih liang yen used described, 144
Liang-ssu-ma: Taiping official, 26
Lin Feng-hsiang: commander for "Northern Expedition", 21
Lin Tse-hsü: high commissioner, 17
Literary examinations: Taiping promise to reform, 36
Lo Ta-kang: convert from Triad Society, 18; proclamation of, listed, 147
Lobschied, William: term for God chosen by, 56; G. 1855 edited by, 143
Lockhart, Dr. William: represents London Missionary Society, 42
London Missionary Society: enters China mission field, 42
"Long-haired Bandits": See Ch'ang-mao-tsei
Lord's Prayer, the: Taiping paraphrase of, 74-75
Lord's Supper: Taiping neglect of, 109
Loyal King: See Li Hsiu-ch'eng
Love: Taiping neglect of Christian emphasis upon, 107
Lu Liu: death of, 14; imprisoned with Feng Yün-shan, 123

Macao: resident missionary work permitted at, 45
MacGowan, Dr. William: translates Taiping documents at Ningpo, 3
McLane, Commissioner Robert M.: prepared for Taiping recognition, 20
Mai-hsi: term for Egypt, 61
Malacca: mission station at, 42; Lassar-Marshman Bible published at, Morrison-Milne

Index   181

Bible published at, 47
Manchus: bases for Taiping attack on, 34; deprecated as aliens, 36
Marshall, Humphrey: refuses Roberts permission to visit Nanking, 6n, 100n; mentioned, 4
Marshman, Joshua: translator for London Missionary Society, 42
Mary, mother of Jesus: disregarded, 79
Meadows, Thomas Taylor: reports impressions of Taiping religion during "Hermes" visit, 122
Medhurst, Walter Henry: translates Taiping documents, 3; pioneer Taiping scholar, 6; represents London Missionary Society, 42; prolific author of tracts, 45; author of Discourse on Theology, 46; mentions possibility of Taiping use of Roberts' tracts, 46; member of Bible revision committee, 47, 143; "Critical Review", available for present study, 47; comments concerning Taiping and Baptist doxology, 72-73; "T'ien-li yao lun" described, 140-41; contents of Ch'üan shih liang yen reviewed by, 144
Memorials of Protestant Missionaries to the Chinese: lists Christian tracts, 52; see Wylie, Alexander
Mencius: dishonored by Manchus, 34; mentioned in "Yüan-tao hsing-shih hsün", 35
Meng-ch'ung: image-breaking at, 123
Meng-shih: term, 61
Milne, William: author of tracts for London Missionary Society, 42; author of tract possibly reaching Taipings, 46; baptism of Liang A-fa by, phrases used in, 113
Milne, William Charles: assisted translation of Delegates' Version, 143
Min Cheng-feng: ordered to suppress God-Worshippers, 17
Min-ning: See Tao-kuang Emperor
Ming, Han emperor: introducer of Buddhism, 68
Missionaries: Chinese language difficulties of, 41; change attitude toward Taipings, 117
Missionary influence: on American policy toward Taipings, 6n
Missionary societies: in China, growth by 1840 of, 42; growth in numbers of, 1843-53, 45
Mo-hsi: term for Moses, 61
Mohammed: followers of, compared with Taipings, 121
Montesquieu: mentioned, 36
Mor. 1823: explained, 48; see Bible: Morrison-Milne Version
Morrison, J.R.: member of Bible revision committee, 47
Morrison, Robert: represents London Missionary Society, translation activities of, 42; uses shen, 59
Mount Sinai: giving of the Ten Commandments, reference to, 60-61; mentioned, 66

Nanchang, Kiangsi: Taiping siege of, 21
Nanking: capture mentioned, 18-19; becomes Taiping capital, 20; unfavorable impressions of, 20; siege of, lifted 1860, 23; Li Hsiu-ch'eng recalled to, 24; final siege of, 24; imperialist capture of, 25; absence of "Ever Victorious Army" at siege of, 26; capture of, connected with Taiping promise, 36
Near East: 41
Netherlands Missionary Society: sends Gützlaff to the Far East, 43
New Testament: development of punishment and reward in the hereafter, 85-86; Chinese title of, changed to enhance

rebel authority, 116-17
Nien-fei: activities of, widen effect of Taiping Rebellion, 11
Ningpo: Taiping seizure of, 24; Taiping ruin of trade at, 25; treaties permit foreign residence in, 45
No-ya: term for Noah, 60
Noah: Taiping reference to, 60
North-China Herald: publishes Taiping translations, 3; comments favorably on Taiping religion, 122; changed opinion of, 122
"Northern Expedition": launched, 21
Northern King: See Wei Ch'ang-hui
Obedience: Taiping emphasis upon, 109
Old Testament: neglect of punishment and reward in the hereafter of, 84-85
Opium: Taiping prohibitions against, 64, 117
Ou-hsiang: used for "likeness", 66
Ou-su: for "graven image", 66

"Pai-cheng-ko": accords with Chinese ethical standards, 35; described, 139-40
Pai Shang-ti Hui: formed, 14; organization of militia for, 15; first clashes with Manchu troops, 17; considered Catholic Christians, 123
Passover, feast of: mention neglected by Taipings, 61
Paul, Apostle: mentioned, 107
Penang: mission stations at, 42
Pentateuch: Taiping borrowings from, 60-61
Pentecost: mentioned, 71
Personal nature of God: stressed by Taipings, 71
Peter: mentioned, 71
Pettee, G.S.: comments on leaders of revolution, 123
Pharaoh: mentioned, 61
Pneuma: New Testament term for

Holy Spirit, 72
Po-pai, Kwangsi: district mentioned, 58
Po-yang Lake: destruction of imperialist flotilla on, 22
Poems for the Instruction of Youth: See "Yu-hsüeh-shih"
Polytheism, in China: situation summarized, 65
Pre-Confucian: influences on Taiping religious ideology, mentioned, 37; tradition, Taiping use of, 35
Protestant Evangelistic literature: methods of distribution of, 44; possible source of influence, 44
Protestant missionaries: responsibility of, for Taiping religion, 41-47 passim; establishment of stations among overseas Chinese, 42; nineteenth century fundamentalist attitudes of, 52
Psalms: stress God to man relationship, 71
P'u-sa: term needed, 84; used for "idol", for Bodhisattva, 66

Quesnay: mentioned, 36

"Rattler": finds rebel attitudes unacceptable, 122
Revelations, Book of: Taiping predilection for, 82
Roberts, Issachar Jacox: denied permission to visit Nanking, 4, 6n, 100n; instructs Hung Hsiu-ch'üan and Hung Jen-kan, 14; influences Taiping treatment of women, 27; likelihood of having given Bible to Hung Hsiu-ch'üan, 43-44; activities of, in Hongkong and Canton, 44; source of tracts possibly used by Taipings, 46; sojourn of, in Nanking, 50n; fundamentalist attitudes of, 52; source of rebel knowledge of Christian rites, 76; compositions of, described, 144-45

Index   183

Roundheads: compared with Taipings, 121
"Rules for the March": quotations from, 36

Sabbath: Taiping observance of, 78
Sacred Treasury: See Sheng-k'u
San-chiao: disparaged by Liang A-fa, 112
San-ho-hui: See Triad Society
"San-tzu-ching": contains story of Israelites in Egypt, 60; described, 137
Satan: See the Devil
Secret societies: influences of, upon Taiping religious practices, 37
Secular Proclamations: available in Chinese and English, listed and annotated, 145-46; available in English only, listed and annotated, 147
Self-baptism: reasons for Taiping sanction of, 77
Seng-ko-lin-ch'in: summoned to oppose Taipings, 21
Serampore: Lassar-Marshman Bible, prepared at, 47
Seventh Commandment: rebel additions to, 117
Shang: term, 61
Shanghai: concerned with loss of trade, 3; first Taiping attempt at capture of, 23; Western representatives decide to resist Taipings at, 23; Taipings attempt conquest of, 24; treaties permit foreign residence in, 45
Shang-ti: Christian use as synonym for Yahweh, 48n; Taiping use of term, 49n; translation of, for present study, 49n; Taiping use of, illustrated, 55; use in T.P. 1853 and G. 1847, 56; convenience of, for Taiping application, 59-60; Liang A-fa's slight use of, 60; worship of, in Chou times, 65; recognized as highest of all gods, 67; absence of Chinese covenant with, 67; reasons given by Taipings for neglect of, 67-68; conferred upon Taoist deity, 68; universality of, 71; Baptist use of term, 73; origin of, 89n; origin in Ch'üan shih liang yen of Hung's theory of, 112; value of identification of, with Yahweh and God the Father, 118
Shen: term for God, mentioned, 59
Shen-chou, Chihli: reached by Taipings, 21
Shen-chu: term for God, used in Morrison-Milne Bible, 56
Shen-hsien: term, 68
Shen-t'ien shang-ti: term used by Liang A-fa, 60
Sheng: term, 61
Sheng-k'u: repository of God-Worshipper property, 16; described, 108
Sheng-ling: term in Taiping and in Baptist doxology, 72
Sheng-pao: summoned to oppose Taipings, 21
Sheng-shen-feng: Taiping and Baptist term for Holy Spirit, use of, 72
Sheol: as concept for Hell, limited development of, 85
Shield King: See Hung Jen-kan
Shih-chiao pool: site of first Taiping baptism by immersion, 76
Shih Ta-k'ai: participates in anti-Manchu planning, 16; given military title, 18; active in Yangtze provinces west of Nanking, 22; rival of Eastern and Northern Kings, withdrawal from Nanking, 22
Shun: term, 61
Shun: sacrifices to, 68
Sin: See forgiveness of sin
Singapore: mission stations at, 42
"Sitting warfare": tactic followed, 19
Siu-tshuen: See Hung Hsiu-ch'üan

So-i ford: Taipings ambushed at, 19; Taiping discipline effective at, 121
"Social gospel": mention of, omitted in Taiping dogma, 108; prominence of, in twentieth century, 113
Songs on the Hundred Instances of Correct Conduct: See "Pai-cheng-ko"
Songs of Salvation by the Basic Doctrine: See "Yüan-tao chiv-shih-ko"
Soochow, Kiangsu: Taiping seizure of, 23
Southern King: See Feng Yün-shan
Stephen: mentioned, 71
Stevens, Edwin: possible contact with Hung, 99n
Stronach, J.: assisted translation of Delegates' Version, 143
"Styx": finds rebel attitudes unacceptable, 122
Su San-niang: woman convert from Triad Society, 18
Supreme Ruler: See Shang-ti
"Susquehannah": visits Nanking, 20; Bridgman aboard, 21, 42; finds rebel attitudes unacceptable, 122
"Sweet dew": See T'ien-lu

T.P. 1853: explained, 48; see Taiping Bible
Taiping approximations of Biblical terms: illustrated, 61
_army rules: quoted, 119
_Bible: used in comparisons, 62 ff.; copy used described, 143-44
_borrowings: Old Testament material summarized, 54; New Testament material summarized, 54; early Hebrew idea of God, described, 54-60; early Hebrew idea of God, terms illustrated by quotations, 55-56; illustrative stories of the Pentateuch, described, 60-61; Ten Commandments, described, 61-65; Old Testament attitudes toward the worship of idols and rival gods, described, 65-69; idea of God in the New Testament, summarized, 69; described, 69-73; accuracy of data concerning life of Christ, 73-74; basic facts of Christ's life, summarized, 73; described, 73-74; teachings of Christ, described, 74-76; conscious choice important in, 74; Christian rites and doctrines, summarized, 76; described, 76-80; neglect of theory, 78-79; Biblical ideas of Satan and evil spirits, described, 80-84; Biblical ideas of Heaven and Hell, described, 84-87; general summary of, 106-7
_calendar: abrogation of lucky days, 120; 1853 version listed, 145; necessity for, 148; preface to 1853 version, translated, 149-50
Taiping Days: See "T'ai-p'ing t'ien-jih"
Taiping designations for God: 55
_discipline: reinforced by promises of heaven, 16, 86; unusual quality of, 27; strengthened by enlargement of Seventh Commandment, 64, 117; use of religion to reinforce, 119-21
_documents: disappearance of, from China, 131; published collections of, 131-32; official papers divided into classes, 132; official religious publications listed, 132-34; Western references to, 135-36; contents summarized, 136-41; repositories of originals of, 136
_factionalism: development of, 20
_iconoclasm: reported to Westerners, 4; initial appearances of, 13; arouses Kwangsi gentry, 14, 123; attracts official notice, 14; supported by use of Chinese history, 35; supported by Ten Commandments, 61, 118;

shown in Taiping versions of first two Commandments, 62-63; attitude toward other gods, 66-69; arguments for, 66-69; embodied in "Yüan-tao chüeh-shih-hsün", 69; source of, 112; mentioned, 56
_idea of God: as merciful, 56; as deity of all people, 56-57; as deity communicating directly with leaders, 57; as helper in warfare, 58-59; failure to follow later Old Testament idea of Yahweh, 59; monotheism prominent in, 59-60; tolerance of other gods, 67
_ideology: neglect of quality and extent of borrowing from Christian sources, 6; nonreligious portion of, discussed, 34; as Chinese in form and ideas as possible, 35; politico-religious linkage of, 119; failure as tool of persuasion, 123-25; reasons for Chinese opposition to, given by Tseng Kuo-fan, 124-25; summarized, 126; ineffectiveness of presentation of, 125; incompetent leadership responsible for nature of, 126
_trade: indifference to possibilities of, 27
_land system: described, 26-27; rules for redistribution, 36
_leaders: organization of, 119; early incorruptibility of, 120; amateurish conduct of foreign affairs, 123; reasons for lack of training of, 126
_monotheism: need for, 65
_neglect of positive program: 36-37
_opposition to opium: approved, 4; mentioned, 27
_political and economic system: described, 26-27
Taiping Rebellion: draws foreign attention, 3; magnitude of, 3; twentieth century view of, as revolutionary prototype, source of military tactics, 5; later Kuomintang neglect of, 5; Communist attention to, 7n; foreign community at Shanghai, hopeful of, 7n; causes of, summarized, 9-11; favorable reports to Shanghai of, 20; high point in military fortunes of, 21; conclusion of, 25; role of foreign powers in suppression of, 25; failure of, reasons for, 27-28
_religion: news of, spread abroad, 3; slight contact with Western missionaries, 3; absence of Catholic influence upon, 4; causes fund-raising for New Testaments, 4; Western enthusiasm for, 4; disappointing to Westerners, 4-5, 20; interesting to missionaries after Rebellion, 5; gives insufficient basis for cooperation, 122; susceptible to development of fanaticism, 122; contained in instructional material and tracts, 136
_religious documents: listed, 132-34; Western references to, 135-36; contents summarized, 136-41
_segregation of sexes: contrast of, with Nanking harem life, 22-23; in Taiping version of Seventh Commandment, 64; mentioned, 27
Taiping Songs on Salvation: See "T'ai-p'ing chiu-shih-ko"
Taiping specifications for religious offerings: 55
_women: equalitarian treatment of, 27
Taipings: ruin trade, 25; promise considerate treatment to Chinese civilians, 36; promise to eliminate Manchu influence, 36; promise to confiscate property, 36; profess Chinese cultural orthodoxy, 36; possibility of contact with Chinese Union, 43; case a-

gainst Manchus, exemplified, 151-54
T'ai-p'ing: term, Chinese use of, 116
"T'ai-p'ing chao-shu": mentioned, 35
"T'ai-p'ing chiu-shih-ko": repudiates Chinese cultural traditions, 117; described, 139
"T'ai-p'ing t'ien-jih": described, 141-42
T'ai-p'ing t'ien-kuo: formal beginning of, 18, 120; origin of term, 116
Taku forts: Anglo-French repulse at, 23
Talbot, Olyphant, and Co.: purchase brig to distribute tracts, 44
T'ang, Shang dynasty founder: worshipper of Shang-ti, 71
T'ang dynasty: burning of temples by, 68; mentioned, 35
T'ang-lang: term, 61
Tao-che: Morrison term for Comforter, 72
Tao-chou: Taiping approach to, 121
Tao-kuang Emperor (1821-51): failures of, 10
Tao, the: mentioned, 67
Taoism: Taiping treatment of, 35; many divinities recognized by, 65; proscribed, 68; attacked by Liang A-fa, 112
Taoist influences: on Taiping religious ideology, mentioned, 37
Taoists: property of, Taiping promise to confiscate, 36; responsible for neglect of Shang-ti, 67
Tatars: Taiping term for Manchus, 151-54
Taylor, Rev. C.: useless effort of, 5; observes Taiping worship, 120; remarks of, on Taiping discipline, 120-21
Ten Commandments: Taiping use of, described, 61-65; comparisons showing Taiping use of, 62-65; Liang's wording of, followed by Taipings, 112; rebel additions to, 117; used to support iconoclasm, 118; called T'ien-t'iao, 120
Testament: fails to impress Taipings in the sense of a covenant, 57
Thistle Mountain: See Tzu-ching-shan
Three Character Classic: See "San-tzu-ching"
Three Dynasties: mentioned, 68
Ti-yü: term for Hell, 87
T'ien: worship of, 65; see Heavenly
T'ien-chu: term for God, 59
"T'ien-fu hsia-fan chao-shu": contents summarized, 58-59; described, 138
T'ien-fu shang-ti: used by Taipings, 55
"T'ien-fu shih": described, 141
T'ien-kuo: See "Kingdom of Heaven"
"T'ien-li yao-lun": tract by Medhurst, reaches Taipings, 46; described, 140-41
T'ien-lu: term, 61, 92n
"T'ien-ming chao-chih-shu": pronouncements during "descents" included in, 16; "descents" summarized, 58-59; contents described, 138-39
T'ien-t'ang: Taiping term for heaven, 73
T'ien-te: used for dating documents, 147-49
T'ien-te wang: See Hung Ta-ch'üan
T'ien-t'i-hui: See Triad Society
T'ien-t'iao: used for Ten Commandments, 120
"T'ien-t'iao-shu": used in comparisons, 62 ff.; emphasizes God as personal deity, 71; discusses sin and its forgiveness, 75-76; details of Taiping baptism, 77-78; explains sin, 79-80; contents described, 136-37
T'ien-wang: See Hung Hsiu-ch'üan

Index

Tientsin, Treaties of; ratification of, 23
Toleration, of Chinese: for Chinese and foreign Christians, 4
Translation: difficulties of, discussed, 53-54
Treaties of 1842-44: foreign exasperation with Manchu observance of, 20
Triad Society: activities of, 11; members of, ask to join God-Worshippers, 15; restricted in joining Taipings, 18; impossibility of Taiping collaboration with, 18, 121; Chiao Liang leader of, 19; Taipings disapprove collaboration with, 119; association with Taipings, effort to destroy evidence of, 170-71; association with Taipings, proclamations containing evidence of, listed, 147-48
Trimetrical Classic: See "San-tzu-ching"
Trinity: Taiping failure to understand, 80
Tsui: explained as Taiping term for sin, 79-80
Tsao Chun: bargain with 68
Tseng Kuo-ch'uan: imperialist leader, 23; siege of Nanking by, 24
Tseng Kuo-fan: Taiping defeat of, 21; leads Hunan militia, 22; campaigns in Yangtze Valley, 23; summarizes Chinese case against Taipings, 124-25; reasons for opposition to Taiping ideology, summarized, 126
Tso Tsung-t'ang: imperialist leader, 23; menaces Hangchow, 24
Tzu-ching-shan: first God-Worshippers at, 14; charcoal from, 16
Tz'u-ku: first Kwangsi preaching at, 14

Universality, of God: stressed in New Testament, 70; supported by native Chinese ideas, 70; identical with Shang-ti concept, 71

Wang, title of: given to military leaders, 19; frequent elevation to, after 1856, 23
Wangs, titles of: shown in document prefaces, 149, 151
Wang: Kwangsi cousin of Hung Hsiu-ch'uan, 14
Wang Tso-hsin: arrests Feng Yun-shan, 123
Ward, Frederick Townsend: anti-Taiping activities of, 24
Wei Ch'ang-hui: participates in anti-Manchu planning, 16; given military titles, 18; murder of, 22
Wen, Chou dynasty founder: worshipper of Shang-ti, 71
Wen, Han emperor: bargain with Kitchen God, 68
Western King: See Hsiao Ch'ao-kuei
Western visitors to Nanking, 1853-54: unfavorable impressions of, 20
Wu-hsuan, Kwangsi: Hsiao Ch'ao-kuei from, 16
Wu, Liang emperor: vows to Buddha, 68
Wu, Northern Chou emperor: proscribes Buddhism and Taoism, 68
Wu K'o-i: mentioned, 16
Wuchang, Hupeh: Taiping recapture of, 21
Wu San-kuei: invites Manchus, 153; mentioned, 149
Wylie, Alexander: lists Christian tracts, 46; lists compositions by Roberts, 46

Ya-lun: term for Aaron, 61
Yahweh, Hebrew idea of: as deity of a chosen people, 56; as deity communicating directly with leaders, 57; as helper in warfare, 57-58; intolerance of other gods, not fol-

lowed by Taipings, 67
Yang Hsiu-ch'ing: participates in anti-Manchu planning, 16; appointed commander-in-chief, 17; given titles, 18; critical of Hung Hsiu-ch'üan, 20-21; ambitious for power, assassinated, 22; sets poor example, 28; yu issued under the name of, 33; examinations to be reformed by, 36; recipient of title from God, 57; identified with Holy Spirit, 72; "descents" strengthen authority of, 148; furnish source of titles for, 148
Yangchow, Kiangsu: Taiping failure to capture, 24
Yao: term, tabulated, 81; mentioned, 86
Yeh-ho-hua: term for God, used by Lobschied, 56
Yeh-huo-hua: term for God, used in Lassar-Marshman Bible, 56; mentioned, 59
Yen: example to Taipings, 35
Yen-lo: needed, 84

Yen-lo-yao: Buddhist Satan, 80; terms for, 81
Yo-chou, Hunan: Taiping victory at, 21
"Young Prince": mentioned, 119
"Yu-hsueh-shih": described, 137-38
Yung-an: title of wang first conferred at, 19; Taiping capture, Manchu siege of, 19; site of "descent", 58
Yung-yen: See Chia-ch'ing Emperor
Yü: use of, 33
Yü: sacrifices to, 68
Yu-huang-ta-ti: designated as Shang-ti, 68
"Yuan-tao chiu-shih-ko": described, 139-40
"Yüan-tao chüeh-shih hsün": quotes Book of Songs and Book of History, 35; embodiment of Taiping case against idolatry, 69; described, 140
"Yüan-tao hsing-shih hsün": mentioned, 35; described, 140